The Circulation of Children

A book in the series

LATIN AMERICA OTHERWISE:
LANGUAGES, EMPIRES, NATIONS

Series editors:

WALTER D. MIGNOLO, Duke University
IRENE SILVERBLATT, Duke University
SONIA SALDÍVAR-HULL, University of Texas, San Antonio

The Circulation of Children:

Kinship, Adoption, and Morality in Andean Peru

Jessaca B. Leinaweaver

Duke University Press

Durham & London 2008

Duke University Press gratefully acknowledges the support
of the Faculty of Arts at the University of Manitoba, which provided
funds toward the production of this book.

*Library of Congress Cataloging-in-Publication data
and republication acknowledgments appear on the
last printed pages of this book.*

Contents

About the Series

Latin America Otherwise: Languages, Empires, Nations is a critical series. It aims to explore the emergence and consequences of concepts used to define "Latin America" while at the same time exploring the broad interplay of political, economic, and cultural practices that have shaped Latin American worlds. Latin America, at the crossroads of competing imperial designs and local responses, has been construed as a geocultural and geopolitical entity since the nineteenth century. This series provides a starting point to redefine Latin America as a configuration of political, linguistic, cultural, and economic intersections that demands a continuous reappraisal of the role of the Americas in history, and of the ongoing process of globalization and the relocation of people and cultures that have characterized Latin America's experience. *Latin America Otherwise: Languages, Empires, Nations* is a forum that confronts established geocultural constructions, rethinks area studies and disciplinary boundaries, assesses convictions of the academy and of public policy, and correspondingly demands that the practices through which we produce knowledge and understanding about and from Latin America be subject to rigorous and critical scrutiny.

Jessaca B. Leinaweaver's study analyzes children's mobility, from fostering to adoption to commercial traffic, in Ayacucho, Peru. Worldwide, children's mobility is clearly affected by the desires and needs produced by capitalist economies and by increasing disparities between rich and poor at both local and international levels. Children's mobility in Peru is also intimately connected to European and North American desires for children that reproduce relations of benevolence and paternalism. In Peru today, children's movements are grounded in traditional and historic communal practices of the Ayllu, but they also interact with the moral codes that structure Euro-American families. This ethnography situates the choices made by Andean families within a broader framework of structural, cultural, and demographic transformations, and documents the social creativity involved, on the part of both kin and state representatives, when arranging the care of children whose social networks have been attenuated under the pressures of poverty and social inequality.

The Circulation of Children: Kinship, Adoption, and Morality in Andean Peru should be read not only by anthropologists interested in kinship in the Andes but also by scholars and students interested in globalization and in the continuing commodification of human lives. It will also be useful for those concerned with ethics, human rights, and the human consequences of an economic philosophy that preaches development and progress as the ultimate horizon of human happiness.

Acknowledgments

It's become commonplace to say, under this heading, how many people have contributed to improving this work and how impossible it is to give each one the sincere thanks they are due. I cannot improve upon this frequently printed sentiment; this is a book that would not have seen the light of day without cooperation, support, encouragement, and constructive criticism from countless individuals. I name some of you here, and to those who I have not named because of space or confidentiality restrictions, I want you to know that I am immeasurably appreciative, and hopefully not too *ingrata*. Errors or infelicities in this text are all my own, and are stubbornly present despite conscientious suggestions for improvement from one or more listed below.

I am grateful to everyone who has read some or all of this work, in one form or another, and shared their comments with me. This book began life as a dissertation for the Department of Anthropology at the University of Michigan (Leinaweaver 2005b), an intellectual environment which I prized for the support among graduate students, the generosity of faculty, and the interdisciplinary cross-pollination that characterized my years there. Powerful examples of these qualities can be found in the Adoption, Infertility, and Gender reading group at the University of Michigan's Institute for Research on Women and Gender, whose members I sincerely thank for a spirited discussion of my arguments and material in 2006, and the University of Michigan's Círculo Micaela Bastidas Phuyuqhawa, a node of Andean-ist collegiality where I first presented some of this material.

Gratitude of the most sincere sort goes to my dissertation committee members, each of whom contributed their own wisdom and style to this project. Bruce Mannheim's deep love and respect for Peru and its people is contagious, and I have long appreciated his support. Gillian Feeley-Harnik gave me extremely close readings of several chapters and drafts, and her warm enthusiasm has been irreplaceable. Marcia Inhorn's thoughtful comments helped me to pinpoint my own contributions to broader conversations on infertility, gender, and love. Sabine MacCormack has constantly been insightful, discerning, and supportive. Nicole Berry was a careful, demanding, and extremely productive writing partner during the dissertation stage and beyond. Jeanine Anderson, Erdmute Alber, Megan Callaghan, Janet Finn, Sallie Han, and Krista Van Vleet also made perceptive and helpful suggestions on some of this material in various forms. Mary Weismantel deserves especial gratitude for pushing me to rethink and rewrite so thoroughly, and I hope I have done her comments justice. Two other anonymous reviewers for Duke University Press provided immeasurably helpful and detailed comments, and I thank them for their thoughtful suggestions. Thanks to Irene Silverblatt for taking a look at this work, and to Valerie Millholland and her staff at Duke for their outstanding competence.

The research on which this book is based would have been impossible without a good deal of financial support. The University of Michigan (in particular the Rackham Graduate School, the Department of Anthropology, and the International Institute) supported research trips in June–August 2000 and July 2004. Twenty-two months of dissertation fieldwork (September 2001–July 2003) were generously supported by the following institutions: the Fulbright U.S. Student Program, the Wenner-Gren Foundation for Anthropological Research (Individual Research Grant No. 6805), the National Science Foundation (Dissertation Improvement Grant 0109060), and the Jacob K. Javits Fellowship Program at the U.S. Department of Education. My most recent visit to Peru, June–July 2006, was supported by the University Research Grants Program at the University of Manitoba, and I also thank the Centre on Aging for awarding me a course release at a critical time, along with my dean and department head at Manitoba who allowed me to arrange my courses so that I had a semester free to revise this book. Thanks also to the Office of the Dean at the University of Manitoba for financial support for this publication.

My gratitude and warm appreciation go to all those in Peru who collaborated with my research. I am thankful to the adoptive families who allowed me to accompany them in their Peruvian journeys, to several contacts in then-PROMUDEH, now-MIMDES, and especially to my dear friend Maria Luisa Bustamante and her hardworking staff at Ayacucho's adoption office. I also gratefully recognize the assistance of the directorship and employees of several orphanages and children's homes in Ayacucho, and of Nelly Alanya, a social worker at Ayacucho's family court. I very much appreciate the help of the dedicated and inexhaustible Sandra Soria at Lima's anti-child-trafficking NGO, who shared with me her vast files and introduced me to José Alvarado at MIMDES. Professors and staff at the San Cristobal of Huamanga National University (UNSCH) assisted in various ways, as did the anthropologist Juan Ossio Acuña, who helped me to affiliate with the Pontifical Catholic University of Peru (PUCP) in Lima. Most of all, I thank my dear *compadres*, *ahijados*, and *amigos queridos* from Socos, Ayacucho, and Lima, who welcomed me into their lives, and whom I cannot name because of my commitment of confidentiality. *¡Viva el Perú!*

My own interests and abilities have been shaped first and foremost by my family, whom I thank warmly and collectively for supporting and caring about me and my scholarly efforts. I am certain that my desire to learn more about adoption as a cross-culturally strong and meaningful way to create family ties grows directly out of being a part of three generations of adoptive families. For teaching me about the importance of adoption and acceptance in North American family life, I am grateful to Emma, Elwood, Mabel, Richard, Edna, Sam, Arlene, Bob, Connie, Jeff, Ellie, Joanna, Alexa, and Marisa. Finally, my partner Joshua Tucker is all over these pages—I thank him for his critical eye as a reader and colleague, and count myself ridiculously lucky to have him in my life.

A Note on Translation

This work is filtered through three languages: the English of this writing, the Spanish of the majority of interviews, interactions, and texts I analyzed, and the Quechua—Peru's most-spoken indigenous language—that the majority of my interlocutors use daily. The rural migrants to Ayacucho with whom I spoke are generally bilingual in Spanish and Quechua. I can operate in either language. My Quechua is passable (although my tentative statements were always revised, in complimentary fashion, in hilarious retellings); I studied Quechua for three consecutive years at the University of Michigan and took intensive Quechua in Cuzco in 1999. In Spanish, though, I am essentially fluent. My father, a theater professor, brought his wife and daughters along on his 1987 Fulbright to Costa Rica. I've spoken Spanish ever since, with reinforcement in high school courses, an undergraduate major, and an undergraduate semester abroad in Spain.

I tried to let informants choose what language they wished to speak in. The preference to speak in Spanish likely reflected both my own language abilities, and the historical and social meanings of speaking one language over another, which I address in the introduction. Though I rarely held conversations of any substantial length in Quechua, my familiarity with the language meant I could better understand the sometimes accented and idiomatic Spanish spoken by my migrant interlocutors. It also meant I was attuned to the multiplicities of meaning that bilinguals bring to the key words under discussion (for instance, the importing of the Spanish *familia* or "family" into Quechua as *phamillay*). Most importantly, my knowledge of and obvious appreciation for Quechua helped me to achieve a good rapport with my subjects.

All translations in the text, whether from Spanish-language books or from interviews, are my own, unless otherwise noted. I include in footnotes the Spanish originals of passages used from recorded interviews. If a quoted passage is not footnoted with the Spanish original, this indicates it was reconstructed from memories of conversations and from jotted notes; in these passages, I include only (and only occasionally) translations of key words because the original reconstruction may not be precisely accurate.

Introduction:

MOVING CHILDREN IN AYACUCHO

"This child is abandoned," argues a legal document filed in Ayacucho's family court at the beginning of the twenty-first century. Its filer, a lawyer for the Peruvian state's adoption office, took pains to spell out the details of the abandonment. The "progenitrix" has mental problems, he argues, and cannot responsibly care for her offspring, so the child has been placed in an orphanage (and note, *por favor,* the woman has other institutionalized children too). The lawyer clarifies: a woman in her sixties, living in an adobe house, has been caring both for the mother and the child and promises to continue to do so once the child is a little bit older. Her nephew, the woman claims, is the child's father. But, writes the lawyer, nowhere is this paternity recorded, so this elderly woman is outside the equation—and certainly not a legitimate caretaker. Furthermore, neither her age nor the condition of her home is appropriate for her to care for this minor. And the progenitrix is at risk of irresponsibly procreating other children, putting this little girl in danger. Finally, it's clear that the mother intends to leave the child with the sixty-year-old, evidencing a "lack of care about her upbringing and future education that proves the progenitrix's lack of moral and mental qualities."[1] These are the reasons, concludes the lawyer, for which the toddler—now nearly two years old—should be legally declared "abandoned" and therefore be made available for adoption.[2]

In the year's worth of adoption files I read while doing fieldwork in

Ayacucho, I found many documents like this one. Abandonment proceedings like this little girl's produce children who are legally adoptable, delight-
ing the hundreds of waiting families eager to embrace their future children.
But the lawyer's language oversimplifies the complex and intricate details of
the little girl's "abandonment," disregarding the many reasons that such
legal interventions are possible, and for whom they might be desirable.

Two themes have motivated my interpretation of files like this little
girl's. First, adoptions need to be understood in the context of the global
political economy. In political terms, international adoptions move children
from Third World sites of tragedy—of war, civil unrest, or disease—to First
World parents in an unbalanced exchange (Briggs n.d.; see also Kapstein
2003). In economic terms, adoptions often resemble a shifting of the resource that is children from poor people, or poor countries, to wealthy
ones. This is an imbalance that does not go unnoticed by young Peruvians
like my teenaged goddaughter Olivia, who remarked, "Here, in Peru, almost no one adopts because they have their own children. Instead, they
give in adoption to others."

Just as important, and perhaps more unsettling, is that adoptions are
produced—as is clear from the file described above—against another set of
relationships that an adoption lawyer must conscientiously define as inadequate. But those relationships—in this case, ties of affection, residence,
responsibility, and kinship between the little girl, her "progenitrix," and her
purported paternal great-aunt—are socially legitimate, and many impoverished Peruvians rely on such connections both for sheer survival and as they
strive for social and economic mobility. In other words, the clarity envisioned in this lawyer's well-meaning but life-changing statement does not
map neatly onto the complex and creative world of kinship and childhood
that I found in Ayacucho. I'll return to the little girl's abandonment narrative at the end of these pages and revisit it in light of this social world.

CHILD CIRCULATION: AN AHISTORY

Reading between the lines of the abandonment file described above, it's
clear that a child has been multiply relocated. She was first cared for by
her paternal great-aunt and was then placed in an orphanage, in what
was probably meant to be a short-term arrangement, before finally leaving

Peru via international adoption. The mobility of the young—their placement into the homes of relatives, state institutions, and adoptive families—
grounds important social relationships between and among individuals,
their communities, and the Peruvian state.

The little girl's first relocation—her reception by her purported father's
aunt—exemplifies a kinship practice that has been labeled "child circulation" by anthropologists working on similar kinds of relationships (Fonseca
1986: 15). In child circulation, as a child physically moves into a new home,
material, moral, and relational responsibilities are also transformed. Young
people accompany (*acompañar*)—or are taken in by (*recoger* or *acoger*)[3]—
their elders. Their transfer also provides children with access to instruction,
education, shelter, or affection. The hallmark of child circulation is coresidence, a physical closeness coupled with sharing the daily tasks of the
home: cooking, sweeping, combing hair. In this book, I focus on child
circulation as an active process leading to the formation, and transformation, of relatedness and sociality. The importance of child circulation to
building up social worlds in the Andes should be better understood before it
serves as the foundation for declaring a child "abandoned."

Moving a child from one house to another is described throughout the
Andean region with emphasis on the active "social work" done in or by the
transfer.[4] For example, the Aymara term for transferred children focuses
on the process of raising them: *wila wawat uywasta* ("raised since birth")
(Arnold 2002: 100). The Quichua term used by the Napo Runa in lowland
Ecuador is *apasha iñachina* ("to take and rear") (Uzendoski 2005). Urban
indigenous people in Ecuador use the Spanish terms *prestar* or *mandar*,
borrow / loan or send respectively, to refer to a similar practice of transferring children that bridges the rural-urban divide and is linked to begging (Swanson 2007). Adoption officials occasionally called such unoffi-
cial child-raising *prohijamiento*, or making-into-one's-child. The practice I
am calling "child circulation" is explicitly contrasted with *adopción*, a legal,
documented procedure. In my field sites, however, the moment of moving
to another household was usually described in a straightforward fashion,
often with the phrase "went to live with," *fui a vivir con*, so "child circulation" is a concept that I have imposed—for analytic and comparative reasons—on the various local terms and interpretations for children's
mobility.

Child circulation in Peru is also "a black statistic," or a complete un-known in terms of numbers, as a highly placed official in Peru's Ministry of Women and Human Development (Ministerio de la Mujer y del Desarrollo Humano, or MIMDES) remarked to me. Our conversation was structured around the official's primary concern, the far more sinister modality of child trafficking, of removing children from their natal homes for destinations unknown. But even for the more morally ambiguous or socially creative movements that I am calling child circulation, there are no reliable statistics indicating its frequency across Peru. I can say that I chose to study it because of the frequency with which I was offered babies on one of my first trips to the region, and also that I found near-ubiquitous confirmation of the practice in Andean ethnographies (e.g., Isbell 1978; Ossio 1992; Van Vleet 2008).[5]

Although child circulation is neither labeled with a discrete term nor quantifiable with censuses or surveys or other instruments of population control, it is nonetheless a widely observable and understandable practice. Producing children as mobile beings whose movements between house-holds can achieve a number of important ends, child circulation is a deliber-ate method of strengthening social ties, building an affective network that will remain key as a child matures into a world of poverty and distinction, and redistributing both the pleasures and constraints of parenting and being a child. Given the importance of family connections and the felt urgency of educating one's children among rural-to-urban migrants, there is an unas-sailable cultural logic to this practice.[6]

"Cultural logic" here implies that child circulation be seen as part of what Andeanists have held up as *lo andino,* practices of regional longstand-ing that, while always adapting to the historical moment, share some com-mon ethic (Gelles 2000: 12).[7] I suspect that child circulation has been part of the fabric of Andean lives, both pastoral and agricultural, both rural and urban, for centuries. The notion of the *ayllu,* the Andean family-based community that has largely faded from scholarly attention (Weismantel 2006), is one basis for imagining a large, flexible network within which children move. Child circulation within the *ayllu* would be invisible; it is only when communitarian groups begin to falter, fractured through their entrance into the political economy of the colony, the republic, or the contemporary neoliberal state, that such practices become marked. But they are largely undocumented and can be difficult to extract from the historical record.

The historical evidence that can be marshaled is spotty. Frank Salomon surmises that native political subunits in the north Andes, under Inca rule, "were linked by a web of nonhierarchical, symmetrical alliances in which such human transactions as exogamy and child loan paved the way for material transactions and, conceivably, military alliance" (1986: 137). The sixteenth-century chronicler Juan de Betanzos wrote that among the Inca, inopportunely born or abandoned children were reimagined as *çapçi churikuna* or "sons of the community," raised by women whose children had died and trained to work in the community's coca fields (1996 [1551]: 102–3). The historian James Lockhart indicates that during the early colonial period, Spanish women living in Peru were expected to raise *mestizo* "orphans" whose Spanish fathers, concerned with their own lineages and responsibility to kin, did not want them raised by their Indian mothers (see also Burns 1999: 16). Such children, called *criadas* or "raised," were often treated affectionately and well, but many were viewed as servants (Lockhart 1968: 185).[8] In eighteenth-century Peru, elite children born under socially disapproved circumstances were similarly labeled "orphan" or "abandoned" as a strategy to avoid public shame, then were integrated into the family (Twinam 1999). Nara Milanich's impressive archival work locates child circulation in late-nineteenth-century Chile, where elite orphans were raised by relatives, but "poor children were often nursed, reared, apprenticed, and 'rented' for service in the households of others" (2004: 313; see also Milanich 2002).[9] No archival smoking gun documents the longevity of child circulation in the Ayacucho region or in Peru more broadly, however, and it remains open for empirical verification.

THE TRAFFIC IN CHILDREN:
COMPADRAZGO AS SOCIAL ANALOGY

An analogous social form found throughout Latin America and Europe, rooted in both precolonial and Catholic morality, is that of *compadrazgo,* or coparenting.[10] *Compadrazgo* was historically described as "fictive," rhetorically distinct from "real" kin, but is now understood as a highly significant and very real way of growing and fortifying one's kindred. In *compadrazgo,*

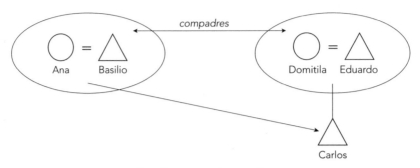

1. Simple diagram of *compadrazgo*.

two families—two houses—are linked through a public commitment and a kind of unbalanced reciprocity. For an illustration, consider the fictional family diagrammed in figure 1.[11] When Ana and Basilio become godparents (*padrino/madrina*) to Carlos (their godchild, or *ahijado/ahijada*), represented by the unidirectional arrow in the diagram, they also become co-parents (*compadre/comadre*) with Carlos's parents, Domitila and Eduardo, represented by the bidirectional arrow. Certainly, Ana and Basilio should spiritually parent Carlos and provide him with occasional gifts, but the most important ties created in this process are those between the *compadres*, the adults involved.

In an essay entitled "The Traffic in Women," Gayle Rubin, following Lévi-Strauss, brilliantly argued that men who exchange women in marriage are at base creating relationships between the distinct groups of men (1975: 174).[12] In *compadrazgo,* the conduit between two groups—the "traffic"—is in children.[13] In the diagram (figure 1), Ana, Basilio, Domitila, and Eduardo have entered into kinship with one another. The forms of address they use with each other will change, and so will the material implications of their relationship. An advantage of invoking *compadrazgo* as a tool for alliance building, over the marriages Rubin and Lévi-Strauss describe, is that *compadrazgo* is a nonexclusive relationship. Women (except in cases of polygamy) only enter one marriage at a time, limiting marriage as a tool for alliance. *Compadrazgo* relationships, on the other hand, can be formed on more than one ritual occasion. For example, in Ayacucho, the same couple may baptize a child, cut her hair for the first time, sponsor her first communion, and stand beside her at her marriage, strengthening their relationship through each event. Alternatively, people may choose different godparents for each occasion, broadening their web of relationships. In either case, a kinsperson's *compadres* may also be treated as kin (Delgado Sumar 1994), so the tie is not limited to the two adult couples and child.

As is typical for foreigners in the region, my partner and I were frequently called upon to become godparents—for first communions, middle-school graduations, and other such events—so we became incorporated into these kinship networks as well. On one such occasion, we agreed to baptize two little Ayacuchanas who lived in Lima. Their parents were kin to our *compadres* in Ayacucho, so it would have been difficult to say no—but upon agreeing, our Ayacuchana *comadre* laughed that we had gotten ourselves into a mess, because the girls are terrors![14]

At first it was difficult for us to grasp why we would be asked to be godparents by near-strangers, since my understanding of *compadrazgo* emphasized periodic visits and continuing social relations, something that would be hard to engage in across the miles. But we eventually came to realize that to "take advantage" of a foreigner in this way was part of the normal course of godparenting and was not immoral—for who could criticize parents for wanting their child to be connected to a godparent in a foreign land? For the Ayacuchanos we knew, acquiring a foreign godparent actualized the sharp class differentials between them and us—but this was a perfectly appropriate strategy. The anthropologists Sidney Mintz and Eric Wolf divided *compadrazgo* into the horizontal (or between relative equals—e.g., asking a neighbor or cousin to sponsor your marriage) and the vertical (across classes—e.g., the extremely common requests for teachers in small towns to become their pupils' godparent) (1950). In vertical *compadrazgo,* the child being godparented facilitates social relationships between adults that would otherwise be impossible (compare Schildkrout 1978). The relationships we entered into would be locally interpreted as uncomplicatedly vertical, owing to our privileged status as foreigners. Although we were often anxious about how little we felt we could provide our growing collection of godchildren, we received a great deal from our various *compadres,* from irreplaceable local connections to plate after plate of lovingly prepared, steaming food.

I saw both vertical and horizontal *compadrazgo* in Ayacucho, and child circulations could also go either way. Note, though, that *compadrazgo* (like child circulation) is never vertical in the "other direction"—the *padrinos* are always of an equal or higher social status than their new *compadres*. If they are of a higher social status, the child or parents may perform specific chores or labors for the *padrinos,* and the *padrinos* may give financial assistance and social guidance to their *ahijado*'s family. (These are "shoulds"— certainly, not all *compadrazgos* continue to be meaningful relationships.) But most of all, as Blanca, a teacher with four godchildren herself, informed me, "I have more family, the family grows, it gets bigger, I now have someone who says to me '*Comadre,* this, that, and the other.' " For Blanca and the other Ayacuchanos I knew, *compadrazgo* is a key producer of social life.

In a similar way, the fluid movement of a child from one house to another enacts a social relationship between those houses. The movement is not typically memorialized as is *compadrazgo,* via a church or civil ceremony,[15] but the transfer of a child—a socio-geographical transfer rather than an entirely spiritual one—is deeply meaningful nonetheless. Unlike the relations of adoption—where children must be legally severed from their natal families before their incorporation into a new and approved family can take place, in what the sociologist Sara Dorow calls a " 'serial monogamy' of national / familial kinship" (2006: 209)—in child circulation, two families are brought into, or articulated more deeply into, kinship with one another.

THE ANTHROPOLOGY OF RELATEDNESS

Over the history of anthropology, "kinship" has been a central trope, one of our most valued tools for discerning how small-scale societies are organized. Early anthropologists drew careful lines demarcating biologically determined genealogical kinship ("blood") from other kinds of relatedness, which are variously classified as "fictive" or "ritual" kinships. Similar to early attempts to theoretically distinguish gender (or the cultural differences between masculine and feminine) from sex (or the biological differences between males and females), kinship studies were grounded in the belief that blood ties are objective difference, and social ties are layered, as culture, on top of this biological and factual basis. In the 1970s, anthropologists began to reconnect the parts of culture that these theoretical distinctions had wrenched apart (Carsten 2000: 2), even as the anthropologist David Schneider informed the field that "kinship," far from an objective tool, was in fact nothing but Euro-American ideas about family, blood, sex, and biology dressed up as theory (1984: 154).[16] Only in the 1990s did anthropology return to questions of relatedness, or the network of relationships individuals draw on in the course of their daily lives, couched now in terms of choice, reproduction, and political economy. Now we're interested in how people conceive of their relatedness to one another, what that relatedness is made to do, and how it is embedded in global ideologies of reproduction (Ginsburg and Rapp 1995).

There is a tension between kinship as simultaneously "a theoretical concept and a social category" (Franklin and McKinnon 2001: 1), which is a source for creativity in theorizing relatedness. "Andean kinship" is a further narrowing of the category, already done skillfully in two key edited volumes (Bolton and Mayer 1977; Arnold 1997). By drawing attention to the specificities of Andean kinship, I hold "kinship" in play as both a locally meaningful notion and an analytical category. "Kinship" here means Ayacuchanos' sense of relatedness as simultaneously given and created, as both unconditional and fallible, and as thoroughly moral. For anthropologists, this book will contribute, above all, to kinship literature. It outlines a sense of becoming kin, over time, that involves the kindling and reinforcing of some interpersonal relationships, and the lessening or divesting of others. The analysis shifts between individuals' emotions and families' goals to the involvement of the state and international bodies, most poignantly portrayed in the adoption stories reconstructed here.

Adoption is a family-formation method that is familiar to many North American readers.[17] As I write this introduction, celebrity adoptions are splashed across the covers of the magazines at the supermarket checkout. The dramatic stories of the rich and famous—and overwhelmingly white—descending upon countries devastated by war, disease, and poverty underscore, like nothing else, the tight fit between adoption and the political economy. Yet adoption may also be familiar to readers from the lives of their own families or friends. Adoption, both transnational and domestic, is a method for creating the most intimate forms of relatedness, yet it is one that is explicitly framed and structured by global relationships, in particular the political and economic relations between countries and regions.

I began this introduction with the legally enshrined narrative of a little girl's abandonment, and though these archival details are all that are available to us, the files show that she would go on to be adopted by a couple who waited for her for many months and who welcomed her into their lives with joyful tears. Adoptions from Peru bring children to developed countries in North America and Europe and are carried out with reference both to domestic law and international treaties and conventions. Despite, or perhaps because of, the dynamics of this one-way flow of children, debate over international adoption engages both supporters, who argue that such adoptions help institutionalized and endangered children, and opponents, who interpret the relations produced in terms of colonialism, genocide, and exploitation (Freundlich 2000: 94). The findings of my ethnographic research in Peru complicate this dichotomy: through an examination of child circulation, the local meanings of institutionalization and the pointed critique of inequalities in adoption are grounded in a sense of this "sending country's" own historic tensions and debates.

STRUCTURAL AND POLITICAL VIOLENCE: HISTORIES OF RACE AND CLASS

Above all, these are debates about the future of Peru. The following chapter goes into more detail on the historic divisions in the country, tensions that can be traced at least back to the Spanish conquest of Peru in the sixteenth century, a colonial period marked by a contest over the cultural legitimacy of Andean beliefs and practices. The struggles that ensued would, under a different form, continue into the early part of the twentieth century in more scientific, even eugenic guises (Stepan 1991). From extirpation to stirpiculture, the history of Peru can be read as layer upon layer of overt and covert oppression of indigenous people.

It's difficult to define indigeneity in Peru, however, for two principal reasons. First, race and class closely intersect: "Indians" are poor. They have been poor ever since they were colonized by the Spanish, forced to labor on the colonists' vast land holdings even as they found their own fields ever shrinking and more marginalized. In 1969 President Velasco officially transformed *indios*, Indians, into *campesinos*, peasants—effectively sealing the link between indigeneity and mode of production (García 2005: 74). This strategy was meant to counteract historical racism; framing them as a class would call attention to the structural inequalities—Indians' position vis-à-vis the land and the national economy—that produced their poverty. Instead, the result was that prejudices and ethnic markers previously related to Indians were transferred to peasants, so that *campesino* became (and remains) a coded term for an indigenous person. While the state engages in some official promotion of indigenous cultures (for instance, maintaining traditional dance performances as part of the public school curriculum),[18] both urban *mestizos* and upwardly mobile indigenous youth eschew the *campesino / indio* subject position. Because it is a position so closely associated with poverty, talk about money and social class often implicates race without discussing it.

Following the link between indigeneity and mode of production formalized by Velasco and still retaining an important discursive role for the Peruvians I knew, in these pages I will refer to my interlocutors sometimes as indigenous and sometimes as working class or peasants. More often, however—and still following this deeply ingrained link—I refer to them as poor. Although race is muted, rarely addressed head-on, in the area where I worked, poverty is on everyone's mind. Although I will go on to interpret child circulation relative both to poverty and to racial mobility, it is worth noting that the Ayacuchanos I spoke with linked it most directly to poverty. In this interpretation, child circulation is partly an effort to build the layers of kinship and connectedness necessary to endure the challenges and tensions of growing up poor and indigenous in Peru. Kinship in Ayacucho, for poor and indigenous people immersed in isolation, indifference, and the violence of the civil war, was and is in no small part about surviving (Medick and Sabean 1984: 13).

A second reason indigeneity is a slippery category is that race and class markers—the visual, auditory, and communicative cues Peruvians use to situate others within everyday hierarchies—are locally defined, relational, evaluated contextually, and changeable over time (Orlove 1998: 202; Romero 2001: 29–30). Phenotypical markers—particular facial features, hair texture, and skin color—are part of this complex, although they cannot easily be read. For example, members of the urban *mestizo* elite in Ayacucho (*huamanguinos*) may appear based solely on phenotypical cues to be indigenous, yet are not locally evaluated as such. Within Peru, their perceived indigenous features only take precedence over other class markers in the context of relatively white Lima. By contrast, my interlocutors in Ayacucho were primarily rural-to-urban migrants, although in general they migrated from towns rather than rural villages. Most of them would have been evaluated as *campesinos* by urban *mestizos* (though would not have defined themselves in this way), because they bore various locally understood markers of indigeneity. Geographical origin isn't the only determinative feature here: clothing, language, food, the identification of kin, and a host of other criteria are evaluated by interlocutors to determine the social position of another. And in the pages that follow, I will occasionally refer to some of these markers in an effort to situate readers in the position of locals evaluating the ethnic position of the person described.

Huamanguinos hold all the cards when at home in Ayacucho and are particularly skilled at reading race and class of those around them. One *huamanguina* friend told me in a confidential manner about how when people come from the *chacra*, "which is what we call places like Socos," patience is essential in the face of their ignorance. Her new maid, from the countryside, had—the *huamanguina* said with kind understanding— urinated into the drain hole in the middle of the bathroom floor, rather than in the toilet. She had had to clean the floor together with the maid, instructing her in the ways of middle-class hygiene and actually sitting on the toilet to demonstrate: "When you are done, call me, and I'll show you how to make it all disappear" (on the interrelations of disgust and "moral hygienics" of the Indian in the city, see Weismantel 2001: 45 passim). Only a few months later, when I met the *huamanguina* in the marketplace, she told me that the "chica" was no longer with them—slowly folding her fingers into a fist in the signal connotative of thievery and accompanying it with a menacing frown. Such are the subtle violences done in the name of distinction.

In a system of vertical *compadrazgo* such as that described above, the new social relations created are unidirectional rather than reciprocal. So for instance, a resident of a small rural village might turn to a rural-to-urban migrant in his quest for a well-positioned godparent for his child. However, that migrant would be more likely to look to one of her children's teachers, or a muddling anthropologist—that is, someone she has evaluated as hierarchically superior on the complex race-class continuum. Yet, once again, the ethnic markers taken into consideration when selecting a *compadre* are not verbalized; these important decisions are never expressed in overt race or class terms. Preferences in *compadrazgo* or in child circulation are framed as opportunities for the child—a chance to become educated—in an association, between education and class, well documented elsewhere in the Andes (and one which will be taken up in chapters 1 and 5). And in this sense, race is mutable: becoming educated is a chance to divest oneself of some of the features that others could use to ascribe indigeneity.

Because these evaluations of race are made reflexively, quickly, without verbalization of the process, race is difficult to talk about and tricky to define. There are times when race does appear discursively, however—during rare moments of reflection, when intellectuals use the terms in self-identification, or, most frequently, in the context of criticizing others. The president of Peru during my fieldwork was Alejandro Toledo Manrique, a man with perceived indigenous features and a storied childhood as a shoe-shine boy who had risen to success via a Stanford advanced degree and a stint at the World Bank. Yet not long after his election victory had been hailed as a key symbolic marker in the incorporation of indigenous people into Peruvian mainstream society, his approval rates bottomed out and citizens disparaged him as an incompetent Indian or *cholo*.[19] In other words, my description of race and class as "relational," above, is materialized when a *relationship* like that between the people and their president is expressed, negatively, in racial terms.

Pejorative references to race do many things, but one of their most insidious effects is the concretization of the idea that opportunity and success are linked to not being indigenous. The other side of this coin is that social mobility[20] partly depends upon sloughing off the ethnic markers described above, the markers that others can use to place someone as Indian. María Elena García has argued that shedding the Quechua language is seen in this way, which is one reason that rural parents reject bilingual education programs that are intended to empower (García 2005). During my time in Ayacucho, I learned that child circulation often engages ideas about social mobility. When a child relocates to a more centrally located home where porcelain toilets are used and only Spanish is spoken, she has made a contextual move toward securing opportunity and, necessarily, divesting herself of certain claims to indigeneity.

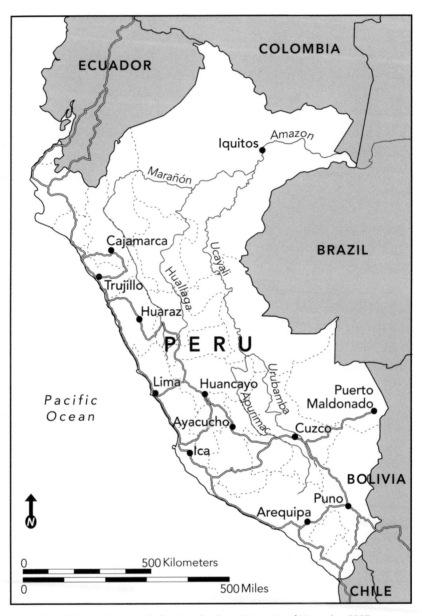

Map 1. Peru. Cartography by Douglas Fast, University of Manitoba, 2007.

A NOTE ON METHODS

I first flew into Ayacucho's small airport on a preliminary field trip in the summer of 2000. Generous funding meant I could live for nearly two years in Peru, from September 2001 to July 2003, with follow-up visits in the summers of 2004 and 2006. Though I spent some time visiting small towns, and a few months in Lima, the city of Ayacucho is my ethnographic home away from home. It boasts a famously beautiful colonial center, more than thirty-three churches admired by all during Holy Week, a friendly small-town feel, and an ever-expanding edge of outlying neighborhoods. Ayacucho is large—125,000 and growing—and is connected to other cities and towns near and far by a complex network of buses, an increasing number of paved roads, and the wires linking Telefónica's green-and-blue boxed phones and dozens of Internet cafés.

I spent most of my time in Ayacucho, but I also accompanied friends back to their villages and to Lima (see maps 1 and 2) and met their family members and village-mates who had remained behind or migrated ahead. I use these spatial metaphors intentionally—migration is concretely visualized as an evolutionary trajectory out of one's village and into the most advanced land of opportunity available, whether it be the city of Ayacucho, Peru's capital, or some faraway land. The rural-to-increasingly-urban migrants I spoke with were a "population" in social scientific terms, not because they all came from the same town or moved to the same city, but because they shared a relationship to jam-packed minivans rattling down dirt roads, and to hasty changes from urban jeans-jacket to old sweater suitable for rural tasks and back again.

My fieldwork methods closely mirrored local methods of communication and interaction, a happy coincidence that made the research a pleasure to carry out and, more importantly, meant that I was able to access everyday kinship practices in a locally understandable and "natural" fashion. For example, I met "subjects" through what network scholars call "snowball sampling" and what my interlocutors saw as introducing one friend to another. And the ethnographic method par excellence, participant-observation (analytically, watching while doing—sharing activities, but taking mental notes at the same time), was extremely effective for informally attending to the quiet realities of family making. Out of these

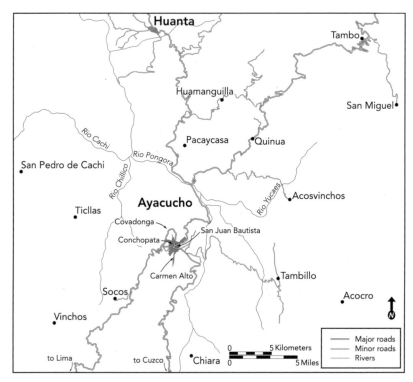

Map 2. Ayacucho and its environs. Cartography by Douglas Fast,
University of Manitoba, 2007.

initial and long-term ruminations, I eventually produced interviews and
surveys, seeking individuals' interpretations of their life courses to back up
my own impressions. Recorded interviews usually took place at my apart-
ment, but everyday conversations might happen anywhere, from sunny
rural cornfields to the roof of an unfinished brick house in a Lima shantytown, while my interlocutor ground bright red peppers or insisted I eat cold
corn kernels with white cheese or shooed a guinea pig away from my feet.

As other ethnographers have pointed out, the Andean region is very
much divided by gender, and it was simpler (and made more sense to my
informants) for me to speak primarily to women. The vast majority of my
interlocutors were also young: with some exceptions, they were almost all
in their early teens to their mid-twenties, by which point some had had
children of their own. Meanwhile, twenty-five when I came to Peru and

twenty-seven when I left, I was of an age that, had I been a rural migrant to Ayacucho, I might well have had children already. My childlessness was particularly inexplicable to many acquaintances because, in Ayacucho, I lived with my partner, an ethnomusicologist researching local music. For many Andeans, childlessness sparks pity; as a foreigner, my childlessness was somehow less painful for others, since I was already recognized as anomalous. A serious explanation for my childlessness—a desire to get established and become financially secure first—resonated strongly with many of the young women I spoke with, who also hoped to finish their studies before reproducing. But with older interlocutors I adopted a more humorous tack. After the first few interrogations, I quickly learned to present my body in agricultural and pastoral terms. "My 'field' is no good," I would say, "my guinea pigs don't reproduce, my cow doesn't give milk." And out of a blend of pity and longing, I received my share of offers—some joking, some seemingly serious—of other peoples' children. I ended up accepting exactly nine of these offers—not, of course, of children to take home as my own, but of godchildren.

My fieldworking relationship with almost everyone who graces these pages was one of friendship. Throughout, I often refer to my interlocutors as friends. Some were close confidants with whom I shared laughter, tears, and dozens if not hundreds of plates of food. Some became relatives through *compadrazgo*. I still e-mail, telephone, send money, and visit, and I miss them all. Anxious about misrepresenting them or compromising them, I have used pseudonyms for everyone except institutional representatives. More seasoned anthropologists of the Andes have set a powerful example by rejecting the protective use of pseudonyms as patronizing—for example, Linda Seligmann's writings on Peruvian market women express her deep desire to make readers understand that her interlocutors are *real* and "we live in the same world" (2004: 11). Although I, too, share this tendency, my reluctance to expose my friends to any sort of harm outweighs it.

ORGANIZATION OF THE BOOK

The book can be read in two halves, each composing one broad stroke explaining the phenomenon of child circulation in the Ayacucho region. The first part is made up of chapters 1–3; it inserts child circulation into different globalized histories, from a Peruvian history of racial conflict and violence in chapter 1 to an international story about children's rights, adoption, and orphans in chapters 2 and 3. In chapter 1, I sketch out the "ethnographic setting," the place under study, beginning with a wide-angle lens for a tour through Peruvian history, and narrowing to explain Ayacucho, both region and city, and how it evokes painful memories and stories of discrimination. In foregrounding the adoption process in chapter 2, I want to engage readers who are familiar with adoption from their own lives, friends, or common knowledge. Chapter 2 takes up not only the adoption process, and the complicated ways that parent and child are mutually produced for one another, but also some of the critiques—such as that of a Peruvian anti-child-trafficking NGO, itself also supported by funding and theory from the developed world. Coupled with the third chapter's description of the workings of local orphanages, chapter 2 shows how familiar understandings of how families are formed in the First World leave many angles of children's stories unconsidered. Finally, the idea of "orphan"— *wakcha,* an Andeanist keyword—is, in chapter 3, shown to be a complicated placeholder that traces a long history and a social definition of solitude. The orphanages in Ayacucho demonstrate that "orphans," just as in many parts of the world today, rarely have deceased parents but instead are the products of poverty, bureaucracy, and a decathecting of social relations.

The second half of the book consists of chapters 4–6, which hold fine-grained ethnography, detailed descriptions, and interpretations of the individual histories that intersect with the global narratives described in the book's first part. Each chapter takes up a keyword or two, a concept which I retain in the original Spanish and which I use to explore different angles on child circulation. Thus, in chapter 4, I approach child circulation from the receiving adult's point of view, showing how companionship (*compañía*) wards off a deeply feared solitude. I also address some of the tensions produced as relationships of child circulation begin: the economics of it, and the slowness of getting accustomed (*acostumbrando*) to a new life and a new positionality. The kinwork described in chapter 4 can be read against the prospective adopters' narratives of their desire for children, recounted in chapter 2, as well as against the unidirectionality of the orphanage, which in chapter 3 is described as nonreciprocal and therefore almost amoral. Next is chapter 5, which deals with the notion of *superarse,* a self-overcoming that should be read in conjunction with a sense of the poverty and structural violence described in chapter 1, and the race relations sketched out above. It is a theme that animates young people's (and their natal families') narrations of their own circulation. Finally, chapter 6 considers Ayacuchanos' interpretations of identity and belonging, *pertenecer,* based on paired assessments of documentation (or knowledge) and emotion. Tugging at themes already introduced in the explanation of abandonment proceedings in chapter 2, this chapter explores how Ayacuchanos know who they are, and where they fit into different social fabrics.

The book concludes with a short essay—chapter 7—that weaves together these disparate threads: violence and postwar poverty (chapter 1); the system of adoptions and orphanages and the specters of child traffic and labor (chapters 2 and 3); and Ayacuchano practices of child circulation, expressed through local theories about the production of relatedness, self-improvement, and their articulations with the Peruvian state (chapters 4, 5, and 6).

I tell two parallel stories throughout the book and return to them both in the conclusion. One is about child circulation as a meaningful social practice for the poor and indigenous both in Ayacucho and more widely in the Andes. Children's mobility is a strategy, though one not without its tensions and ambivalences, and the transfer of children achieves real and important social ends for everyone concerned. The other story is about the ways in which the state, NGOs, and the international arena critique and intervene in the practices I am calling "child circulation."

In the first story, child circulation is a way for receiving households to recruit labor, for sending households to negotiate the economic pressures of childrearing, and for young people to contribute to family goals and to mediate, forging dense and valued connections, between social groups. Child circulations occur within and help to shape the Peruvian political economy: buffeted by violence, aggressively globalizing, criss-crossed by migrants, overlaid with a wash of social connections meant to be drawn on in both good times and bad. The stories of individual children and their movements trace the broader history of the recent civil war, the interpersonal affections that tug at young people as they undertake new lives, the tensions of parental expectations, and the larger narratives of socioeconomic, racial, and geographic progress.

Running parallel to this ethnography is a second story, one in which the Peruvian state ignores, tolerates, or condemns child circulation. The history of race and class relations in the Andes, recounted above, makes the state's underlying motivation very clear. Child circulation is a practice endemic to Andean households—in this, it is one of the markers signaling "poor Indians." This is true even though child circulation binds together the rural indigenous poor and their urban kin or social patrons, and even though (or especially because) child circulation is perceived as a strategy to emerge out of the Indianness of poverty. In other words, child circulation is associated with the kind of people that the state has routinely mocked, despised, or slaughtered, most appallingly in its response to the Shining Path uprising. The kinship I take up in this book has been irrevocably colored by the material presented in the following chapter: Ayacucho's colonialist history, its economic isolation, and most recently its central role in the devastating civil war.

One.

AYACUCHO: HISTORIES OF VIOLENCE AND ETHNOGRAPHY

Lupe came over to my house for her interview with her husband and young son in tow. I served them the strange kinds of foods I liked to eat on a daily basis and they liked to sample out of morbid curiosity—this lunch included bruschetta and potato soup with dumplings. Afterward, we parked her husband in front of the VCR with a video I'd made of a fiesta in Lupe's father's hometown, and she brought her little son into the kitchen with me. He got on her lap and promptly fell asleep, as I switched on the recorder and Lupe began to tell me her life story.

She described the different relatives she'd lived with after her mother died when she was only a toddler: how she had felt in each home, the relationships and events that she remembered. One typical reminiscence went like this:

My aunt . . . hadn't yet finished high school, so she began to study high school, but at night, at nighttime. Sometimes I went with her, and sometimes I stayed alone in the house. During those times I cried—well, I was alone in the house, and it was dark, you know? It was scary, those were scary times, it was the time of danger, there were blackouts, there was no electricity, all that, and I stayed there crying by myself, I locked myself in my room and cried there, alone, missing my mother.[1]

Other people whose stories I recorded mentioned this "time of danger," the *tiempo de peligro*, in a similar way: a backdrop to a story, a few words to evoke a past time, a hastily sketched reminder—Lupe's "all that"—of a shared historical period. By the time I first traveled to Ayacucho in 1999, the blackouts and fear Lupe speaks of here had largely come to an end. And so I experienced my interlocutors' memories of Ayacucho's recent history only inasmuch as they wanted to share.[2] Though many people shared stories and testimonies with me almost urgently, others declined politely, and still others criticized the whole process of remembering and discussing it at all (Theidon 2004). And now, sorting through my jotted impressions, notes, and transcripts, I am reluctant to leave anything out, worried that to do so will be to diminish my friends' suffering and struggles. Sure that I won't be able to do their experiences justice, I can at least begin at the beginning.

A BRIEF HISTORY OF VIOLENCE

"When exactly did Peru screw itself?" a character asks in the Peruvian author and presidential also-ran Mario Vargas Llosa's well-known book *Conversation in the Cathedral* (1975 [1969]: 3). Many have tried to compose a satisfactory answer, beginning with Vargas Llosa, who has another character conclude, "This country got off to a bad start and it's going to end up bad" (140). The claim refers to the defining event in Peruvian history: an unequal meeting of indigenous South Americans and conquering Spanish. In public school, my friends learned that Peru once comprised all of Inca territory, and that every country carved from it was a robbery. Think how different Peru would be if the Spanish hadn't come, I was told: "much richer, and much bigger!" Thus Peru's poverty is historicized and politicized, imported back into a past everyone can share.

As Vargas Llosa suggests, the violence of that original encounter has also colored subsequent Peruvian history, which is marked by a series of bloody conflicts periodizing class and ethnic tensions. The Taki Unquy (singing sickness) movement, which began in 1560, revived pre-Inca gods and promoted pan-Andean solidarity in a critique of Spanish colonialism (Salomon 1999: 33). But in a recurring theme of Peruvian history, continuing ethnic fragmentation eventually defeated the movement, aided here by Viceroy Toledo's "reductions" of the natives via consolidation into Spanish-style villages (Stern 1982). José Gabriel Condorcanqui "Tupac Amaru" 's 1781 rebellion against oppressive Spanish rule also failed due to in-group tensions (Walker 1999) but did nothing to allay elite fears about Indian uprisings. Unruly natives had to be kept down, and racism became one of the cornerstones of nationalism and of postcolonial governmentality.

Peru attained what Peter Klarén refers to as a "reluctant independence" (2000: 99) in 1824. The internal conflicts that characterized failed rebellions during the colonial period were reproduced in the 1824 Battle of Ayacucho, where Peru's future citizens contested its independence on a plain outside the city of Huamanga (Walker 1999: 85, 107). In honor of this event, Ayacucho gained its postindependence moniker, shedding the colonial name Huamanga. (Today, locals use both city names interchangeably, as well as Ayacucho to refer to the department and Huamanga for the province. As I mentioned in the previous chapter, elite families of long standing in Ayacucho are still called *huamanguinos.*) Centralism prevailed over other possibilities (Walker 1999: 86–88, 106–8; Mendez G. 1993), producing a Peru where Indians continued to be separated from white elites. Relations of inequality were foregrounded once more in Peru's cataclysmic participation in the War of the Pacific (1879–83), which continues to resonate in the Peruvian national imaginary. The Peruvian upper classes ultimately sided with Chile precisely because they feared the loss of their property, to mobilized peasant masses, more than they feared the loss of national territory to Chile.[3]

Throughout this history a particular formulation of "the Peruvian nation" emerged, based in Lima: an exclusively *criollo* nation which monopolizes commerce and politics, even as it attempts to maintain indigenous peoples as a distinct and separate class. Whether Indians are portrayed as passive victims of state violence or as dangerous threats to the established order, they are painted as "a world apart, excluded from the nation, beyond the frontiers of the civilized" (Flores Galindo 1988: 301). This pervasive racism has excluded Indians from attaining full citizenship and inhibited the articulation of alternate senses of "Peruvian-ness."

The reified and incommensurable Indian / elite ethnic division, sharply drawn in early nation-building projects, continues to persist through discourses of geography (highlands / coast—see map 1), language (Quechua / Spanish), and culture (tradition / modernity, or Andean / *criollo*). This division is patently false on some levels—witness the ethnic, linguistic, and cultural heterogeneity reflected in the internal conflicts that tore apart resistance movements in the colonial period—but so much is rooted in it that it carries the weight of reality. Enrique Mayer (1992; see also de la Cadena 2000: 314) has pointed out that the homogenized and undifferentiated image of Indians is so difficult to contest because it is so widely accepted by opposing sectors of society, from the elite intellectual Mario Vargas Llosa (1983) to leftist revolutionaries of the Shining Path (Seligmann 1995: 9). The poverty of Andean Peru and the appalling levels of discrimination against indigenous Andeans are not recent phenomena; nor is it particularly surprising that this intense inequality bubbles over into horrific and periodic violence.

RINCÓN DE LOS MUERTOS: AYACUCHO IN THE PERUVIAN IMAGINARY

Every time I returned to Ayacucho, whether from a short visit to Lima or a longer stay with family in the United States, my bags were bursting with delicacies and amenities unavailable in the highlands. On the nine-hour bus trip, usually endured overnight, this was not usually an issue, but on the small planes that traversed the Andes a few days a week, extra fees were often required to compensate for the weight of my culinary indulgences. So I was especially glad to meet Rubén as we both waited in line at Lima's airport to check in for a flight to Ayacucho, when he kindly offered to share his weight limit with me.

Rubén introduced himself as an employee of the Ministry of the Interior in Lima, carrying only a small bag as he was coming for a day-long meeting. On the plane, as we flew over thirsty brown fields, he asked about my research. When I described my questions about child circulation practices and kinship strategies, he shook his head critically, arguing that my ethnographic contribution would be severely skewed—artificially misrepresenting the child circulation practices both quantitatively and qualitatively— simply because of my choice to work in the Ayacucho region.

Rubén was referring to two decades of Shining Path (Sendero Luminoso) insurrection, violent military reprisals, and human rights abuses that rocked Peru from the poorest highland communities to wealthy Lima suburbs. This period of danger and fear is what many Peruvians think of when Ayacucho is mentioned. The region's name is often translated from the Quechua as *rincón de los muertos* or corner of the dead (*aya* means corpse, *kuchu* is corner): a true descriptor during the 1980s and into the 1990s as Ayacucho came to signify terrorism, violence, and death. A character in the Peruvian author Santiago Roncagliolo's novel *Abril rojo* remarks of Ayacucho—remembering the warlike Chancas, the indigenous rebellions, the independence won on its soil and the still-fresh pain of Shining Path—"This place is condemned to be forever soaked in blood and fire" (2006: 245).[4]

The Shining Path movement began in Ayacucho. It was born and raised inside Huamanga's Marxist-identified public university, and led by the Maoist philosophy professor Abimael Guzmán,[5] who held a great deal of power within the university itself (Degregori 1997: 42, 48). Politically engaged students soon ventured into the countryside as teachers to convert rural youth to the revolution's aims.[6] Shining Path announced itself during the night of May 17, 1980. Disdainful of the newly recovered electoral system and of the state itself, armed insurgents burned the ballot boxes in Chuschi, a small town in central Ayacucho, and in so doing declared war upon a nation that barely noticed this first foray.

The movement grew rapidly, but although the war would spread throughout the country, the Ayacucho region bore the brunt of it. Seventy thousand Peruvians were killed or forcibly disappeared during the twenty years of violent political conflict between counterinsurgency forces and Shining Path, and a full one-third of them were from the department of Ayacucho (CVR 2003: Annex 2, 19).[7] The poor and indigenous suffered disproportionately; 75 percent of victims spoke Quechua as their first language (CVR 2003: 13). The effects on the poor are painfully ironic, given that Shining Path ostensibly intended to alleviate a sharply unequal distribution of wealth (Degregori 1997: 34). Instead, the war exacerbated poverty in a region that has long been one of the poorest areas of the country. One important effect of the violence was to increase migration out of the area (Skar 1994: 86); over 150,000 people in the Ayacucho region were displaced, moving from countryside to city, or from Ayacucho to Lima

(Revollar Añaños 2001: 18). Many thousands of children were orphaned during those years.[8]

The worst of the violence came to a close in the mid-1990s, after Alberto Fujimori was elected president and imposed a draconian series of policies diminishing civil rights. Guzmán was captured on Fujimori's watch, and the movement lost much of its influence. The effects of the violence—displacement, devastating loss, poverty—still linger throughout Peru and beyond, and strains of Shining Path are still present in Ayacucho's jungles today, having allied with the drug trade.

Enrique Mayer, in contrast to Vargas Llosa's stark statement, states, "I do not think that it is necessary to go back hundreds of years to find out when Peru screwed itself . . . Peru's inability to understand the Sendero Luminoso uprising and its inability to deal with Sendero Luminoso in realistic terms are at the heart" of the persistence of Peru's problems (1992: 207). That is, the Peruvian state, centered in coastal offices and ministries,[9] continues, to a large degree, to maintain a willful ignorance of Andean society as indigenous and irrelevant. And when a place like Ayacucho does come to the attention of the Limeño elite, it is often disparaged as backward and blood-soaked. One young woman with whom I spoke remembers, as a child, hearing then-president Alán Garcia say on television that the best way to fight terrorism would be to blow up Ayacucho.

In his critique, I understood Rubén to mean that the massive killings and migrations of the 1980s and early 1990s would have left thousands of Ayacuchano children orphaned, and families less able to pull together and care for them. Thus, by the ideals of objectivity and proper sampling strategies, both of which tend to be foregrounded in much of Peruvian social science, my research design was inherently flawed. Certainly, he was correct that the violence of the last two decades of the twentieth century affected the ways in which the kinship strategies under study could be used. But the history recounted here suggests that this was not the first time or place that child circulation practices have been adjusted to Peruvian sociopolitical realities. I chose to work in Ayacucho because I thought that a study of the interaction of historical and political processes with practices of kinship and social relations was essential for understanding the broad and overarching effects the war had on Peruvian lives.[10]

SOCOS, PROVINCE OF HUAMANGA, DEPARTMENT OF AYACUCHO

The horrors of the civil war devastated families and entire communities, and though several years have passed the memories persist in stories that are told and retold by survivors and their interlocutors. I especially saw this process of blending, shifting, altering stories in the community of Socos, less than one hour outside the city of Ayacucho. Unlike many communities in Ayacucho, Socos was never eradicated, so it never had to go through the politicized process of repopulation and return. But like many other towns in the region, it is a community marked by the experience of a massacre.

While doing preliminary fieldwork in Ayacucho in 2000, I met Madre Covadonga, a Spanish nun who has spent the better part of her life in Peru, and whose compassion during the violence is the stuff of local legend. I asked her about whether orphans were taken in by others during the violence, and she replied with the inspiring description of Socos, a community that had refused to parcel out its orphans and instead chose to raise them in the community. The story of the events that turned many Soqueños into orphans was fictionalized by the filmmaker Francisco Lombardi in his *Boca del Lobo* (1990), and it is also recounted in the documentary *State of Fear,* accompanied by the photographer Vera Lentz's images of the aftermath (Onís 2005). The Truth and Reconciliation Commission (Comisión de la Verdad y Reconciliación [CVR]) paid a visit to Socos in 2003 (see figure 2), and its findings, based on interviews with the victims' families, are recounted in the final report (CVR 2003, vol. 7, 2.1: 53–63).

In the years to come I would hear this story several times, both from adult community members and from their children who were too young to remember. It came up on one occasion in March 2003, when after a delicious lunch of semolina soup, *puca picante* (potatoes in a peanut-beet sauce), and *mote* (boiled corn kernels), conversation turned from upcoming travels to the war in Iraq. My college-aged friend Sarita commented that she wouldn't have believed people could kill other people until she saw it for herself, "en Sendero, en terrorismo." Turning to her mother, who was clearing the table wearing a comfortable green skirt and plastic flip-flops, she invited her, being *antigua,* to tell the stories. Her mother obliged, taking

2. Truth Commission worker with victims' families at massacre site, 2002.

a seat at the wooden table and recounting a story that by then I'd heard a few times over.

Love was in the air in a purportedly "red" neighborhood in Socos. A man and woman had run off together, and her parents wanted him to make things official. This meant a *yaykupakuy* ceremony, which would culminate in the young man traveling to her house and publicly asking her parents for her hand, in the traditional way. In November of 1983, the groom asked permission at the police post to hold this wedding-related event one night, and the whole neighborhood turned out to celebrate. Late that night, after most people had gone home, the police suddenly arrived, wearing masks. Perhaps they had originally forbidden the party as too dangerous, or perhaps the drunken partygoers began to criticize them in Quechua (a language they did not understand) for abusive police behavior typical of the era. The police forced the attendees to walk down into a crevasse by a stream (figure 2), perhaps ten or fifteen minutes away from the center of town, and shot them—old people and babies alike, entire families.

Community members might not have ever known what happened to their relatives, except for the seemingly miraculous survival of one old woman, who is no longer living today. She fell into a hole and wasn't shot;

hours later she dared to come back to town and denounce the police. What happened next varies depending on who is telling the story. Some say that police, disguised as Shining Path, took part in further killings—of insistent relatives demanding to know the fate of their loved ones, or of possible witnesses—"so that they could erase what they had done." Others mention the arrival of a kind of Truth Commission, to whom no one spoke out of fear of police reprisal.

Not until the early 1990s, after nearly ten years of police abuse, would the community create a *ronda* or self-defense committee. In the meantime, those who could moved or sent their children to Ayacucho, fearing death. Community members also took in the numerous orphaned children, who are all now grown: in a small agricultural community where children represent current and future laborers, the possibility of losing them to orphanages or adoptions went unconsidered. But for every uplifting outcome like that which occurred in the community of Socos, there were also many instances of children being scattered to the winds.

IN MEMORY: JOSEFA

In the stories I heard, memories are inscribed on the landscape. A town plaza became the setting of the torture and killing of teachers and town authorities, whose wakes townspeople did not attend out of fear of reprisal. A path between fields became the site of an accidental meeting with a terrorist column, which, uninterested, marched on by. Animal corrals or caves became hiding places where parents stashed their children when escaping from insurgents or military. Houses or entire towns became just memories, as people were uprooted from homes and families, having to leave suddenly in the middle of the night or after a threat. And some people's memories of home are colored by the recollection of clinging ineffectively to a mother's skirts when soldiers arrived, so that no one would take her away.

Flora, a slim and well-dressed secretary in her late twenties, became one of my closest friends during my time in Peru. I read her story before she told it to me; she had been encouraged by her employer to submit a typed testimonial in memorandum form to the Truth Commission. Later, I would interview both Flora and her younger sister, the protagonists of this narrative. Finally, bits of the story came up in conversations, as Flora and her siblings would refer back to the events of this day to explain parts of their personality, reasons for decisions made later in life, and feelings toward members of their extended family who didn't behave as they should have.

Flora was ten years old on the summer night in 1984 when a soldier came to her house, a cozy set of adobe rooms in another "red" town less than a day's journey from the city of Huamanga. Her mother, Josefa, was a widow whose husband had died of alcohol poisoning a year before, leaving her with four small children: Flora and her sister Tania, aged ten and seven, and their two little brothers, aged five and three. Josefa was known throughout the small district capital as an excellent cook, and in previous months she had cooked for both insurgents and military personnel. The soldier politely asked her to come and cook for the captain's birthday, but when she turned distractedly to look for her apron, he told her she wouldn't need it. She disappeared into the night, and did not return to her adobe house.

Flora, Josefa's eldest daughter, went to the barracks to ask after her mother. There, she was told that Josefa was in jail. Though this concerned them, the children were mainly relieved to hear she wasn't dead. But the next day, townspeople observed the soldiers digging a hole inside the barracks. When Josefa's children asked about it, they were told it was for a bathroom. Their dog, who loved Josefa dearly, lingered by the barracks until the soldiers shot him dead. Flora cried bitterly over her dog's corpse, but soon after this, when they were finally told that their mother had been killed, she found herself unable to cry. The soldiers refused to let the children see Josefa's body, saying it would traumatize them, so an aunt went to identify her instead. On her return, their aunt reported that sixteen people had been tortured and killed that night, and that pieces of Josefa's skin had been removed in the torture.

The aftermath of this devastating story, with whom the children stayed and what happened to them upon their orphaning, told much about how painstakingly constructed social networks became more fragile in wartime. Their mother's *compadres*, who had promised to care for her children if anything were to happen to her, now refused. Four days after Josefa's murder was revealed, the children's grandmother came to care for them for a time, but she was too elderly to bear this responsibility for long and so she eventually dispersed them among their older half-siblings. Each of the four has his or her own tale of the difficult days that lasted until the orphanage opened and they became part of its first cohort.

Josefa's four children are kind, generous, happy people today, but they have had to pass through difficult times in their struggles to stay together as a group. Periodically, fear, worry, or grief caused them and several others of my friends to weep openly. Tales of anorexia, abuse, and ongoing fear were couched in relation to these traumatic experiences and memories. The word *trauma* was adopted in the postwar vocabulary as a previously unavailable way to index such events without even having to give details, and people who have lived through these years often frame themselves as traumatized. The fear, trauma, and suffering caused by the internal warfare were ever-present in Ayacucho's landscape and the memories and conversations of people I met.

AYACUCHO AS ANTHROPOLOGICAL SITE

Unhappy histories like these have become the source material for an influx of foreign scholars like myself, each investigating various angles of Ayacuchano postwar existence. During the war, however, much of Peru was considered too dangerous for foreigners to conduct fieldwork. Fortunately, Peruvian scholars (e.g., Degregori [1997]; del Pino H. [1998]) and journalists (e.g., Gorriti [1999 / 1990]) produced a strong body of literature denominated "Senderology" at this time, presenting their perspectives on the violence. As Steve Stern has written, the sheer impact of Sendero forced scholars of the Andes to rethink their teleological historical approaches in an atmosphere of constant surprise and wonder (1998).

The disarray of the Ayacucho region also became symbolic of a disconnect between foreign social science and Andean realities. Holding up Billie Jean Isbell's ethnography of Chuschi (1978) as an example of work framed around an American anthropological paradigm of social maintenance, the anthropologist Orin Starn argued that "residues of paternalism and hierarchy persist in Andeanist discourse" (1992: 156). Starn's critical portrayal emerged from the general crisis of representation in anthropology and called for depictions of Andeans to become more complicated and sensitive to change. More recent scholarship takes a more measured position, such as

Paul Gelles's political assertion that relegating romanticizable parts of Andean culture to the margins is indefensible (2000: 12).

Prior to the violence, the Ayacuchano setting was never an especially prominent scholarly topic, by comparison with the Inca capital of Cuzco, which occupies much of Peru's intellectual landscape. The colonial-era efforts of Felipe Guaman Poma de Ayala, the indigenous artist and chronicler who called the region home, and the lyrical folkloric / ethnographic / novelistic / memoiristic work of the twentieth-century writer José María Arguedas are two notable sources of information about Ayacucho. But between them, there was little scholarly attention to this isolated and famously mestizo city, or its indigenous countryside. As Arguedas wrote in one ethnographic essay, Ayacucho is a very different site from those cities that produced the Peruvian *indigenismo* movement of the early twentieth century: *huamangino* architecture and dress "transmits the living sensation of how the Hispanic stamped its seal on Indian culture . . . with a capacity to convert that was much greater than in other highland cities of Peru" (1981 [1975]: 157).[11] If readers familiar with race relations elsewhere in the Andes find my portrayal of them in Ayacucho unfamiliar, it is likely because this city is defined both by its residents and by outsiders as peculiarly "Hispanic."

It was not until the much-heralded 1959 reopening of Ayacucho's Universidad Nacional San Cristóbal de Huamanga (UNSCH), which had closed during the War of the Pacific (1879–83), that social scientists, both local and foreign, would return to the region in force. By the 1970s, foreign graduate students like Billie Jean Isbell, John Earls, and David Scott Palmer worked alongside local scholars like Ulpiano Quispe and Salvador Palomino in the Ayacucho region. This expansive ethnological moment coincided with the Velasco land reform and efforts to integrate indigenous communities in Peru, events which created a demand for anthropological work on indigenous peoples (Salomon 1982). A central aim of Andean studies during the 1970s was to locate similarities throughout the region and elucidate a sort of Andean culture complex, *lo andino*, including traits shared with their Inca and pre-Inca ancestors, focusing mainly on ecology and social organization. Scholars at Ayacucho's university also met this demand, with more overtly politically engaged and critical work (see especially Díaz Martínez 1969) rooted in the structural, socioeconomic inequalities they saw on an everyday basis (Orlove response in Osterling and Martinez 1983: 353). Several of these Ayacuchano researchers would go on to play key roles in Sendero, which was finding its feet during this period.

COMING TO TERMS

In postviolence Ayacucho, the work of local social scientists can still be categorized broadly as either problem-focused (emphasizing the developmental and applied aspects, a choice which reflects both the kind of work available for anthropologists in Peru, as well as the kind of projects that can be funded locally) or community-based (as are many of the anthropology theses that come out of the university). Arce Castro's work on youth gangs (n.d.: 68–71, which lists eighty-three gangs in the city) exemplifies the problem-focused ethnography. Though the gang activity seemed minimal to me (in comparison with that present in North American cities), Ayacuchanos perceived it as a real threat, and many of them connected it directly to the years of violence, convinced that gang members were orphaned by the war.[12] But the researcher Cordula Strocka has conducted field research with youth gangs in Ayacucho and found no direct connection between violent family disruption and gang membership—the links between the war and contemporary gangs are indirect ones, in that the violence exacerbated poverty and filled the city with migrants, increasing unemployment and, she argues, blocking a transition to adult status that is possible mainly through wage labor (2006). Research on gangs and other perceived echoes of the war is one way in which Ayacuchanos are coming to terms with their recent and tragic past.

During the period of my fieldwork, at the turn of the twenty-first century, I witnessed several other ways that Peruvians are coming to terms with the years of violence. This happens poignantly through artistic expressions of every stripe, from the provocative wood-and-plaster *retablos* that chart the events of the violence (Toledo Brückmann 2003), to the sometimes daring lyrics of Ayacuchano protest music (Tucker 2005; Ritter 2002), to the stunning photography exhibited in Lima's Riva Agüero house in 2004 (Forero 2004), to the cinematic efforts of the local filmmaker Palito Ortega Matute (2006, 2000, 1997) and his peers.

But the most notable project of coming to terms is that carried out by the Truth Commission, established in 2001 during the transition presidency of Valentín Paniagua. The Commission takes an almost postmodern approach, seeking the moral or practical truth about the events of 1980–2000, situated in science, narrative, and intentionality (CVR 2003: 32). Between 2001 and 2003, a period coinciding with my fieldwork, the Commission held public audiences, collected the testimonies of survivors, and raised awareness through educating students in the classroom. It also sponsored public events, such as a free Concert for Memory, featuring performers whose works chronicle the social upheaval of those years, and an open-air allegorical performance by the Lima-based theatrical troupe Yuyachkani, both of which I saw in Ayacucho's central plaza. The findings of the Commission are brought to life in the stunning documentary *State of Fear* (Onís 2005).

Olivia was one of the high school seniors whose homeroom had been instructed by representatives of the Truth Commission in the tragic history of the violence. Her quick, blurry summation gives a sense of the gap between the Truth Commission's best intentions and the way they are received by Ayacuchanos:

> There was this guy, Abimael Guzman. I think Abimael Guzman was a student or teacher at the university here. Abimael Guzman wanted to change the government of Peru to a communist one, because there was a dictatorship. So they talked to the peasants and got them to help fight for this. But then things went bad and they started killing people who didn't agree with them. They killed everyone in Chuschi because they wouldn't tell the soldiers about Shining Path. Or maybe that was the soldiers who did that. And in Uchurraccay[13] they killed eight journalists who had gone to report on something. Shining Path killed them because they didn't want people to know about what was going on.

This level of uncertainty about the events reflects a broader sense of ambiguity and confusion. In the photographer Vera Lentz's words, "everything was unknown, there was no information . . . people did not always tell you what they were thinking because they were also scared" (Onís 2005). The state was initially reluctant to disseminate reports about the conflict, and many treated what little information they had with both skepticism and hope, sharing what they knew and imagining what they did not. Paradoxically, this heightened state of disinformation actually allowed Peruvians a broader range of options in choosing how to deal with fear and threats. Information that countered the logic of any one decision could be strategically disregarded in the face of uncertainty and deliberate obfuscation of events.

Given the vexed relationship to "information" during those years, Ayacuchanos' responses to the Truth Commission's anti-forgetting crusade are noteworthy. Several people adamantly defended their right to forget and to silence the events that had happened.[14] I often found this difficult to understand, having brought with me to Peru the perspective that attitudes toward the recent conflict were borne of the centuries of oppression and disenfranchisement of the indigenous, and that addressing this openly might lead to positive changes on a national level. But there is both a shame felt by those who were victims, who may choose to forget or elide their past as a conscious strategy for recovering—as well as a parallel embarrassment felt by those who did not overly suffer. The middle-class Ayacuchanos who were discriminated against in Lima, assumed to be terrorists, and prevented from traveling would prefer to forget the embarrassment of rural indiscretions like war; and it is *this* forgetting that the Truth Commission situates as especially problematic.

Nonetheless, during the period of my fieldwork there was a growing tension between the Truth Commission's insistence that Peruvians not only remember but reveal, and survivors' desires to forget or to remember only on their own terms. When its regional office opened in Ayacucho, expectations were high; many gave testimony imagining that it would open the door to individual reparations. As it became clear that material benefit would not accrue out of the structured remembering, the initial sense of hope felt by people in the area was quickly doused, and many who had lived through those difficult years declined to give testimony, saying that the wounds have healed and should not be reopened.[15] Palito Ortega's newest film, *El Rincón de los Inocentes* (Corner of the Innocent, playing on the translation of Ayacucho's name), tells yet another story of the violence— but caps it off with a cynical twist, the appearance of the "Truth Delegation," which turns out to be sloppy, uncaring, and self-interested (2005).

The city of Ayacucho today is a bustling regional capital of over 100,000 souls—though it remains oppressed by poverty, infrastructural problems, political crises, and social issues. By the time I arrived in Ayacucho, memories of the worst of the violence were nearly a decade old. People didn't focus on the war above all else in conversations: it wasn't the primary referent for most people I talked to, and many almost implied that times were harder now. The violence, in retrospect, was one crisis of many, and although it was devastating it paled against the constant of the struggle against poverty, discrimination, and disenfranchisement. Despite the recountings above, then, this is not a book about the violence. It's about how, in the context of the lines that are sometimes violently drawn between political power and indigenous oppression, families hope for a better future for their children. In the following chapter, I analyze the process of legal adoption as one careful and highly regulated way in which claims about a "better future" are enacted.

Two.

INTERNATIONAL ADOPTION:
THE GLOBALIZATION OF KINSHIP

In 2001, a couple arrived in Ayacucho from Europe to meet their new son. A taxi loaded to the gills with the couple, the man who represented their adoption agency in Peru, Ayacucho's adoption office social worker, and an eager anthropologist made its way to Huanta, a small city about an hour away from Ayacucho, where one of the region's children's homes—named after Pope John Paul II—sits just blocks from the central plaza (see map 2).

I tried to imagine what it was like for these new parents, seeing the road to Huanta for the first time. I noticed how dry the hills were, whites and browns and yellows, with a flash of green from each cactus or eucalyptus, and the bright yellow of the iconic broomflower. I took in the sight of animals young and old with fresh ribbons in their ears following the recent *herranza* ceremony. I saw the taxi driver driving on the wrong side of the road to avoid the potholes; and as we got to the police post on the road, the driver slung a fake seatbelt over his chest, announcing to me as I awkwardly straddled the gearshift, "Lady, I've been driving without one of these for forty years." As we barreled along, the social worker leaned back to advise the couple's representative to reserve a daytime return bus trip to Lima rather than overnight: that way they could see the scenery, and oh yes, plus it's safer. There had been another robbery—highwaymen stopping an interdepartmental bus and robbing its passengers—early this morning, and she was worried about them returning to Lima by night.

In Huanta, our group disembarked at the convent's unlabeled door, paying the taxi driver the established fare of S/.5 each—about $1.50 at the time. One of the nuns opened the door and welcomed us inside. She showed the couple to the bedroom of their small suite, which was furnished with a double bed, a large crib, and a private bathroom: the nuns offer reasonably priced room and board to the couples who come to Huanta to adopt their children. The couple put down their bags and the husband pulled out his video camera; I offered to run it so that he would be free to meet his new son. And so I saw the rest of the encounter through a black-and-white viewfinder, cinematically following the couple's half-block walk to the orphanage, down the narrow stairs, across an open patio, and into the room where the young boy was presented to his new parents. His mother instantly started to cry, and the couple took turns holding him.

For me, this whole experience was a cross between awkward and fascinating. I'd been introduced to the couple only moments before the trip by the adoption office social worker, who informed them I would be accompanying them on this major life event. Despite the presence of other nuns, another child, the social worker, and the representative, I felt that I didn't belong there observing this private and personal moment. Oddly, it reminded me of when I worked as a medical translator one summer and had to tell a woman that the baby she was carrying had died: like I ought not to have been there. At the time, I thought I was seeing the couple and their new son traverse that terrain from stranger to relative in a matter of moments. Reflecting now, it's clear that the couple already felt like parents during much of their long wait. Later, one of the nuns commented that the boy had been told for days prior to the arrival of the couple, "Your parents are coming for you!"—so he, too, was beginning to be constituted as the child of those parents before they would even meet.

After the emotional first meeting, several of us took photos, and the mother asked how to correctly pronounce the boy's name. As we all headed back to the convent, she told the social worker that he would keep the first name he had been given. I remarked to their agency's representative what a wonderful experience it had been to witness this, to see firsthand the joy on the couple's faces. He and the social worker both replied, stating their frustration that local foes of adoption do not see this and think that people just want to adopt to get laborers or organs.

Back in the living room of the couple's suite at the convent, we sat around and admired the child as he played with some of the toys the couple had brought from Europe. Eventually the boy fell asleep in his crib, and as his mother admired him, he shifted position so that his hands were behind his head, and she said with amazement, "That's how my husband sleeps!" Later, she told us that some time ago they had taken in a sickly stray kitten that has since grown quite large and healthy, with good food and care. "You adopted her," said the social worker, and I don't think anyone missed the deliberately drawn parallel.

Of course, a great deal had to happen before this couple could come to meet their child. The following sections trace the steps that may already be familiar to readers through personal experience or media representations. On one side of the equation, the couple had to go through a lengthy process designed to determine whether they would be appropriate parents. On the other side, the child had to be made available for adoption, which— whether he was orphaned, abandoned at birth, or removed from his home as a protective measure—would have involved a legal process extending over several months. And all of this—the detailed analysis of the parents, the legal production of a child for adoption, and the process through which they were matched together and finally legally made a family—is governed by national law and international conventions binding together Peru, the European country that the new family calls home, and the larger sphere of legal adoptions and children's rights. Adoption is not the only arena where the state and international standards intervene in kinship-making practices. It is merely one of the most obvious ones.[1]

JUMPING THROUGH HOOPS: HOW ADULTS BECOME POTENTIAL PARENTS

The files prepared by potential adoptive parents,[2] both international and domestic,[3] are a deliberate statement about their suitability as parents. When read against the narratives of child abandonment they're paired with, they support the construction of birth parents as unsuitable at the same time as they naturalize, or at least justify, adoptive parenthood. Hopeful adopters perform their appropriateness as future parents through the detailed documentation of their moral uprightness and through narratives of desire.

Parental worth is demonstrated as pre-adopters (the term given them by the adoption office) collect together all the required documents. They prove their identity through photocopies of passports and birth certificates. Letters of recommendation from friends and colleagues, coupled with clean police and judicial records, demonstrate their moral solvency. The pre-adopters document their own economic solvency through records of employment, pay stubs, or property tax receipts. They will include certificates of physical and mental health, produced by medical professionals. A written application includes a recounting of their respective educational histories (at least one parent is required to have completed a high school education). The adoption office evaluates the suitability of their home via a collection of photographs, which must include "the room of our future son and / or daughter."

The breadth of these documentary requirements is frequently frustrating to pre-adopters, who often see themselves as naturally worthy of receiving children (see Fonseca 2002b).[4] "There are no unplanned adoptions," adoptive couples like to say. Such a sentiment is echoed in one social worker's report on a couple that stated "I think that this case merits giving the opportunity to people who *truly deserve to be parents*" (emphasis mine). The conclusion of this portion of the file is that its producers deserve to be parents, in implicit contrast with the child's birth family.[5]

Applicants chart their desire to become parents through producing all the documents required, but this desire shines most brightly in the couple's narratives and in the reports prepared by social workers and psychologists who have interviewed and observed the couple. Ostensibly, the goal of these reports is to document that the prospective parents are emotionally stable, realistic, and open toward children and adoption. But these reports depict much more than this—they speak of desire, emptiness, and longing.

These emotions are conveyed under the clinical heading "Motivation for Adoption." The vast majority of people adopting internationally have suffered infertility, and this is usually cited as the reason for adoption. For example, one psychological report concluded that a couple had borne "disagreeable third party donor attempts to allow Mrs. S to experience the joy of conceiving a child" and considered that ultimately the couple had understood and discovered they could feel "truly father and mother to a child who came from another country." Mrs. S's struggles with infertility are coupled with an impassioned defense of the desire to have children, grounded in a happy family full of love to give a child. Nowhere is parental suitability performed more explicitly than in these narratives.

Such narratives position adoption as second best—that is, as a choice arrived at only after infertility treatments aimed at producing genetically related offspring have failed—but this positioning actually achieves something fundamental.[6] Appropriate parents are individuals who have demonstrated, through great personal sacrifice and pain, their intense desire to be parents. Paradoxically, the discursive positioning of adoption as second best makes a powerful claim about the person's deep desire to parent. Because parenting is understood within Euro-American folk ideology to be rooted in biology, having undergone such processes in the name of a never-conceived child demonstrates, even more clearly than turning immediately to adoption might, the desire to parent. That is, recounting unsuccessful fertility treatments is an important part of performing an urge to be a parent. This desire, in turn, is the foundation for approval of one's adoption application: the government's *Guide to Adoptions* explains that the only valid motivation for adoption is "when a person or couple wants to adopt a minor *out of love*" (PROMUDEH 2001; emphasis in the original).[7]

PRODUCING ADOPTABLE CHILDREN

Who are these children, the profound desire for whom animates each prospective parent's narrative? Above all, they are children who must be legally identified as "abandoned" or otherwise without parents. The process of locating, investigating, and labeling such children as abandoned is a joint endeavor, carried out in the intersections between the police, the courts, and the network of orphanages.

In 2006, I was permitted to interview three Ayacucho police personnel about their involvement with children. The most common issues regarding children that the police deal with regularly include glue sniffing and family violence; only a couple of children per month pass through their doors on the way, ultimately, to a stay at the orphanage, I was told. If they encounter a child, the brigadier informed me, they follow a specific process: notify the prosecuting attorney, interview the child about his or her provenance, and have the medical examiner inspect the child for signs of mistreatment (if the exam reveals indications of abuse, a *denuncia* will be filed against the parent). If the police cannot locate the child's guardians, they then file a report with the courts describing the child's moral and material abandonment, and the courts take over from there, interning the child in one of several children's homes.

The courts' role in producing adoptable children is carried out largely by staff social workers. I spoke with one of these, Nelly Alanya, who had worked for several years at Ayacucho's family court. She and a colleague carry out the guardianship investigations for the court; they do more than a hundred of these per year. (Adoption office staff are also involved with, or sometimes conduct, these investigations.) The guardianship investigation begins, Nelly told me, when the prosecuting attorney makes a formal *denuncia* or complaint. Confirming the police brigadier's explanation, she stated that at the time of the *denuncia*, the child will be placed into a children's home (or hospital, if the child is ill) for protection.[8]

In the investigation, the courts request statements from the police, Missing Persons, and the doctor who has attended the child. The case is announced via news and radio sources, seeking information or relatives. A social worker familiar with the child's case prepares a report, based on an interview and a visit or two (Nelly surmised this might represent around three hours of contact) and collects declarations from relatives or "interested parties," like the person who found the child, as well as from the child if he or she is old enough. The investigations take at least six months. (This means that if an infant is abandoned at the orphanage gates, he or she is not legally adoptable until at least six months of age.) The hardest part of this process, Nelly said, was finding the relatives: "I'm proud that we've never given up, we've searched house by house by house, and there's always someone who says, 'She was pregnant and she isn't any more.'"

Nelly's boss, a local judge, gave me permission to accompany Nelly on a guardianship investigation in 2003. An infant had been abandoned in an outlying neighborhood of Ayacucho and had been placed for protection in a local children's home. Nelly's job was to collect the child's history. As we sat together on the public bus that lumbered its way out of the downtown,

Nelly told me that on the preceding day the infant's young mother had come to her office and spilled out her entire story. She had gone to Ayacucho's jungle region in search of temporary work, a strategy employed by many young and impoverished people from the highlands, and one that this young woman probably embarked on to be able to afford what her baby would require. She was able to engage in this strategy in the first place because her sister was willing to take care of the infant. But when he began to cry, and the sister had no money for milk, she took the baby to the home of his presumed father. The young man's mother yelled angrily at her, and the sister was so frightened that she put down the baby and ran away. Later, when she sent a neighbor to retrieve the baby, she discovered that his grandmother had already taken him to the police and reported him abandoned. When the young woman returned from the jungle, she was horrified at what had transpired and went to the children's home where the baby had been installed, asking to be allowed to breastfeed him. She told Nelly that she had been denied this—that the officials at the home thought she might take the baby if she were allowed to feed him.

Nelly and I got off the bus and walked up a steep hill looking for the house. As we dodged the soccer ball that the neighborhood kids were kicking across the paved street, she told me that, the day before, she had informed the young woman that this was a wake-up call. Nelly insisted to the young woman that she get her child's father to legally recognize his son, which would not only give him a documented father,[9] but also the possibility for child support. "Sometimes bad things happen for a reason," she said she'd told the young woman.

Locating the house at last, Nelly knocked and we were ushered in by a small boy, who brought us to the room rented by the young woman. We sat together on a wooden bench, and I noticed how a partition made of woven black plastic shielded the sleeping area (where stacks of homespun cloth sacks and old sheepskins did double duty as mattresses) from the room's door and window. The room smelled good; Nelly asked if the pot bubbling on the gas stove contained the tuber *olluco*, and when the answer was yes she carefully recorded it in her hardcover notebook.

Nelly asked the young woman's sister, a young, thin, and shy-looking girl, for the details of the day in question. She recounted the story, adding that the baby's grandmother had angrily thrown water on her and gotten the baby wet, and that the father's brothers were there and "wanted to hit me," so she'd put down the baby and run away. Over and over, Nelly asked how she knew they wanted to hit her, but she simply repeated again, *"Me querían pegar."* Later, when I asked Nelly why the girl hadn't just held on to the baby when she ran away, she replied matter-of-factly that the girl had felt cornered and that she wouldn't be able to escape them if she were carrying the baby.

Nelly asked the young woman if she wanted her baby, and the answer was yes. She followed this with some guiding comments: how truth is best, and she should have told her mother about the baby; and how to handle the baby's father if he should try to get out of paying child support. In closing, Nelly invited the young woman to come down and talk to the free attorney provided by the courts, and we took our leave.

This case reveals much about the process of legally removing a child from its birth family. First, it's surprisingly easy to get a child placed in a children's home or orphanage. Police stations are key points of entry, following the process the brigadier described to me—they are nodes of the state, liberally scattered throughout the city and into the countryside. Also, the sour relationship that led the child to be temporarily classified as abandoned says a lot about the ease with which Peruvians employ state apparatuses in their own personal quarrels.[10] Second, the role of the social worker is paramount. Those I knew in Ayacucho, like Nelly, were generally from the region, competent in Quechua, and aware of the social dynamics that might cause a young woman to leave her baby with her sister, or to put down a baby before attempting escape. They aren't out to get as many adoptable babies as they can—perhaps obviously, they are there to help. Still, the scope of their influence is instructive, and a child who has inadvertently entered a children's home via the police station can, conceivably, end up adopted.

This investigation of a child's guardianship, only a small part of which I observed with Nelly, is converted into archival form and, if the child is ultimately declared abandoned, will form the child's half (complementing the prospective parents' dossier) of each complete adoption file. The case just described ended in a court-sanctioned reunification of birth mother and child; other cases end by terminating that relationship. In one such file, described at the beginning of this book, a child was deemed abandoned because of her mother's mental illness (and, apparently, associated promiscuity), the mother's willingness to leave her child with a caretaker, and the caretaker's lack of documented relationship with the child, advanced age, and rustic adobe home. These archives prove a child's abandonment, essentially through maligning his or her natal family, home conditions, and social network or community.

Take the file of Fiona, nine months old when she was taken by her two aunts and her mother to the orphanage in Vilcashuamán, a town located a few hours south of Ayacucho on a bumpy dirt road. Her aunts, described in the file as married, Catholic, illiterate farmers, told orphanage staff that they were surrendering this child because they, as principal caretakers, "have precarious finances and it is not possible for them to maintain said minor."[11] They informed staff that they did not know the identity of the child's father, as "the mother of said minor is mentally deficient, and it's possible she was tricked, but according to what the mother says, the father of the child is P——."[12] Legal documents in Fiona's file reflect that the courts opened her investigation less than two weeks after her aunts brought her to the orphanage, and requested a psychological exam on the mother, police reports of any complaints, the child's birth certificate, and publication of the proceedings in a legal newspaper. (The absence of any discussion of the child's paternity in the file suggests that the say-so of a mentally deficient peasant was not sufficient cause for social workers to pursue the identification and consultation of P——.)

Nearly six months later, the adoption office lawyer reiterated in documentary form that failing to carry out these tasks was a violation of the law and reminded all concerned parties to do their part. This seemed to do the trick, as shortly afterward the local hospital produced a psychological report on Fiona's mother (who, they explained, was "temporally disoriented"). This, coupled with the lack of visits by Fiona's mother or any of her kin to an orphanage a few hours' walk from their small village, was sufficient information for the adoption office lawyer to request that she be declared abandoned. The entire investigation took just over a year from the date on which Fiona was brought to the orphanage.

Thus, if a child's father is unknown, or she receives no family visits once interned in the orphanage, or her caretaker is elderly, or her mother is mentally ill, or her parents or extended family cannot, for lack of economic resources, "adequately maintain the child," the courts may argue that her current conditions are unsuitable for her upbringing. While many of these features of a child's life can be traced to her family's profound impoverishment, under Peruvian law, poverty cannot be the justification for removing a child.[13]

If children cannot be removed from their natal families simply on the basis of poverty, though, poverty's many expressions may certainly be marshaled to buttress a claim that a child is "morally and materially abandoned" —the legal catchphrase required in these cases. Police officers defined this term for me in 2006: it means, for them, that a child's parents are unconcerned, inattentive, do not provide the needed care or even engage in exploitation of a child by making him or her beg or work.[14] I pried further— was it possible, in their minds, for a child to be abandoned materially but not morally? The answer was a resounding no: "If I'm poor," said one officer, "I'll still take my child to the soup kitchen so he gets fed."

The police officer was arguing that because such minimal resources do exist—though in urban areas only, and only for those willing to take on the discomfort of receiving charity—poor parents alone bear responsibility if their children are not receiving adequate care. In this framework, a determination of a child as malnourished (and therefore "morally and materially abandoned") relies on surveillance of individual children's bodies in lieu of a sustained critique of the neoliberal structural adjustments of the 1990s that led to a notable decrease in children's consumption of calories and protein (Vásquez H. and Mendizabal O. 2002: 78). To deem a child abandoned is to criticize his or her parents, and their poverty, from the perspective of a neoliberal state that has proceeded to divest Peru of social infrastructure.[15]

Since poverty cannot be the basis for removing a child, the political economy of parental support is transmuted, in these files, into children who are "morally and materially abandoned" so that the act of removing a poor person's child can be normalized as moral and beneficial.[16] Of course, thousands of children live in similar situations: in homes that are not "legally constituted," in poverty, with older or only distantly related family members. Yet most of these children are not declared abandoned, because they do not officially come to the notice of the state. It is only once a child has appeared as "abandoned" on the state's radar (whether through temporary placement at an orphanage or entry into the police *comisaría*) that he

3. Family Planning billboard: "To plan your family is to love life."

or she is at risk of being permanently removed from his or her natal family, in the name of "the best interests of the child."

Setting aside the deeply disturbing racism and classism embedded in the judgment about which houses and families are appropriate, all of this might be less troubling—since it is, after all, explicitly done for the child's protection—if it were not carried out simultaneously with Peru's problematic national family planning program (see figure 3). Hundreds of thousands of women, primarily poor and indigenous, were sterilized in the 1990s, some against their will or in exchange for badly needed food or medicine (Leinaweaver 2005c; Sims 1998). The juxtaposition of the family planning program and the strategies for obtaining abandonment decrees suggests an underlying disdain for the reproductive practices of the poor that permeates the relationship impoverished Peruvians have with the state.

THE SETTING: WHEN PARENT MEETS CHILD

As an undergraduate, I worked summers in the social services, including a couple of stints at a program in Colorado designed to provide emergency Medicaid to low-income pregnant women. The first time I walked into Ayacucho's regional branch of the government-run adoption office, it brought me back to those social work days: low-budget surroundings lovingly spruced up by the staff. The adoption office itself, though part of the national-level government, was a small room wedged into the downtown building that housed Ayacucho's regional government offices. The stucco ceiling looked like it was on the verge of crumbling, the dented metal desk was made more appealing with a red cloth cover, and the weak yellow overhead lighting completed the image. A wooden cabinet with glass doors held the year's adoption files, to which the office coordinator gave me full access.[17]

The office was decorated with posters produced by the head office in Lima. These included my own favorite image (figure 4), a cartoon drawing of a worried-looking pregnant woman holding a child's hand, captioned "If you don't think you can assume your responsibility as a mother, don't listen to bad advice! Come to us, and together we can find a legal solution." Another announced the "Campaign of Birth Certificate Recording for Children and Adults," taking place during September and October of 2001, with impassioned pleas both in Quechua and in Spanish exhorting parents to officially register their children: "I exist, I want a name," "Without a name, what are you?" and "Citizens or shadows?"[18]

Approaching the front door of the regional government office, parrying the occasional flirtatious remark from security personnel ("Going to the adoption office, are you? Well, if you want to get a little baby, I can help you with *that*"), I visited that office dozens of times during my stay in Ayacucho. It was always bustling: the three-person staff had a lot of work on their hands. The director, social worker Maria Luisa Bustamante, could usually be found in her private office, partitioned off from the remainder of the small room. Two desks in the main part of the small office housed an on-staff lawyer (although she would later resign, to move with her partner and son out of the city, and a psychologist would take her desk) and a secretary, the latter of whom was "tipped" minimum wage by the salaried staff rather than having a contract of her own.

Señora Bustamante was the primary gatekeeper for information about adoptions in Ayacucho. She'd worked at the office for years and was widely admired in the city. A member of the first cohort of university students to graduate from Ayacucho's university when it reopened in 1959 after decades

4. PROMUDEH poster: "If you don't think you can assume your responsibility as a mother . . ." PROMUDEH (Ministerio de Promoción de la Mujer y del Desarrollo Humano / Ministry of Promotion of Women and Human Development).

of closed doors, she seemed to know everyone she passed on the street. She lived with her husband and youngest daughter in an attractive flat close to the center of town. Her warm smile, kindness, and Quechua language skills made the clientele of the adoption office, from angry parents whose children had been interned in the orphanage to young women seeking advice about how to reveal an unplanned pregnancy to their families, open up to her as if they'd known her for years. She is a respected community figure, almost a local matriarch, and was consistently generous and supportive to me. In fact, all members of the Ayacucho-based staff (figure 5) were friendly and helpful to me throughout my stint in Peru, and I left with a powerful impression that they truly care for the children and wish the best for them. They feel fortunate to have been entrusted with the mission of placing

5. Members of the Ayacucho adoption office staff raising awareness in the plaza.

children into families for their own protection and well-being, and their moral and professional excellence bolster the admittedly imperfect and potentially manipulable adoption process.

I remain very favorably impressed with the kindness, competence, and good sense of the staff I knew during my fieldwork and am sorry to report that all of them have since moved on. Staff positions in Peru's government offices are notoriously unstable. Every time polls are low or a new government is installed, offices are restructured and workers are shuffled, with what might almost be the weekly introduction of a new and lengthy acronym to describe some aspect of government. The branch of government overseeing adoptions is no exception, having metamorphosed from the Technical Secretariat of Adoptions (Secretaria Técnica de Adopciones, or STA) in 1992, to the Ministry for Promotion of Women and Human Development (Ministerio de Promoción de la Mujer y del Desarrollo Humano, or PROMUDEH) in 1996, to the Ministry for Women and Social Development (Ministerio de la Mujer y Desarrollo Social, or MIMDES) in 2002. These name and staff overhauls create local confusion over the work done by the office. They also contribute to a climate of job insecurity for the employees of the local adoption office, which was exacerbated by the effects of being chronically underfunded; the "tipping" of the secretary is indicative of a work environment where the state cannot even provide the most basic clerical support for a busy office doing the important work of, as the brochures advertise, "forming families."

This project of family formation—the adoption office staff's real labor—begins when a child's abandonment file is matched with a couple's dossier. This union occurs in a closed meeting that I was never permitted to observe, among six "persons of recognized moral and professional solvency," drawn from the legal, social work, and psychology fields and serving on an unpaid basis. This duly formed *consejo* reviews the files of at least two applicant couples for each child, meaning that there is an element of choice, expressed as a search for the better match. The parents' and child's files were created in separate instances and in separate time frames; they are only brought together through the efforts of an office, but the archival juxtaposition of parent and child information in the same file gives a teleological spin to the adoption, as if they were always meant to be together.

This sense of destiny is also observable at the first meeting between parents and child, which itself is codified by the observing social worker in a document titled "Empathy Report." The empathy reports I read drew on similar words and images: punctuality, nervousness, excitement, anxiety, emotion, happiness. It is read as an explicit performance: "The Adopters complied with their parental role, changing her diapers and preparing her bottle," read one. The child's reactions depend on the age, but in general the child is described as surprised, tranquil, and eventually smiling. Empathy is shorthand for behavior that indicates belonging, appropriate treatment, and the deliberate naturalization of the relationship that the anthropologist Signe Howell has referred to as "self-conscious kinship" (2001). These empathy reports are almost uniformly positive.

The adoption office staff is responsible for overseeing the remainder of the twenty-one-day, legally outlined process of adoption. The parents must sign a Decree of Transfer, officially accepting the child that was designated to them, which begins the period of Family Placement (*Colocación Familiar*) during which the child resides with them in their lodgings. The adoption office coordinator reports on this period as well, based on visits and interviews. The Family Placement Reports I read typically indicate that the child's incorporation into his or her new family has been easy, quick, and natural. These reports are also overwhelmingly favorable, and if so, are followed by the formal documentation of the adoption (an Administrative Resolution of Adoption) and the issuance of a new birth certificate, solidifying the child's new identity.

THE LEGAL BACKGROUND: BEST INTERESTS

"Historically, international adoption has sprouted in the aftermath of wars" (Kapstein 2003: 115), and in 1990, while still embroiled in the civil war described in the previous chapter, Peru was third only to South Korea and Colombia in the number of international adoptees it sent to the United States. In 1991, international outcry and political troubles made Romania the number-one sending country for one year only (see Kligman 1992), but as Peru had surpassed Colombia it remained in the number three position. But 1992 saw a new adoption law passed by the Peruvian legislature setting forth more stringent regulations, and Peru's numbers began to drop—it fell to fifth place, and in 1993 to eighth. By 1994 the flow of Peruvian adoptees to Europe and North America had been reduced to a trickle.

The three-week process just described is set forth in this new law, Peru's 1992 Code of the Child and Adolescent (Law 26981).[19] The Code states that adoptions in Peru shall be directed by the principle of the "best interests of the child and adolescent" (Article 9). As the inclusion of this well-worn phrase makes abundantly clear, Peruvian adoption law is shaped by numerous external codified statements. These include the Hague Convention on Intercountry Adoption (1993; see U.S. Committee 2000), the legal requirements of the ten foreign countries approved to receive Peruvian children in adoption, and the 1989 United Nations Convention on the Rights of the Child (CRC) (United Nations 1995).

Peruvians perform their state as modern by publicly and roundly celebrating these Rights of the Child—in the way so many things are celebrated —on one designated day with school decorations and a parade. A few weeks after arriving in Ayacucho, while in the main plaza on my way to the

6. Children's Rights Parade.

adoption office, a large parade of children spilled out into my path bearing a banner emblazoned with their kindergarten's name. They were divided into groups of two dozen children each, each group celebrating a specific Right of the Child: the right to play (children dressed as clowns, some on tricycles that faltered when going up the hill); the right to food (children dressed as vegetables and cans of evaporated milk); the right to a family (bearing signs like "I'm happy because I have a family" and "Mom, Dad, don't abandon me!," some dressed like grownups and pushing baby carriages); the right to a name (with signs in the vein of, "I'm happy to be named JUAN") (see figure 6). Though on more cynical days I would come to see such displays as a thinly veiled excuse to avoid teaching obligations, many Peruvians do take these rights, and their participation in celebratory parades thereof, very seriously; these are not empty gestures.

Despite the local enthusiasm, it's also clear that the CRC is written in the global language of "best interests" (Article 3) (Alston 1994).[20] Reflecting the numerical dominance of Western states and NGOs in the drafting of this document (LeBlanc 1995: 33, 42), that principle itself draws quite heavily on North American social work. Because, as LeBlanc has noted, "the drafters of the convention were primarily concerned with making the provisions compatible with their own domestic laws and not the other way around" (281), the Western states involved with the initial drafting of the convention found little to contest in the unqualified usage of the principle. The anthropologist Sharon Stephens has noted that claims to universal rights are problematic in terms of cultural relativism: Western principles of childhood can be perceived as antithetical to social norms in other cultures (1995: 36–39). So Peru's Code is a social "policy graft" (Kim et al. 2000: 139). Rather than drawing explicitly from local morality and materiality, it closely mirrors the universalizing frame found in the CRC. As Señora Bustamante explained to me, the basis of all of the efforts carried out in the adoption office is "the best interests of the child."

Stephens also argued that international declarations of children's rights such as the CRC can do real good in the lives of children who are in danger or who are oppressed on ethnic or religious grounds (1995: 40). In the arena of Peruvian adoption law, as well, the CRC has another important benefit: it provides a powerful tool for silencing critics. It suggests that Peru experiences parity with the rest of the global adoption scene, and that its laws are modern and progressive. The delays in adoption caused by careful adherence to the law prove to impatient waiting couples that the process is above-board. Constant references to the law stave off critiques of the adoption system and banish thoughts of corruption, randomness, and irregularity. Recourse to the CRC-based Code, for actions that may at times feel both questionable and almost immoral, is emphasized in order to suggest that the adoption process is regular, regulated, orderly, trustworthy, and valuable.

As adoption office workers throughout the country interpret and act upon Peru's Code, itself based on the United Nations' CRC, they are instrumental in fusing together international standards and national law. Through this carefully worded law, and every child abandonment or adoption that is justified in its name, the Peruvian state is engaging with the reproduction not only of families but, as seen in abandonment proceedings, of existing social relations of exploitation and domination.[21] And this legal and international basis for adoption represents a global ideology of reproduction that can sometimes come into serious conflict with the local forms of social reproduction practiced by impoverished highland Peruvians, as will be seen in the pages to come.

NEGOTIATING THE IRREGULAR: A TRAFFIC REPORT

In a historical moment in which "privatization synergized with other facets of structural adjustment to create a climate where nearly all quadrants of the Peruvian landscape were for sale" (Kim et al. 2000: 135), and in a globalized world where "the rich countries of the North have a great demand for our children in the countries of the South" (Ludeña Gonzalez 2000: 117), adoption staff work hard to minimize the impression that children, too, fall into one of those commoditized quadrants. The staff are quick to tell visitors that the adoption services they provide are free, and to criticize foreign adoption agencies that charge exorbitant fees and make money off the formal transfer of a child. They dismiss organ-trafficking rumors out of hand, thanks to the legal requirement that photos of adopted children be sent to them twice a year for the first few years.

But the rumors persist. One day, when I was out shopping with my godchildren, a shoe salesman came running out after me, blurting, "Señora, señora, is it true that foreigners take children away to cut them up?" He may have been joking, but there is no doubt that such things are widely believed (Briggs 2006). Days later, one of my *comadres* told me that she had read in the paper about how foreigners take Peruvian kids to raise, and when they grow up they are their servants. Organ trafficking and forced labor:[22] a pair of unhappy assumptions about adoption that resonate with Peruvians who wonder why outsiders are so eager to take in their children (see Fieweger 1991; Tate 1990).[23] Perhaps unsurprisingly given the history of their relations with the state, a sense of distrust seems to permeate the idea of adoption for many poor and indigenous Ayacuchanos.[24]

Not only do foreigners appear thrilled to adopt Peruvian children into their homes, they pay for the privilege! The economics of adoption are not well understood among the general public, and what is known comes not from government sources but from the media. For example, in a locally famous case (but one that is not among the worst offenders), the Spanish singer Isabel Pantoja adopted a Peruvian child and during my fieldwork was found to have paid the now-disgraced spymaster Vladimiro Montesinos thousands of dollars in connection with the process.

Rumors floated that in the early 1990s Ayacucho's orphanage personnel sold dozens of babies in adoption, against the will of the children's relatives. The nuns who run Ayacucho's main orphanage, perhaps understandably, rarely allow journalists inside today. In 1993, the press reported widely on a North American, James Gagel, who was said to be selling babies in Lima (see Constable 1997). I found it hard to believe that similar things might still be happening, given the careful tightening of the laws, but they are: during a recent visit to Peru the front pages were splashed with details of the police roundup of a doctor in Lima who convinced women not to abort, then sold their babies to French adoptive couples for a few thousand dollars, smoothing over the illegalities with the help of a corrupt judge or two (Salazar Vega 2006).

Thus, despite the diligent work of adoption office and family court staff, and the frequent discursive use of Peruvian law and the CRC to frame adoption proceedings as legitimate, critics of the process remain vocally unconvinced. Because of legal loopholes or infrastructural weaknesses, irregular adoptions can still slip through the cracks in the generally sound and well-intentioned Peruvian system, and this is one area of concern. A broader concern is with the fundamental inequalities underlying adoption everywhere, in that it involves transferring the children of poor people into the homes of those who are better off.

"Irregular" here means any movement of children that is not explicitly mandated by state authorities. Two factors lead to the production of irregular adoptions: time and intention. Time pressures frustrate adoption office staff and prospective parents alike, each of whom may interpret legally mandated delays as unnecessarily hampering the quick placement of abandoned children into loving families. But if a parent has placed a child in the orphanage only temporarily, and lives several days' walk from the nearest paved road or telephone, the slowness of the proceedings can be necessary to protect the parent's and child's interests. Intention refers to the spaces where legal guidelines and local realities diverge, or where the law does not offer an obvious answer. At these sticking points, each case is dealt with individually, and the results depend at least in part on the personal judgment of adoption office staff, leaving Peru's children to rely on their trustworthiness. To paraphrase one conscientious and thoughtful adoption worker, the law can be bent, to accommodate local realities, without breaking.

The inequalities that support adoption are visible, according to Gerardo Ludeña, an Ayacuchano lawyer who has written extensively on the subject, in Peru's lack of resources, infrastructure, and trained professionals (2000: 298–99). I had to agree with him on the issue of infrastructure: one file I read described a boy whose social worker requested that he be interned in a provincial children's home, "which is so full, the child should be adopted."

Ludeña's concerns about the legitimacy of adoption from a country that cannot afford to provide for its own children are echoed in the work of Sandra Soría, director during the period of my research of the Institute of Childhood and Family (Instituto de Infancia y Familia, henceforth IDEIF), a nongovernmental organization founded in 1989. IDEIF is housed in a two-story concrete house on the outskirts of Lima, on the very edge of the La Molina neighborhood, backed up against gray gravelly hills in an empty gated community. It represents Peru in an international campaign entitled "Stop Child Trafficking" (figure 7), spearheaded by the international federation Terre des Hommes.

IDEIF follows the Peruvian public at large in linking legal adoption practices with child trafficking. For Soría, the same procedure of seeking relatives prior to a declaration of abandonment, a procedure that can frustrate adoption office staff with its built-in delays, is uncomfortably rapid: "The child is put in a glass case to be seen and sold. He's labeled: adoptable child. In record time he is designated to a couple."[25] Soría was quick to say that her organization is not against adoptions—they think kids should have families that love them—but there are many irregularities that merit observation and repair.

Foes of child trafficking object to adoption, and relocations of children more generally, on moral grounds that take strength from economic and social critiques. Their objections rely—in a now-familiar trope—on international definitions and regulations. Until January 2007, Peru did not explicitly outlaw child trafficking; during my fieldwork, Peruvian laws against kidnapping only condemned obtaining a child through force or trickery, with economic ends.[26] "Nandito," essentially the IDEIF's poster boy, was stolen from his mother while she worked in a Callao market. Three months

7. Anti-child-trafficking poster at immigration on the
border with Chile. Photo by C. Joshua Tucker.

later he was found, being raised by a fellow marketer—a case which did not involve economic ends, so it could not be defined as "traffic" and the kidnapper's sentence was minimal. The IDEIF, Soría informed me, wanted child trafficking to be defined more broadly—in such a way that it does not rely on economic considerations.[27]

The challenge I faced in evaluating IDEIF's work was that the worst ends of child trafficking—sex tourism in jungle, tourist, and border departments, and labor exploitation for mining, adobe brick production, and gold-washing—appeared to be lumped together with historically and socially valid forms of child labor. Like her complicated position on adoption—reluctant, partial acceptance—Soría's position on child labor is vexed as well: "The child should not work. But he works, that's our reality." Therefore some forms (such as the "natural" labor in the fields, under a parent's guidance) are acceptable, and others should be regulated to ensure children can study and be fairly paid.

CONCLUSIONS: THE WORKINGS OF ADOPTION

Concerns about exploitative child labor are more closely connected to international adoption than it might first seem. Adoption and child trafficking are, respectively, official and extralegal forms of relocating a child within historically constituted and globalized social geographies. The state adoption office grounds its activities in a legal realm, while its critics emphasize the irregularities and economics of that realm and link them to a broader discourse critical of child trafficking. The most problematic tensions involve removing children from their families if those families are not judged to be appropriate. This is hardly unique to Peru—it can be found anywhere that "the imposition of hegemonic principles of fitness and stability on families organized according to alternative principles" reigns (Strong 2001: 480). This is an alarming reality in a national context in which the indigenous poor are devalued to the degree of forced sterilizations in the 1990s. In this context, the Peruvian government's involvement in reproduction has the unseemly appearance of either preventing the reproduction of the poorest and most indigenous, or—if this is not possible—systematically displacing their children into orphanages and ultimately channeling them into new and more socially appropriate families.

There are no unblemished characters in this larger process, but there are no real villains either. The anthropologist Ilana Gershon has written that adoption too often involves "a context in which state bureaucracy—a familiar villain for many anthropologists—intervenes negatively in a process that is in itself so flawed as to make most of the people involved unhappy" (2003: 442). It would be relatively easy to place the blame on the Peruvian state and its eagerness to jump on the bandwagon of international law and convention despite lacking the infrastructural muscle to fully back it up. Easy, too, to criticize the CRC itself for its ethnocentrism and structured inability to respond to the cultural idiosyncrasies that may arise in its implementation. But given Peru's position within the global political economy, I came away from my two years in the field cautiously optimistic.

On the ground in Peru, individual adoption workers are sharp and competent; they sometimes try to bend the global around the local, and they do so creatively and with their understanding of the children's needs always foremost in their thoughts. Court-appointed social workers aren't out to collect a quota of babies; in the home visit I observed, the social worker astutely ascertained the complex family situation, provided emotional and supportive guidance, and emphasized to me afterward how, in her view, if Peru could provide economic supports for the poor, there would be no abandoned children.

Prospective adoptive parents have a not uncomplicated desire for Peruvian children that may derive from Peru's image abroad, the reputation of its adoption program, or perceptions about the "quality" of the children available there. Their painstakingly assembled dossiers implicitly critique the parenting abilities of anyone who would abandon their beloved children-to-be, while those birth families, as I've suggested here, surrender their children either against their wishes—judged by a state that implicitly asserts the poor's inability to appropriately reproduce—or in the depths of poverty and social disenfranchisement.[28]

When I described the European couple's adoption that opened this chapter, which I'd found moving and illuminating, to a Peruvian friend, she responded, "It's sad that he can't be with his parents." Reacting quickly and defensively, I told her that the child had been abandoned on the orphanage steps. She said, "What a mother!" and resigned herself to the baby's trip overseas. Adoption is not an unknown in Ayacucho's social landscape; those I spoke to used it, more than anything, to talk about family connections and roles. My studies of adoption in Ayacucho opened doors to understanding more about how the families of children who are adopted might comprehend the process itself.

Three.

PUERICULTURE AND ANDEAN ORPHANHOOD

The lengthy process of declaring a child abandoned, described in the last chapter, can partly be interpreted as a response to the laws of the foreign countries approved for placement of Peruvian children. My own country, the United States, defines a child as an "orphan" for immigration purposes if:

(a) The child has no parents because of the death or disappearance of, abandonment or desertion by, or separation from or loss of both parents; or
(b) The sole or surviving parent is incapable of providing proper care and has, in writing, irrevocably released the child for emigration and adoption. (U.S. State Department 2004).[1]

"Orphan," a term that in the North American popular consciousness refers to a child whose parents are dead, thus legally means—for the purposes of transacting U.S. citizenship—a child whose parents are dead, absent, missing, or incapable. And the orphanage, an institution that first appeared in the Ayacucho region to deal with the smallest casualties of war, now contains children who, for the most part, have living parents. The best way to identify an orphan, in this new framework, may in fact be to look within the orphanages that were created to contain them (following Foucault 1965).

Both of these current realities can be traced, first, to the violence that drenched Ayacucho in the late twentieth century, and second, to the socioeconomic troubles that have plagued the region since—two conditions that are themselves rooted in a historic disenfranchisement of Andean peoples and cultures. Yet it was not so long ago that—as documented by shelves full of Andeanist ethnographies from the 1970s—the idea of "orphan," or *wakcha* in Quechua, meant something very much broader.

THE BIRTH OF THE ORPHANAGE

"The orphanage" in Ayacucho during the period of my fieldwork referred to one iconic institution: that which today sits on the city's outskirts, the Puericultorio Juan Andrés Vivanco Amorín (JAVA) (figure 8). Its namesake, a local politician and benefactor whom the orphanage's residents knew mainly as "Papá Andrés," envisioned, raised money for, founded, and directed this institution during the decade of the 1980s (figure 9).[2] Prior to that period, there were no orphanages in Ayacucho.[3] It was (and remains) common for Andeans to take in related children, so orphanages were unnecessary. But the war wreaked havoc on relatives' ability and desire to help, and orphanages soon sprang up to receive the smallest victims of the violence.

Papá Andrés's project took time to build, staff, and expand. A soup kitchen was inaugurated in 1980 to serve 250 children, and beds were installed for Josefa's children (introduced in chapter 1) and the others in the first cohort of 180 "true" (i.e., both father and mother had died) orphans who would soon enter the facility. Their needs were met by ten aides and social workers who had trained for three months in Lima's orphanage. The orphanage was supported financially by an impressive roster of donors: I was told that Peru's first lady laid the first stone in 1982, the Ministry of Agriculture donated the land on the outskirts of town, and each neighbor along the narrow passage out to the property was persuaded to donate the front portion of their property to widen the road. In 1986, the Peruvian author and politician Mario Vargas Llosa, shortly after having served on the commission on Uchurraccay (Vargas Llosa 1983), donated his sizable monetary Príncipe de Asturias prize to build a strong wall for "Señor Vivanco's orphanage."[4]

The violence colored the experience of the first few cohorts of orphans much more so than it does today. One orphan told me that the public was

8. The approach to Ayacucho's orphanage.

9. A mural of Papá Andrés has pride of place on the orphanage wall.

scandalized when a local newspaper published photos of the children play-ing cops-and-Shining-Path. I also heard that the staff was frightened when babies were left on the steps in baskets, accompanied by torn rags in the reds and yellows symbolic of Shining Path. And all the children knew very well why they were there; from time to time, they were instructed to share their stories with the other orphans. (Nélida was running with her mother, and a grenade fell on them, and then she was running without her mother. Elmer's parents' throats were slit in front of him and his siblings. Samuel developed a nervous stutter after watching his father being killed with an axe.)

Flora remembers a visit by President Garcia's wife. She had been in-structed to kiss the first lady in greeting, but she was so traumatized that she hid behind the door instead. Seeing the suspicious behavior, a guard concluded that she was a terrorist and held a gun to her head. The or-phanage director gritted her teeth, and after the first lady's entourage had departed, she informed the children that the first lady would not be wel-come again. In less than five minutes, said the nun, the first lady—by bringing with her an atmosphere of fear and a guard who would hold a gun to a child's head—had made them all feel like terrorists.

Papá Andrés's goal was to take in and care for these *huérfanos de ter-rorismo*, these orphans of terrorism. He strongly believed that the children ought to be raised in Ayacucho, learning professional or technical skills in the orphanage so that they could leave at age eighteen, independent and successful, and enter society. He was therefore deeply resentful of for-eigners who would arrive to legally adopt orphans and take them away, and he announced to the children that he didn't want anyone there to be adopted. The children, who loved him dearly and considered him their father, saw that it upset him and didn't want to be adopted either, although many were. More than fifteen years after his death (in memory of which a mass is celebrated annually), the children today still know who is respon-sible for them being there: if asked, they will chime out "Papá Andrés!"

In 1987, Papá Andrés, dying of lung cancer, reluctantly turned over administrative duties at the orphanage to the Santa Ana sisterhood of nuns. This sisterhood, led by Madre Susana (who would become the or-phanage director), had previously been headquartered at the San Juan de Dios church near the center of town, and Ayacucho's monsignor assigned them to the work of the orphanage. Ever since, the *madres,* everywhere identifiable by the light blue scarves fastened to their hair and the crosses pinned to their chests, have cared for the children. These new maternal figures were quite a contrast to the sometimes-chaotic civilian management of the loving Papá Andrés. The grown orphans I spoke to implied that the nuns were more orderly but less emotionally giving: contradictory figures, at once maternal and cold. In contrast, the orphanage social worker pronounced the nuns to be ideal caregivers: "They have no competing interests. A secular worker will always be most concerned with her own home, but not the *madres,* they're like mothers."[5]

From the early 1980s to the present, then, orphans have been confined and separated from the population at large in a philanthropic effort to aid them. Michel Foucault has written that philanthropy is unstable, in part because it masks the origins of the problems that it addresses (1965: 232). In essence, because state support of orphans and abandoned children is not guaranteed, they rely on the kindness of strangers—on donations from adoptive parents or wealthy patrons, and especially on the sponsorship of adoption agencies overseas. But because the donations have continued and the orphans are relatively isolated, Ayacuchanos generally do not perceive any weaknesses in the model.

Nine institutions that support orphans in Ayacucho proper, and five centralized children's homes in provincial towns, were active during my stay in Peru. They are mostly privately run, by the Catholic Church, willing volunteers, or other interest groups, and are funded by governmental, nongovernmental, and foreign aid. At least three institutions offer support rather than lodging: MIVED (a Protestant institution where war orphans receive tutoring), Wawakunamanta (a ten-year-old institution providing workshops and other support for street children), and the Albergue de Niños Inti Raymi (which teaches handicrafts to children). In Ayacucho, adolescent children may be housed in Inabif "Urpi" or Los Cachorros, and disabled children are often placed in two new homes, Los Gorriones and Casa Luz. Children are also occasionally placed at or through Ayacucho's Mormon churches. But the Puericultorio Juan Andrés Vivanco Amorín, the largest and oldest institution in town, is particularly iconic of these institutions that shape the characters and futures of the children held within their walls at the beginning of the twenty-first century.

A TOUR OF THE PREMISES

Take a bus or taxi out the same dirt road that leads to the airport, cemetery, and prison. A bus would cost fifty céntimos, the price of a local pay phone call or half an hour in the Internet *cabinas*; a taxi would run you S / .3, nearly one dollar at the time. The surrounding neighborhood is tinged in adobe browns and the dusty reds of new brick constructions that locally mark upward mobility, but that resemble poverty to the newly arrived international adoptive parents eager only to be united with their child.

If you've taken a taxi, you'll direct your driver to turn down the dirt alley marked by a sign painted on a brick wall advertising the primary school located within the orphanage (figure 8). As you turn down that alley, you'll see Mario Vargas Llosa's adobe-and-stucco wall surrounding the property, and two large metal doors painted dark green. The doors are bookended by murals depicting Papá Andrés and the Virgin Mary and are vigilantly guarded by a *watchiman* or guard in a brown uniform. At night he stays awake listening for the cries of babies who are left outside the doors, wrapped in blankets or tucked into fruit crates; but it's daytime, so opening a small portal in the center of the doors, he'll check your identification and call in to the orphanage to find out whether you've been cleared to enter the compound.

As you enter JAVA, you'll find the grounds to be spacious and open. Farm animals wander through the vegetable garden, and children play on the metal playground equipment donated by the Backus brewing company. The compound holds several buildings, whose walls are painted with images of children and biblical sayings. The buildings are clean and proudly modern, made of cement (referred to as *material noble*; see Colloredo-Mansfeld 1994 on architecture and Andean upward mobility), rather than the earlier adobe. The orphanage continues to be funded by private donors, although the state provides support in the form of numerous personnel, such as schoolteachers.[6]

By any local measure, JAVA is reasonably well funded, and gifts from foreign adoption agencies and adoptive families are gratefully accepted. Yet the donations are oddly skewed; a classroom of four- and five-year-olds was well supplied with toys but had no pencils. In October 2006, a mother of two Peruvian children posted to Yahoo's PeruAdopt listserv:

When we were in Peru we were instructed by our agency and the PRO-MUDEH [MIMDES's previous incarnation] to please not donate clothing to the orphanages. We thought we were helping by doing this. But, at least in the 3 orphanages we visited in 2000, they had a surplus of clothing. Yet they were doing without food in some cases . . . they put my [husband] to work sorting donations. The entire 3rd floor of one building was full of clothes, shoes and toys. Yet, they had trouble with school supplies. They had requested we bring a good can opener, as they were trying to prepare meals for 120 children with inadequate kitchen utensils (something I certainly never thought of) . . . Buying clothing for children is so much fun, and it feels like helping. But, I learned from this to call first and make sure it is helpful.

This mother critically analyzes her own good intentions—as she notes, bringing small clothes "feels like helping" but does not respond to the orphanage's felt needs.[7]

The nursery is located on the second floor of one of the buildings, its open door blocked by a child's gate. Two large, sunny rooms hold babies; on my visit (again, as I accompanied an adoptive couple who would meet their new son for the first time) the first room contained babies lying in strollers, and the second held pink and blue cribs. The first floor of this building holds offices (including one for a social worker), an infirmary, and a simple chapel with large windows along both sides, filled with wooden chairs and decked out with the proper accoutrements for Catholic worship.

The other buildings are dormitories, segregated by sex and internally divided by age, as Papá Andrés envisioned when he first dreamed up this orphanage. Within these lodgings, discourses of kinship flow freely. Age- and sex-sorted children share suites, a couple of bedrooms with bunk beds and a bathroom and playroom. The suite doors are labeled with a sign defining the inhabitants as a "Family." They're called this because, as the orphanage social worker told me, "it's like a family, where one lives." For example, "Familia Santa Ana" contains eight six-year-old girls. The different Families take turns performing the daily chores (wiping down the table, setting out the silverware). The orphans are casually referred to as siblings. In one adoption file, I saw a photograph of two adoptees posing with the other children and a nun, the image captioned "With all their siblings at

JAVA and the *madre* that cares for them." Leaving the orphanage is a move-ment toward the severance of these family ties; a photograph of the same two children at the orphanage after their adoption was captioned "At his first communion, with all his friends from the orphanage" (see Bouquet 2001 on the conventions of family photography).[8] While siblings abound, parental figures are lacking; despite the title *madre*, the nuns are not mis-taken for parents, and despite the occasional presence of male teachers or priests, there are no obvious fathers to fill Papá Andrés's shoes.

The children residing at the orphanage are well-dressed, thanks to the donations that flow in from around the world. There are more clothes here than staff know what to do with, as the mother quoted above expressed, so the children are bundled up till they sweat, yet they often don't fully wear out their clothes as the poor kids outside the walls must do. Clothing for special occasions is carefully stored, so that no additional expense is borne during frequent mass baptisms or confirmations. On such occasions, rela-tionships are formed between the orphanage residents and wealthy families or orphanage staff and associates, from which group the children's god-parents are drawn. In years to come, those godparents will be contacted in the summer with the children's clothing sizes, ensuring that Christmas presents will arrive in a timely and fitting manner, and guaranteeing that the orphans will never be underdressed.

In the orphanage, or *puericultorio,* children are cultivated: like the im-plications of the suffix in the words "agriculture" and "horticulture," "puer-iculture" is the act of raising, grooming, and tending to children. And puericulture, it turns out, is a term that has a weighty history in Latin America.[9] While the Puericultorio staff today may not be fully aware of their nominal links to eugenics, puericulture in fact means "the scientific cultivation of the child" (Stepan 1991: 77). A term developed in France at the turn of the last century, it connoted the application of scientific knowl-edge to the mother-child unit—both prior to and following birth—in order to promote the health and growth of the nation's population (ibid.).[10] As Nancy Leys Stepan writes, "Children especially were thought of as biological-political resources of the nation, and the state was regarded as having an obligation to regulate their health" (78). But while the original puericulturists conceived of women as essential to the proper rearing of their children, today's Peruvian *puericultorios* work with detached children.

The careful and thoroughly pedagogical cultivation of orphans leads to their socialization, via institutionalization and isolation from the "outside world."[11] They are cautiously protected as they are slowly permitted into the exterior realm of education, as the orphanage school offers instruction only through fourth grade. But other children in the few public schools orphans are channeled into (policing one another on the bus rides to and from classes) rarely include them in their socializing, meaning that adolescent orphans have schoolmates, not friends.

If the young residents are not adopted or retrieved by a relative, they eventually reach the age of majority (an age that seems to depend as much on the whim of a *madre* as on the youth's opportunities or chronological age) and leave to make their way in the world (Leinaweaver 2007b). Whether financially and emotionally unsupported, kept on as a part-time worker at the orphanage (boys do manual labor, girls care for children), or placed into the official foster care (*colocación familiar*) system (a kind of couched support resembling a household help position in a wealthy family's home),[12] leaving the orphanage is almost always a difficult and sudden change. One young orphanage "graduate" commented that only six women from the orphanage's first cohort are still childless and added that while she is grateful for everything she received there, she believes that the nuns fail to teach the children how to live once they leave. Out from under the protective umbrella of the institution, many young adults are faced with real challenges (unplanned pregnancy, homelessness, arrest) that the nuns had deliberately elided.

ORPHANS AND PERFORMATIVITY

One such challenge: figuring out who you are. Orphans who have left the institution are faced with several possibilities of how to identify, with various allegiances to be taken up, alliances to be forged and dismantled. For many Ayacuchanos, the expression "poor little orphan" (*pobre huerfanito*) is indelibly associated with a local cinematographic effort, the self-proclaimed "jewel of Ayacuchano film," ominously titled *Dios tarda pero no olvida* (God Takes His Time, But He Doesn't Forget) (Ortega Matute 1997). Such images of orphanhood do not go unnoticed by the youths they define; they shape the local understanding of these children into their adulthood.

The municipal auditorium was packed full on the October night in 2001 when I eagerly settled into my hard wooden seat to discover this cinematic jewel; more than a hundred people had paid the S/.5 ($1.75) admission to see a film that had been screened in the city many times before. (Local films share billing with Bollywood most weekends at Ayacucho's cinemas.) Said to be based on true events from 1984, the version I viewed in 2001 had a new format situating it as a local and historical classic: it had been expanded to include bookend shots of and voice-overs by the now-adolescent actor who had starred as eight-year-old Cirilo.

Cirilo's home is a tiny town, several hours on foot from the city of Ayacucho. The violence echoes throughout the first moments of the film, as he overhears his mother mention that people were killed in a village above theirs. Later, he dozes off in class (a nice touch of realism) and awakens only with the ringing of the church bell. To Ayacuchanos, hearing bells on a school day in the 1980s would instantly index the arrival of the *terroristas*, and in fact gun-toting, black-ski-mask-wearing toughs await them in the plaza. Once the villagers have assembled, the Shining Path militants yell at them, demanding money, livestock, and revolution against the government. A female Senderista shoots and kills Cirilo's father, and Cirilo and his mother weep.

When the Senderistas leave, villagers advise Cirilo's mother to take him to Ayacucho for safety. As she cannot leave her harvest duties, she sends him on by himself. He walks for hours, singing a song about an orphan, and musing, "I'm alone now, alone in life, and it's very sad." In Ayacucho he soon finds his aunt, who promises to help him study. His aunt also tries to bring his mother to join them, but she discovers that Cirilo's mother has also been killed by the Sendero. The rest of the movie depicts the orphaned boy's suffering. In Ayacucho, people make fun of his indigenous peasant attire: a *poncho* and a *chullu*. It is clothing associated with the countryside, rarely worn in this urban setting, and the cruel mocking further tightens the associations between rural/urban, indigenous/*mestizo*, poor/elite. The husband of Cirilo's city-dwelling aunt is a mean drunk who forbids Cirilo to go to school, instead making him sell gelatin treats and shine shoes on the streets. The uncle ultimately becomes abusive and Cirilo runs away, living in an abandoned house (another poignant sign of the times) and begging for food and work. Finally, Cirilo goes into a chapel, is touched by God, and becomes an altar boy, finding his family in the support of the Church.

This film, so familiar to working-class Ayacuchanos old and young, cements an image of the orphan's life that continues to compel audiences, years after the film's release. Cirilo is sad, alone, and poor; he eventually lives on the street, abandoned by his living relatives, and his only possible salvation—in a Peru which only provides hardships—is a religious one. Cinematic portrayals like Cirilo's entered popular consciousness to such a degree that a certain image of orphanhood had become solidified by the end of the war. This kind of orphanhood—poor, unkempt, and humble—is presented and performed as what the social theorist Judith Butler would call a prediscursive reality (1999 [1990]), that is, an already existing possibility for identity, and one with which those who have passed through Ayacucho's orphanage must decide how to engage.

Yet the children who most often perform as dirty and sad are likely to fit into a category which can overlap with, but is not congruent with, that of orphans. These are street children (niños de la calle, or callejeros, strays), children who are thought to be homeless and to sleep in the streets. The picture of an unkempt child beggar is one that resonates with donors and NGOs alike. But the vast majority of the youths who evoke orphanhood and homelessness in this way actually bring their earnings home to their parents every evening (Green 1998: 61).[13] By contrast, the residents of Ayacucho's orphanage are, for at least as long as they live there, taught to be clean, well-dressed, and polite.[14]

In a postwar context characterized by the struggle between forgetting and revealing, a child whose parents were killed in the war is now a young adult with conscious decisions to make about how to self-define. The identity of "orphan" can be strategically mobilized: a documented orphan status can enable the receipt of a deceased parent's state pension or give an advantage in the university application process. But this requires calling on tropes of victimhood, accepting shame that may come with asking for charity, and negotiating the public image of orphans as dirty and sad. Meanwhile, other orphans consciously refuse to use their status for political ends. One orphan who declined to join any political organization told me that "people have the right to forget the bad things that have happened to them." The alternative to strategic mobilization of the orphan identity thus becomes the silencing of the stigmatized past (following Goffman 1963) as a conscious strategy for surviving with dignity in the present.

A SOCIAL HISTORY OF PERUVIAN ORPHANHOOD

The orphans described here are classified and defined by possessing particular traits. Their parents are dead—most likely killed during the 1980s and 1990s in Peru's bloody civil war. They reside in one of the institutions built to shelter such children. And either they're sad and dirty, begging on the street, as many locals might tell you—or they are polite and nicely turned out, defying expectations but taking on a different burden, that of having to perform their identity in other ways, if they choose to make it public.

These characteristics may not surprise many middle-class North American readers, whose conception of orphans may come from characters like Little Orphan Annie or Oliver Twist who inhabit literary or cinematographic domains. Yet they are quite surprising when viewed in the light of what orphanhood used to mean throughout the Andes. The Quechua word *wakcha* is doubly defined as meaning both "orphan" and "poor."[15] Billie Jean Isbell's writings echo those of many other Andeanist ethnographers in her claim that the members of "the family that cannot mobilize reciprocal aid . . . are truly orphaned, not just materially poor" (1978: 76). *Wakcha* implies that someone without frequently enacted family connections is both socially and economically bereaved, epitomizing what Medick and Sabean have called "the relationship between emotional needs and material interest" (1984: 10).[16]

One of the earliest travelers to the Andean region took note of the term, shortly after the Spanish conquest. Juan de Betanzos recorded that *wakcha* referred to, among other meanings, the offspring of Inca men and nonroyal women (1996 [1551]: 71). This definition derived from Inca marriage policy, which blended social groups in gendered ways to produce children loyal to their mother's Inca line but respectful of their father's recently conquered group (Betanzos 1996 [1551]: 52, 58; Julien 2000: 33). Children not born of approved unions were ignored by their progenitors, referred to as "sons of the community," and raised by others. Prior to the Spanish conquest, family ties were ranked according to social position, and "orphan" meant relative to someone undesirable: as Betanzos puts it, "relatives of unfortunate people and low offspring" (1996 [1551]: 71). The close linkages between economic poverty and social undesirability seem to have held, as status—defined by birth—fed into and produced socioeconomic position.

This possibly autochthonous meaning of *wakcha* took on new meanings in the first decades of Spanish colonialism, when "the terms 'mestizo,' 'illegitimate' (*hijo ilegítimo, hijo natural*), 'orphan' (*huérfano*), and 'abandoned children' (*expósitos*) were synonymous. Orphaned *mestizos* were considered poor, not only because they had no money but also because they had no family connections" (van Deusen 2001: 40). The connection between orphans and illegitimacy is also noted in Montecino's work on postconquest Chile. *Wakcha,* she suggests, "comes from the Quechua *Huachay* [*sic*], to commit adultery. It designates the illegitimate child and the orphan. It is also used to refer to the animal that has been separated from its flock" (1996: 43n11).[17] Mannheim suspects the presence of a *mestizo* cultural translator somewhere in the chain that produced Montecino's claim, because "adultery" and "illegitimacy" are not concepts native to the Quechua language (personal communication). Instead, what is being glossed here as "illegitimate" actually refers to, in Betanzos's words, relatives of unfortunate people and low offspring.

A nineteenth-century dictionary of "Peruvianisms" defines both the word *wakcha* (*huacho* in the author's transliteration) and the word *botado* (thrown out) as "*expósito, hijo de la piedra* [abandoned, child of a stone]" (de Arona 1974 [1884]: 102, 235). *Expósito,* a word still in legal and popular use today to describe abandoned children, comes from the Latin term *expositio,* which is often "translated as 'exposure,' but this conveys a sense of risk or harm—'exposure' to danger, dying of 'exposure'—which is absent from the ancient terms . . . [which] meant simply 'putting out' or 'offering'; 'exposition' (e.g., as a display, or as the elaboration of an argument) is closer to their connotations than 'exposure' in the sense of 'suffering' . . . 'Exposing' a child was simply placing him outside the home, usually in a public place, where he would be noticed" (Boswell 1988: 25).

These layers of meaning, from the pre-conquest relatives of the unfortunate to the critiques of illegitimacy and racial mixing imported from Europe, in turn infuse the term today. For instance, Gavin Smith's writings on the pastoral community of Huasicancha document that, because wealth in a herding community meant owning animals, a *wakcha* was one who had *inherited* no animals (as a result of having no kin or being poor) and who had to obtain some as payment for labor (1989: 35).[18] Although scholars of the region continue to define the term as an individual who is simultaneously impoverished and kinless, it's clear in a closer read of the material that *wakchas* are not so much kinless as they are abandoned, ignored, or simply poor.

Throughout the history of *wakcha* in the Andes, the concept seems almost entirely unrelated to the image of a child whose two natal parents have died.[19] Such a loss would certainly be devastating, at any age, but it would not automatically entail poverty and loneliness, since everyone but those constituted as *wakchas* had relatives ready to take in a child. I have seen more than one elderly woman publicly weep as she lamented that her parents had recently died and she was therefore alone in the world—but the word chosen to describe this was the Quechua *sapalla,* all alone, rather than *wakcha.* Such mourners do not think of themselves as cut off from all kin, but they do need a way to voice their overpowering senses of loneliness. As Blanca (who lives with her grown daughter and often sees her siblings and nieces and nephews) put it, "I don't have a father, I don't have a mother, I don't have a husband: I have nothing."

On one chilly morning in a town not far from Ayacucho, my *comadre* Margarita fed her piglet, pitying it: "Poor little piggy, your belly is so full, you don't have a mother, you don't have a father—I'll be your mother." Then a moment later, she commented that her piglet's mother is enormous. Ever the literalist, I observed aloud that her pig in fact did have a mother. She replied matter-of-factly, "Yes, but *here* she's an orphan." In this sense, although the word *wakcha* is not customarily used to describe someone whose parents have died, it is employed metaphorically, as a much wider interpretation of what it is to be apart—physical separation from living parents, distance from home and homeland. This is best seen in a pair of musical examples, songs that are frequently heard in the city and its environs. "Huérfano pajarillo" (Little Orphan Bird), a classic Ayacuchano *huayno* song (dating to the early twentieth century, if not earlier), uses the Spanish word for orphan to represent a young person who's traveled far away and whose parents mourn his absence.[20] "Wakchaschay" (My Little Orphan), a Quechua-language *huayno* from the Cuzco region, paints a picture of a *wakcha* who has been purposefully abandoned by living parents.[21] In other words, *wakcha* refers not to an orphaned child—who in any case would be taken in by kin or community members—but, more poignantly, to someone who has lost all the support of his or her family.

The interpretation of *wakcha* as a state of apartness led at least one scholar with whom I spoke to argue that there is no word for *huérfano* in Quechua. Fermín Rivera, a professor of anthropology at the university in Ayacucho, retorted (when I tentatively proposed the word *wakcha*) that *wakcha* means poor, or possibly "a person who is being punished by his community and has no one to call on for help in the fields." In the social context Rivera described—an extended family, where uncles and aunts also share parenting rights and responsibilities, and where the word *tío,* uncle, means much more than it does to a monolingual Spanish speaker—even if *parents* die, no one is ever really orphaned. For Rivera, the only orphan, therefore, is one whose whole community (since communities are kin-based) has perished.[22]

Rivera's spirited negation of the possibility of orphanhood must have carried less weight during Peru's dirty war, when tens of thousands of children lost mothers and fathers. Many, most even, followed the traditional path to a relative, including to the baptism godparents whose duty it is to take in orphaned godchildren. But some communities were completely wiped out through massacre and migration, leaving no one to receive a child. Some relatives, while they might be willing to take in one child, could not commit to the care of three or four siblings together. Most pertinently, the war created new conditions of fear and want, which led more people to decline the responsibility of receiving a related child. And it was in this way—not when parents actually died, but when relatives would no longer take in a child—that orphans were created during the war, and that the meanings of *huérfano* and even *wakcha* were crystallized.

THE POSTWAR ORPHAN

Now that those years are beginning to fade into memory, it may be surprising that Ayacucho's orphanage still stands. But the orphanage has not only failed to close in the postwar context; it has veritably bustled and has been joined by ever more children's homes. During the two years that I was in

Ayacucho, three such homes opened to take in even more children of poverty and circumstance: one run by a French-Belgian couple, another by Argentine Protestants, and a third by a Dutch woman who had been adopted from Peru. In 2008, the international organization sos began to build a new home in the outskirts of Ayacucho.

The numerous children's homes in the region are no longer there to raise the children whose parents were killed during the violence. Instead, the relatives of today's young residents may have discovered a niche for the orphanage in the landscape of their survival strategies. Just as Milanich has argued for nineteenth-century Chile, in Ayacucho the orphanage and the "extra-institutional" practice of child circulation are not opposed but rather are closely linked, each supporting the other (2004: 321). That is, in many cases, young people are placed in orphanages as a relief for temporary hardship and will ultimately be retrieved by a parent or other relative. The Ayacuchano orphanage, built to house the products of war and fear, thus now serves almost as a babysitter (compare Fonseca 2002a: 402 for Brazil; see also Kligman 1995: 245 for this "pawn shop strategy" in Romania).[23]

When I attended a baptism for twelve orphanage children, I was puzzled to see four police in attendance. An older orphan explained to me that they were escorting jailed parents to attend their children's baptism. Older children will often enter the orphanage because their parents or responsible relatives are prevented from caring for them, whether through imprisonment, the economic need to migrate for labor, or the delicate negotiations brought on by remarriage. Babies might be abandoned at the orphanage door and never recorded officially. Other common sites of abandonment include hospitals, bars, or the airport (perhaps in the hope that a tourist could give the child a better life). These locations share the quality of being places where a baby will be quickly found and taken to the police, who notify the courts, where the child's future placement is determined. Both small and grown children enter orphanages in one of two ways. They are either delivered there directly by individuals (usually kin) or institutionalized through official (i.e., police and judicial) channels.

I view the abandonment of babies as a somewhat different (though not unrelated) phenomenon from the placement of older children at orphanages. Many of the same reasons given for entering into child circulation—such as a parent needing to find full-time work in order to ultimately provide for the child he or she is temporarily letting go—are echoed by those who use the orphanages. Señora Bustamante, the adoption office social worker, recounted to me numerous tales of young people whose entry into the orphanage made sense in the terms of child circulation. One young girl, Yessenia, was brought to a local children's home by her brother and guardian, who was worried about her coughing—it eventually turned out to be tuberculosis—and who saw the orphanage as the best place for prompt medical treatment. Another, Luci, spent much of her youth in the orphanage, so much so that it was a safe haven for her when she was being beaten by her brother's wife—on escaping from the house, she informed strangers that she was from the orphanage and needed help returning. Both Yessenia and Luci were already "circulated"—they were both being cared for by elder siblings—prior to entry into the orphanage.

Regular visits from relatives mean that a child cannot be declared legally abandoned and thus does not enter the adoption program, instead remaining in the orphanage until collected by a relative. But in some cases, visits may slowly decline and cease altogether. As the orphanage's social worker explained to me, "The mother must promise to visit weekly, Saturdays or Sundays, so the family tie isn't lost. And what happens is that at the beginning these mothers come three times a week. A month passes and they're now coming once a week. The next month they come every two weeks. There comes a moment when they no longer visit. Finally the mother disappears—and the child is a year and a half old, and is adopted."[24] Slow abandonment has explicit moral dimensions; unvisited children are "practically forgotten," poor single mothers ultimately "don't worry about them any more," and disabled children or those who are the product of incest or rape are "rejected by their progenitors" (Ludeña Gonzalez 2000: 161n157). A decline in visits means that a child can be declared legally abandoned, as described in the previous chapter; the postviolence orphanage is filled with those who have encountered this new concept. But quick declarations of abandonment are only feasible for infants; the abandonment paperwork of older children is frequently delayed. Despite the appearance of full orphanages, adoption workers must tell prospective parents that there are no children available for adoption. Children may reach adolescence before visits decrease enough that they may finally be declared abandoned, and at that point they are typically too old to be adopted.[25]

João Biehl's study of a Brazilian home for abandoned adults sensitively disentangles how social abandonment can come within the purview of common sense. What Biehl calls "amputations of a family member" are done overtly and without shame (2005: 296). Abandoned (or what Biehl calls "socially amputated") adults, of course, carry a different valence than do abandoned children. While the residents of the home Biehl studied, conceived of as being at the end of their life trajectories, are deemed value-less while simultaneously and ironically affirming the value of the human-ity tending to them (52), children who are legally deemed abandoned—to borrow the ugliness of Biehl's analogy, children who are "socially aborted" —are at the same time given value as ahistoric beings suitable for interna-tional adoption. They are also scored as endangered within a broader and equally international discourse of risk and childhood.

The contemporary orphanage is thus an option with its own risks and benefits, to be calculated against others. The benefits include the assurance of food, shelter, medical care, and education; the dangers include the pos-sibility that temporary can lead to permanent, if social workers and psy-chologists determine that the child receives too few visits or the parent is too poor ever to be able to reclaim the child. Children also see both risks (the orphanage is like a prison, there is no affection or love) and benefits (a stable source of food, a parent's diminished worry) of entering the or-phanage. The risks and benefits are not dissimilar to those entailed in temporarily placing a child with a relative, as in child circulation; and, for some, they are preferable (compare Rugh 1981: 231 for Egypt).

I reviewed records for the year 2002, maintained in the Ayacucho branch of the adoption office, revealing the numbers of children interned in the various children's homes dotting the region. The records also document exactly how many children received visits from relatives, and how often. JAVA held 103 full-time residents, 66 of whom received visits from relatives. The Casa Hogar "Juan Pablo II" in Huanta held 24 children, 11 of whom received visits. The Casa Hogar "Juan Pablo II" in Vilcashuamán held 19 children, 10 of whom received regular visits. The Hogar "Señor de Naza-reth" in Tambo held 32 children, 26 of whom received visits. Ayacucho's Inabif Hogar "Urpi" held 47 boys, 30 of whom received visits. The percent-age of children receiving visits went without note at the Casa Hogar "Juan Pablo II" in Huancapi (31 resident children), the Casa Juvenil de Ayacucho

(7 resident children), and Ayacucho's new Casa Hogar "Los Gorriones" (18 resident children).[26] In 2002, then, 281 children (about 45 percent male and 55 percent female) were wards of eight orphanages in the department of Ayacucho.[27] And of the institutions that reported visits, two-thirds of the resident children had some sort of regular contact with family.

The children in these homes and others today are orphans too—although many of their parents are still living. Situating them as orphans makes sense when viewed in light of the social history of the term *wakcha*. Despite, in many cases, having living parents, these children are orphaned when their ostensible kin become unable or unwilling to assume the responsibility of caring for a child. The inability to do so may happen through poverty—*wakcha*'s other meaning. The aftermath of the violence and the effects of globalization are blamed for the crushing poverty that continues to hold the Ayacucho region in its grasp. Peru effectively has no social welfare system, and the option of the orphanage is seen as a kind of social insurance, a backup or emergency plan for when crisis strikes or it is determined that the child needs something that a responsible kinsperson cannot provide. Social workers and adoption agents alike opined that if there were a widespread social welfare system to fight poverty at its source, rather than parceling out children to the patchwork collection of agencies that hope to help, there would be almost no need for orphanages and their kind at all.

CONCLUSIONS: PHILANTHROPY OR RECIPROCITY?

The historicized meaning of orphanhood in Peru suggests that orphans are those whose social network refuses to provide them with support when it is needed. This occurred more often during the years of violence, as Peruvians came to experience greater depths of poverty and insecurity, which necessitated the emergence of orphanages in the wartime social landscape. But this definition of orphanhood is also seen in the postwar period, when the persistence of labor migration and poverty means that people sometimes cannot care for their children.

The creation of orphanages, and the state pronouncements and practices of kinship this entailed, had significant effects on Ayacuchano families.

The orphanage is an isolated site of state support, directed only toward children of a certain age (and by extension, toward their social networks). Ayacuchanos, forced during wartime to accept the orphanage as a beneficial and philanthropic establishment, recognized the risks of incorporating orphanages into their postwar survival strategies.

One of the risks of temporarily using the orphanage is that it is one-way rather than an exchange. The use of state or philanthropic facilities does not provide a site for the child or her parents to reciprocate these immense gifts of food, shelter, care, and education. To use the orphanage is, in this sense, amoral. Where Andean morality is rooted in reciprocity, in the give-and-take of exchanges and connections and deeply embedded relations (see Alberti and Mayer 1974), an orphanage only gives. This is a serious social loss, although it is not always worded as such. The neglect of reciprocity that use of the orphanage entails is not at all at issue in the "extra-institutional" forms of child care and exchange to which I now turn.

Four.

COMPANIONSHIP AND CUSTOM:
THE MECHANICS OF CHILD CIRCULATION

When I first met teenaged Reyna, in my second month of field-work in Peru, I thought she was Cristina's maid. As I reread my field notes I can see myself wondering who she is. The notes describe her as "acting like a *muchacha*, answering the phone and the door and running to buy stuff, but also a loved one, who sits around with the group when she's not doing errands—is she related? what is her position? where does she live?"

Slowly as I continued to visit the extended family, I observed more of Reyna's life. She laboriously hand-washes the household's laundry, including her own school uniform, and she stays home when others leave so the house isn't unattended and the pets are cared for. She knows where the key is that unlocks the telephone's wooden cover, preventing its costly unauthorized use for dialing out. When I asked Cristina's niece Olivia if Reyna was her cousin, she answered, "Yes . . . no. Not by blood, but by treatment. Not by last name, either." And Olivia's brother called Reyna "Aunt Cristina's . . . well, like her granddaughter. But she *is* a relative, because Reyna's father is Aunt Cristina's godson."[1]

Within the context of Peru's complicated racial landscape, described in the introduction, Reyna bears many of the markers upon which urban *mestizos* would draw to define her as indigenous. She is a pretty young woman whose Spanish is tinged with a strong Quechua accent. Her parents and five siblings live in a small town two hours from Ayacucho, where her mother keeps house and raises three young children (Reyna's two older siblings are married and travel around the province to work) and her father, Carlos, finds work where he can, including laboring on the construction of a new natural gas pipeline.

Reyna's father, Carlos, is Cristina's godson. By the logic of *compadrazgo* described in the introduction, then, Cristina and Carlos were kin. Over the years, their relationship had grown and strengthened: she had taken him in when he moved to town to study as a youth and housed his sons years later when they wanted to study in the city, and she provided a city "home" for his family whenever they needed it, in return for their help in various labors. To Reyna, Cristina—her father's godmother—was like a grand-mother, a city-dwelling, reasonably bilingual woman with several grown children.

Cristina, a widow in her mid-sixties, had been living in Ayacucho for probably thirty years; before migrating to the city, she had lived in her small town, which today is only an hour from Ayacucho thanks to paved roads and fairly regular bus service. She wears braids, a felt hat, and a heavy *pollera* skirt—ethnic markers which inform strangers in the city of her indigeneity. What's more, she speaks Quechua more often than Spanish, and she will chew coca on occasion. She also participates in the urban economy, owns a telephone, and speaks proudly of her six adult children—four of whom have migrated to Europe. "Shame comes from leaving elderly parents without young people to help around the house and to bring joy to it" (Weismantel 1988: 170), so, as befits responsible Andean grown children, her own children sought ways to remedy her solitude. First, a grandson accompanied her while his parents worked to carve out their new life in Europe. But when he turned seven and began telling his parents that Cristina was his real mother, they came and collected him in order to nip this in the bud (Leinaweaver n.d.). This left Cristina unaccompanied once more, a situation that her children felt was untenable.

Cristina's sons took steps to see that she would not be alone for long, asking Reyna to accompany their mother. As Cristina's teenage niece recalled, Reyna came to Ayacucho three years ago "well, because my aunt was alone." Because of the rules of Andean godparenting, Reyna was a reasonable target of this request. Her father, beholden to Cristina for the layers of supportive reciprocity that had built up for years to form a strong relationship, would be reluctant to say no.

So Reyna moved into the house of the woman she now addresses as "Ma," in a dusty hillside neighborhood of Ayacucho. (Although the neighborhood is a poor and marginal one, Cristina's house is brick and concrete in contrast to some of its adobe neighbors, and it boasts electricity and running water.) This action was not a completely selfless one in any sense— a second and equally important reason for Reyna's move was so that she could take up studies in a high school in Cristina's neighborhood, which would provide her an education far superior to any attainable in her small town. At the time, she remembers, her father told her, "Yes, it's good that you study, that you accompany Cristina." Years later, her father told me that the two reasons Reyna came to Ayacucho were "to become educated and to accompany" and asked me to encourage her to study hard and take advantage of her situation. That is, Reyna is stated to be where she is in order to "accompany" a kinswoman who is in a position to help her become educated, both in school and in city life.

Reyna's experience gives a sense of what child circulation means to Andean kinship. Her relocation from her parents' home to Cristina's represents both companionship for someone perceived as related and the opportunity to make something of herself, an opportunity which her parents conceive of as an investment. This chapter takes up the question of companionship—the social relations forged and strengthened through child circulation, relations that are impossible in the orphanage setting.

ACOMPAÑAR: THE MORALITY OF ACCOMPANIMENT

Acompañar, "to accompany," is how Ayacuchanos describe what happens when a young person goes to live with an older one, in a role somewhere between child of the family and household employee. Although the younger person may have many reasons of her own to relocate, the word "accompany" emphasizes what she is doing for the older person: warding off solitude through coresidence and companionship. *Acompañando* (accompanying) involves the meaningful sharing of social and physical space over time.

While I usually heard about *acompañando* in the context of child circulation, there was one exception that is worth mentioning, because it explains some basic truths about accompaniment. After hearing my fiercely independent *comadre*'s life story—how her husband had struggled to convince her to marry him—I asked her if getting married had been the right thing to do. She replied that it absolutely was, because it is imperative to have a child to accompany you, and "people with no children suffer so much more." She told me she had once advised a male friend, "Get married or not— that's up to you—but definitely have a child, whether or not you are married, because *you can live with that child*, married or not" (emphasis mine).[2]

The companionship she describes is mutually constituted, a physical and social contiguity between parents and children.[3] Through this contiguity and accompaniment, parents support their children, and children alleviate the suffering and loneliness of their parents. This key characteristic of kinship usually goes uncommented, because it is self-evident, taken for granted. Only when adults have not yet reproduced children—or children and parents have been separated through migration or strategies of betterment—does companionship come to the fore in people's conversations and recollections. Companionship, or accompaniment in a more literal translation, is thus characteristic of the deeply interdependent parent-child relationship. Its invocation as one of the key bases of child circulation suggests that it, too, makes kinship.

"People with no children suffer so much more," said my *comadre*. The suffering that she refers to may be partly economic in nature—the problem of having to do all the household upkeep oneself—but what I think she really means is unbearable loneliness. The aloneness of the *wakcha* or the orphaned adult who feels *sapalla* hovers beneath the surface of this desire for companionship.[4] Being accompanied is a basic need which is only articulated when it is lacking. Accompanying another person is equivalent to caring for them, and the fact that children are so often called upon to do this for adults turns the typical North American focus on child care on its head.

Among the urban migrants I worked with in Peru, I clearly saw a strong ethic of love and value for children. One young woman told me she wanted "as many kids as came," and I had an acquaintance who had suffered two dangerous miscarriages but rejected her doctor's recommendation that she abort a third pregnancy. (The doctor sent her to a specialist in Lima, where she had a precipitous C-section, and the baby—now a much-adored toddler —spent two months in an incubator.) Even the smallest children are also valued as economic beings, contributing members of the household, whether through unpaid labor that offsets the need of adults to remain at home (going to the store, washing clothes, carrying heavy loads, watching younger siblings) or through paid labor as a maid (*muchacha*, literally "girl") or a *cobrador*, the child who takes fares and calls out the route on the buses.

THE COMPLEX PRECEDENTS OF *ACOMPAÑAR*

This desire for children—as beings to love and bring up, who are expected to collaborate with family economic and social efforts—coexists with other kinds of relationships to childbearing and fertility. In particular, the Peruvian state's own vexed relationship to fertility deserves some comment. Official policies on family planning and an ideology of population control have effectively linked lower fertility to modernity.[5] A seemingly untempered desire for children thus takes on specific moral connotations: government-sponsored billboards around Ayacucho announce that "family planning helps us to live better" (see figure 3) and a set of university preparation course notes I reviewed define family planning as "a basic human right consisting in that the couple reproduces in a *rational form*" (emphasis added).[6] In fact, in 2000, about 50 percent of Peruvians used "modern" contraceptive methods (INEI 2004), and many of the young people I spoke to adamantly stated that they would complete their studies before having children.

These two sometimes disconnected relationships to children—the desire to have children and the imperative to have only those that one can afford— interact complexly in the scenes that follow. Because Peru's government "does not assume in any way, shape, or form the protection of and attention to children" (Ludeña Gonzalez 2000: 76), impoverished couples who reproduce "irrationally" have few sources of support when it comes to raising numerous children. In this context, child circulation becomes potentially a response to population-control policy: a large number of children can be parceled out to kin with fewer children, distributing both the burden of providing for them and the benefits of their company. At the same time,

given the generally strong desire for and valuing of children, child circulation is also a potential tactic for satisfying this desire for (more) children[7]—
more affordable than medical intervention,[8] more recognizable and trustworthy than legal adoption.[9]

Companionship sounds idyllic—but the care entailed in this companionship is perceived as flowing in only one direction. Reyna left Cristina's
house six months after I left Peru, and I was unable to track her down
during a brief return visit in 2004. As Cristina told me, "Her father, her
mother, are other [than me]. It can't be prevented" (she used the word
atajar, in the sense of interrupting Reyna's trajectory). *Acompañar* "just isn't
the same as being with your own family," I was told by young people and
their parents alike. And perhaps I should have expected Reyna's eventual
departure, because during our interview Reyna articulated her loneliness to
me in no uncertain terms. She missed her mother, her father, and her little
sister. "Just me, by myself, I do everything . . . they go, they return late,
sometimes I am alone and don't even want to eat either, I'm alone, I feel all
alone."[10] The affection Cristina gave Reyna "just isn't the same" as the
affection of her own mother. Her loneliness even extended to the bed-
chamber: rather than sleeping in the same room or even the same brick
building as Cristina in the co-sleeping customary among indigenous people
throughout the Andes, Reyna had her own separate adobe room with a
lock on the wooden door. The terrible irony here is that accompanying is
intended to obviate solitude, and yet the companion receives no parallel
emotional succor.

Acompañar is produced out of two perceived failings in the workings
of Andean kinship, as the mother of nine-year-old Diana could tell you.
Diana's family moved to Ayacucho after her father, the captain of a *ronda* or
town defense group, was threatened by Shining Path and dropped out of
sight, vanishing for several years. Diana's mother, terrified of what Shining
Path might do when they couldn't find her husband and unsure of how to
make ends meet, brought her children to the city to live with her sister
(Leinaweaver 2007a). Diana's mother now works long days and nights col-
lecting the fare on an interprovincial bus and has strategically dispersed her
children around the region: the eldest daughter lives in her mother's house
to make sure no one robs it, the second daughter resides permanently with

her aunt and uncle, and the only boy works with another uncle in the jungle region.

The practical reasons for Diana, the youngest daughter, to accompany a neighbor thus are many, but her mother still must justify letting her child go.[11] The twists and turns of her justification suggest an underlying shame:

> Once, I was so sick I lost consciousness; the *señora* helped me then, cured me. So my Diana must have thought, "You know, Mom, she saved your life, the *señora* isn't well, I'll help her. I'll be there just as a way of accompanying her, I'll be there," she told me. "But Diana, when I am at home, you have to be at home." "Yes, Mom." So she's just there. The *señora* also: "Let her just accompany me, I'm lonely here by myself, I'm missing people, there's no one in my house," she told me.[12]

Acompañar has a moral cost, for the family loosening its hold on a child, and especially for the mother of that child. There is a gendered morality of parenthood, a sense that maternal love should have some bearing on whether a child is sent away. Diana's mother's justification is set against the backdrop of newspapers filled with lurid tales of *madres desnaturalizadas*, "unnatural mothers" who abandon or abuse their children in a strike against the very nature of motherhood.

Diana's mother deflects this tension skillfully by turning the critique around and suggesting that the real immorality here can be found in the *señora*'s home:

> It's as if the *señora* doesn't exist for her children . . . it's said they don't even talk to her. Sometimes they close themselves in their rooms while they watch TV or sleep . . . Because of this she drinks also, so when she's talking with Diana she's distracting herself and isn't thinking of drinking. Sometimes her daughters cook, each one going into her room and eating, not even capable of giving a plateful to their parents, and they just leave their plates outside of their rooms for their mother to collect and wash. So their mother: "My children aren't for me, if Diana accompanies me I won't mind so much."[13]

Here then is another moral cost of companionship. If children are barriers against loneliness, then *acompañar* springs from an ethical absence of grown children. A person who effectively lacks children, whether it is a physical absence (Cristina explained that Reyna lives with her because her children are not *a mi lado*, "at my side") or an irresponsible failure to comply with filial duty (like the *señora*'s children, despite their physical contiguity), requires proactive accompanying.

THE TASKS OF COMPANIONSHIP: CHILD LABOR

Lupe is an experienced companion whose mother died in childbirth. Her father Wilmer was a construction worker who was unable to care for her due to the demands of his job. Wilmer brought his infant daughter Lupe, along with her toddler sister, Laura, to his parents' village home. A few years later he remarried and brought the girls to live in his small town with him and his new wife, and soon with their three young children. When Wilmer's father died, Laura was returned to the countryside to accompany her lonely grandmother, while Lupe, who had reached school age, was sent to live with Wilmer's brother and sister-in-law in Ayacucho. For the first year she missed her grandmother and the fields desperately, but after that "more or less I got accustomed, and when I went to my field I didn't cry very much any more, I left calmly."[14] Lupe's tearful, emotional connection to the fields and her grandmother waned as she grew accustomed to city life. The front room of her aunt and uncle's house was a small corner store, and the doors were always open to attend clients. Lupe liked the freedom of the open doors, being able to play with her friends outside while keeping an eye on the store.

Eventually Lupe's aunt grew tired of her company and told her she had to leave. Lupe remembers thinking, "if I were to stay with my aunt, I know they might have separated, or fought." She had grown accustomed to living with her aunt and uncle and worried that it would be difficult to get accustomed to living with her father, but said, "I have nowhere else to be." Although she was resigned to the change, both her stepmother and her half-brother phrased this as a realization on Lupe's part (see Alexander 1978). Her half-brother told me that Lupe "no longer felt comfortable there, as it wasn't her house. She realized this on her own. She became tired of it, maybe they yelled at her, and for this reason she came to live with us."

And Lupe's stepmother explained, "Lupe must have realized, because she wanted to live with her father."[15]

This change was not an easy one for Lupe:

Being at my father's side meant a closed house, closed, closed, and I didn't get accustomed to that environment . . . I wanted to go back up to my aunt's. I didn't get accustomed with my siblings either, they didn't understand me. It's hard when you don't grow up with a person from childhood. Well, I don't know what you think about that, but it's like that for me . . . I was always sad, missing, it wasn't the same, I don't know how to explain it to you, I wasn't very accustomed to my father,[16] and I didn't get accustomed to my other mother. I liked to be up where my uncle was even if it bothered them.[17]

Lupe's description of life "at my father's side" places his house and him on a par, equating shelter with sentiment. She found it truly difficult to get used to life with her father, suggesting that kinship in the Andes is perceived to be largely, even primarily, the product of long-term cohabitation. With these challenges in mind, Lupe strategically planned her own "circulation."[18]

Blanca, a teacher, was godmother to Lupe's half-sister. When the two of them would visit the teacher, Lupe helped out in Blanca's house, "little by little, earning her confidence" until one day Blanca said, "You can be with me; you can accompany me, help me; I'll be here at home during vacations." (Notice in this quote that Blanca emphasized her own presence in the house—in contrast to a maid's lot of working and minding the house in its owner's absence.) As Lupe recalls:

I told her "Teacher, tell my father that you want me to be with you." And also the teacher was going to give me like a tip, I wouldn't go just for free. I didn't want to say no to her, she was a good person, so I said, "Okay Teacher, I'll be with you," and she told my father. But it was my decision, my father didn't tell me "Go, go be with her." It was my decision, but I had to ask my father's permission, I couldn't just go on my own. It wasn't a job; it's a small house, I just washed her clothes, cooked like in my own house, it was very calm and normal. I never lacked for food, we all ate together like equals and went out together too.[19]

Here, Lupe describes her situation in terms that explicitly differentiated it from domestic service. The "tip," the eating together, and the chores that were just like those in her own house—these are all markers of a family-like arrangement. And this is not inappropriate; a sister's godmother is thought of as family. There is labor involved in this arrangement, but it's the kind of chorelike labor that people at Lupe's income level perform in their own houses anyway.

Accompanying looks like an active coresidence, or to put it even more plainly, like child labor.[20] The vast majority of relocated children end up performing household chores for the family that has taken them in. I have seen transferred children cooking, washing dishes, and doing laundry by hand. These are chores that would normally be done by children in a working-class or peasant household but in the new context come to resemble the work done by a maid in a middle-class home.

THE PRICE OF COMPANIONSHIP: THE *PROPINA*

Circulated children are not exactly paid for the work they perform, but their school supplies or new clothes may be purchased by adults in the new household, contributing to the idea that this movement can lead to a socioeconomic "betterment" that is charted in apparel and education. Furthermore, as Lupe was, they may be given a *propina*, a word that can be translated as "allowance" or "tip"—in other words, a small amount of money. This payment situates child circulation in an ambivalent gray area, somewhere between kinship and domestic service, both of which it resembles.

On one hot summer day I had taken a bus two hours out of the city of Ayacucho to visit Reyna's family. My arrival coincided with Carlos's project of building a corrugated tin roof to cover the patio. He balanced on a board that had been placed on an old chair, reaching up to hammer the wooden supports for the tin roof, and as I looked on, one of his young sons entered the house compound. The boy crossed the open patio and went straight into the kitchen, and his father called after him, "You don't help me, you don't get a *propina!*"

Here, as in many North American households when allowances are discursively presented as "payment" for a child doing chores, the father was equating his son's participation in household tasks with the allowance he would later receive. So the *propina*, which in this context corresponds to "allowance" in English, represents a sum given to children within the family environment, including by godparents (Palomino Vall 1986: 85).[21] In this case, however, the boy didn't help his father; he had a more important task, which was to obtain money from his mother, run to the corner store, and purchase a round of cheese to dress up the lunch of boiled potatoes for the unexpected and important *gringa* guest.

If the *propina* is an economic practice located at least partly within the sphere of kinship, it's not insignificant that circulated children receive similar sums. The *propina* is given in the context of social relatedness. Though parents set it up as a "payment" for chores completed, and Lupe presents it as something that gave her presence in Blanca's household some sort of value (saying "I wouldn't go just for free"), participants in such relationships nonetheless never use terms like *sueldo* or *salario* (salary) or *pago* (payment). Wages are for the impersonal workplace; *propinas* belong at home in the context of interpersonal relationships.[22] Nara Milanich has come to a similar conclusion, studying child circulation in nineteenth-century Chile: that wagelessness signals kinship (personal communication).[23]

This analysis runs the risk of making *acompañar* into an idyllic stretching of boundaries, a previously undocumented category of relatedness bridging family and labor. But as Roger Sanjek has suggested, "One should be suspicious of analyses in which everyone benefits" (1990: 57). There is a great deal of ambivalence here, expressed in the acute details of a child's chores, and of the exploitation of kinship in order to avoid paying a real wage to a laboring child. And, significantly, the economic relationship between patron and domestic worker is also frequently expressed in *propina* form.

Ximena Bunster and Elsa Chaney researched the lives of domestic workers in Lima, Peru's capital. They recounted the story of one such worker, Maria, a twenty-eight-year-old who came to her *señora*'s home at age eleven and has worked there since. Maria—like many maids throughout Peru and beyond—has always been described by her employer as "just like a family member." Bunster and Chaney write: "What María receives she calls 'propinas' or tips, a common recompense for younger servants just beginning their work life, and still found here and there among older women. María says, 'Well, they don't pay me anything, I don't earn anything. The señora buys my clothes, shoes, and apart from that, sometimes gives me a tip'"

(1989: 52). This resembles Reyna's financial situation. Cristina's niece said that Reyna "sort of" gets paid. Cristina's grown children, who live in Europe, told the young woman, "We'll help you with clothes and everything, but accompany our mother." When they visit their mother, they bring Reyna small gifts and "tip" her to wash their clothes. As Reyna herself said, "No, they don't pay me, I only accompany, that's all."

Any hard-and-fast unlinking of kinship and domestic work in the Andes is thus difficult to sustain under close scrutiny. Parents give tips to their children, employers give them to their maids; kinship terms are employed to describe both kinds of relations. Critical analyses of employers who say maids are "like a daughter" suggest that this terminology "soften[s] the edges of exploitative capitalist wage relations" (Colen and Sanjek 1990; see also Loza et al. 1990: 26–27).[24] And so it does—but this analysis should not be limited to relations of domestic work alone. The *propina* hints at inequality and exploitation in the safe and loving family environment, too.[25]

There is a certain kind of relationship that is being expressed through the *propina*. The "gratuity" suggests spontaneity, rather than obligation, and represents gratitude (López Basanta 1997: 462–63; see also Mauss 1990 [1954]: 3–5, 13; Kopytoff 1986). Similarly, the connotation of work in the private sphere, as Grace Young has written in an article on domestic servants in Peru, is that it "is of a voluntary nature, given of love and devotion" (1987: 368). Within the space of the house, labor is felt to be given voluntarily. This is the case whether a son is helping his father with the corrugated tin roof, whether a young woman is accompanying a teacher and helping her in her household, or whether a domestic servant is performing her duties. And the *propina* is felt to be given voluntarily to recognize that voluntary labor.

In this, the *propina* can be aligned with a distinction charted by the anthropologist Ben Orlove (2002) elsewhere in the Andes. In the diaries of Bolivian peasant men, recorded for a development project in the 1970s and 1980s and reconsidered by Orlove, all manner of men's activities were described as "work," but the majority of women's activities (chores, meal preparation, tending to animals) were described as "help" (Orlove 2002: 101–7). The division was not economic, as many of the men's work activities were unpaid, and some of women's helping included selling vegetables at market. Instead, helping connotes a voluntary kind of labor—the kind that would be recognized with a voluntary payment like the *propina*. Importantly, the very idea of helping implies the presence of another person, and thus a social relationship. And, as Orlove's analysis suggests, helping occurs within the domestic sphere—within the thoroughly gendered space of the house.

The giving of a *propina* to circulated children positions them within particular social and relational geographies. It represents both voluntary pay for voluntary labor and the furthering of social relations. The neutral reciprocity described as *ayni* throughout the Andean region (Portugal Catacora 1988: 68–69; Alberti and Mayer 1974; Skar 1982: 213) does not apply to the parent-child relationship (Anderson 2004), perhaps because parents can never be certain that their material and affective "investments" in their children will ultimately be reciprocated in the form of help in the household and fields and care for aged parents (Van Vleet 1999: 170). In the short term, then, parent-child relationships appear deeply unequal (Bloch 1973: 76–77), with parents giving everything and receiving little in return.

Though the *propina* is popularly claimed to be voluntary and spontaneous, I maintain that it is more accurately about reinscribing social relations, simultaneously framing these relations as voluntary while at the same time making them habitual, patterned, and regular. The *propina*, appearing on the surface as a one-way gift, is really a statement reminding children that they are subordinate—that they must accept this gift, and that they must repay it one day. Here, a gift—of money—is being used to symbolize and produce hierarchy.

Sarita, who spends her school vacations helping out in her uncle's house in Lima, explicitly described the *propina* in these terms. Rather than saying, "I cook for them, and at the end of the summer they give me a *propina*," she said something very different, something like: "It is humiliating to have to accept this treatment in exchange for getting the tip, but I don't want my parents to worry about school expenses." In an interview, she repeated this sentiment, directed now at an aunt and uncle in Ayacucho: "Sometimes people in Peru, when they're going to give you something, no matter if they're your relatives, if they're going to give you their money it's because they want you to do things right, the way they like them. So to receive a little money, since we don't have any, we basically have to humiliate ourselves and accept what they say to us. This is what's sad about society."[26]

Sarita sees her *propina* as a payment for humbling herself. When a young person accepts a *propina*, this reaffirms for the giver that he or she retains social superiority and control. The *propina* marks imbalance and charity, making the inequalities contained within one shared social space tenable, both constituting and muting them through economic practice.

When the relations made material through the *propina* are exposed to the scrutiny of the state's representatives, however, they don't hold up—it becomes a clear case of domestic service, and the connotations of reciprocity, dependence, and imbalance fade into the background. Ayacucho's adoption office coordinator, interviewed on a local radio station, explicitly stated that *acompañar* is definitively not adoption, nor should it be considered a family relationship:

Q: Do people take [i.e., adopt] kids for service in the home? Do they want to take a child for service?

A: No, no, no, no, no . . . A couple is disqualified if it's for that. Because many times fifty- or sixty-year-old people, who already have children, come [to the adoption office]. They want a companion; it's not for company. We tell them, "You don't want a son or daughter, what you want is a companion." Now, for this, there are persons that can serve you, hired, but no. So the focus is, is it a child they want, a son or daughter? Not a person that can serve them, you understand?[27]

Her reference to "hiring" a companion discursively pushes *acompañar* toward employment, distancing it from kinship. Those who are involved in the relationship would never use "hired" to describe it; the coordinator is explicitly doing so in order to set up adoption as a legitimate kin-making practice, the same as family and therefore necessarily distinguished from *acompañar*.

Similarly, *acompañar* makes little sense to persons of a higher social class. One well-off woman who worked for the Fulbright Commission in Lima commented that when people bring their godchildren to live with them, they may treat the children a little better than they would treat an *empleada*, but they do not treat the godchild like their own child, because they make him do chores, and this is wrong. For her, there can only be coddled children or maids; anything between is ambiguous and exploitative. *Acompañar* is uncomfortable or even unacceptable to outside observers.

The inequities contained within the few coins of a *propina* underscore the class distinctions of giving and receiving children. Households that can afford to take children in will do so; those that struggle to provide for their children may distribute them (Weismantel 1988: 169; Fonseca 1986: 17). Nara Milanich asserts that in nineteenth-century Chile "the circulation of poor minors was inseparable from the market for women's domestic labor" (2004: 314), because live-in domestic workers were usually not allowed to raise their children in their employer's home. The sharp tensions of need and opportunity play out in gendered, classed ways on the terrain of child circulation. While children receiving the *propina* as an allowance may only vaguely grasp the messages about inequality it contains, circulated children are more often positioned in a structural context of inequality. If a poor child moves into the home of her social superior, the *propina* can, in essence, remind her of this indisputable fact persisting somewhere beneath the surface of a voluntary transaction.

Lupe described how, when she moved in with her father's family, six months passed before she got used to it, and "from then on my father took me into account, since I had come to be at his side. He bought me my notebooks, paid for my graduation party, all my school costs."[28] Circulated children are attentive to who pays for what—Reyna and Sarita each took care to let me know that, although they were living with or had lived with relatives, it was their natal parents who paid for clothes, school supplies, and other expenses. Their insistence on this suggests that such expenses are typically borne by the adult responsible for the child (see Goody 1982). But if the child's entire economic upkeep is not the main reason for the transfer (that is, if a parent is not too poor to pay for the child's school supplies him- or herself) then other, noneconomic, intangible aspects are clearly felt to be more central: educational opportunity, the possibility of learning Spanish or a useful trade, the hope for self-improvement. Tony Whitehead has suggested that such economic transfers may even provide incentive for an adult to receive a child (1978: 824).

Lupe's story of how she came to live with Blanca deserves a closer look. She paints it as her own decision, but one that must be set up as a request from Blanca to Lupe's father. She then describes herself responding to this request: "I didn't want to say no to her, she was a good person." And finally, she denies that her move to Blanca's was something her father told her to do. Lupe avows that the move was her choice, framing it as a strategic plan on her part, but the complex set of reasons suggest some level of implicit coercion.

Reyna's move to Cristina's house played out very similarly. Reyna told me that Cristina's grown son Vladi told her she would be needed, and she then told her father, presenting it as a fait accompli: "Vladi says I'm going to accompany." Reyna said that her father responded, "You decide." But she also said that she had already told Vladi, "Okay, uncle."[29] Furthermore, she said that her father had "already" told Vladi she would accompany. She implied that the move was her choice, but she also referred to how her father and others had supported, taken for granted, and ultimately agreed to the move.[30] Reyna's relocation occurred within a context of long-term social relations complicated by class differentials.

This volatile combination is articulated by the young people concerned in terms of duty—*deber* in Spanish, which also means "chore," and, as a verb, means "should" or "must." When a social superior who is also already connected to your family—Blanca, a teacher and Lupe's sister's godmother, or Cristina, mother of four migrants to Europe and godmother to Reyna's father—makes an initial request for companionship, a dutiful response is both necessary and prudent. The framing of social responsibility and hierarchy as "duty" is a strategic portrayal of kinship. Kin feel a sense of duty to one another—strangers do not. But "duty," like the *propina*, is also a nice strategy for deploying the terms of kinship in order to bind a young person to the work of companionship.

I asked Lupe what happened when she moved to Lima as a young adult, after her time with Blanca—was what she did there accompaniment? She said:

> No, I worked there, I was like a maid. I lived and slept in the house, and went out on Sundays to visit my aunt. I worked there, I did everything. But people there treat you like a maid—there, they can't treat you like family, like when you work in another house [another versus your own, I think]. I liked it. I never lacked for food, the Señora was very nice, it was a small house, I liked to clean well and quickly.[31]

She was telling her story, and I didn't interrupt, but of course I regret never asking her directly what she meant when she said that Limeños treat you like a maid and can't treat you like family. But the important point is that, while analysts may perceive child circulation and domestic service as suspiciously identical, Lupe experienced them as different. She *accompanied* Blanca, but she was a maid in Lima. The process of being welcomed and getting accustomed is at the root of this difference.

THE PROCESS OF KINSHIP: GETTING ACCUSTOMED, BECOMING FAMILIAR

Yosselin lives next door to her mother-in-law, yet she never eats with the rest of the family, never gives her mother-in-law "a piece of fruit or a plate of food—she should really make more of an effort with her husband's family," said one in-law. It would be "no big deal" for Yosselin to give her mother-in-law a plate of soup or main course, but she doesn't, "she's not like that." Yosselin "doesn't seem like family, she removes herself, it's not right."[32] Her mother-in-law's relatives complained, one after another, that Yosselin was not *familiarizada*.

The in-law relationship is another kind of circulation—marrying into a family means entering into a new set of social relations that must be delicately negotiated. The tensions that inhere in in-law relationships can be soothed by active efforts on both parts to become familiarized—that is, to get along, to graciously share space and food, and to earn each others' trust, confidence, and affection (see Van Vleet 2002: 578–80). Familiarization is an active and engaged effort toward becoming family, a process that hints at the tenuousness and constructedness of kinship.

Diana's older sister, Juana, reminded me in an interview how she had gotten to know me:

> Bit by bit I have been, since you are very friendly and understanding, and so because of this, bit by bit I got closer and we are going along accustoming to one another, we went along accustoming to one another, and then we came to visit you on your birthday, and from there bit by bit we have been accustoming to one another, and I think up until now, right?[33]

This transformation wasn't described as familiarization but rather as accustoming. *Acostumbrar* is that slow, surprising transformation in behavior, treatment, comfort, and sentiment that results in friendship or kinship. The actors are effaced, and the process appears passive—it happens *to* people. Accustoming represents getting used to new practices, to an active inter-action with persons or objects within a new or rearranged social space.[34]

To an anthropologist like myself, this process of getting used to life inside someone else's house resembles nothing so much as the slow ha-bituations of fieldwork, the developing relationships we like to call "rap-port," and the subtle methodological shift from heavy-on-the-observation to immersed-in-participation. I remember my anxieties when I first came to Ayacucho, most of all not knowing what or where was safe to eat, and resenting the stares that a white woman walking down the street on her own naturally drew from curious townspeople. A few years later Sarita would describe to me how her relationship to her aunt and uncle changed slowly over time:

> In the first weeks I went to my town every weekend, and it was very hard to get accustomed . . . One or two years I must have felt like that, dying to go back to my parents and grandmother every weekend . . . After those two or three years, by then I had gotten accustomed, with my uncle and aunt. In their house I didn't feel such a hurry to return to my town, I went when I felt like it. That is, I had already gotten accustomed.[35]

Sarita referred to two unique statuses, unaccustomed and accustomed, and deflected attention from the accustoming as it actually takes place. It re-minded me that I, too, had already gotten accustomed to life in Ayacucho. Though the stakes weren't as high for me, I thought I knew what she was getting at. *Acostumbrar* happens when you aren't looking.

In Zumbagua, Ecuador, Mary Weismantel recalls a man, feeding his newly "adopted" son, who staunchly proclaimed: " 'I *am* going to be his father . . . Aren't I feeding him right now?' " (1995: 690). His words under-score the recognized importance of a serious investment of time and the active social sharing of the spaces and practices of the domestic sphere in producing the desired conditional relationship. *Acostumbrar* is a slow pro-cess of becoming, situated in and responsive to a web of relatedness, taking place "bit by bit." This slowness must be one of the most striking differ-ences between companionship and adoption, for older children who have experienced both. A colleague who is an adoption psychologist remarked excitedly on reading these words that *acostumbrar* sounded like what he, in his profession, would call "attachment" (Karen 1998)—this material from Peru suggests that attachment, complex and deeply essential though it may be, can indeed take place after infancy. Yet *acostumbrar* is rarely so complete that the former status is entirely rejected. Psychologists researching adoption call this "boundary ambiguity"—is the incorporated person in or out of the family? (Fravel et al. 2000: 425).

In child circulation, a young person starts life in one household or family and then moves to another. Although participants may immediately begin to use the words and acts proper to relations of cohabitation, they only become naturalized and embodied over time. When self-aware young people move or are moved into different households, at first there is fear and careful self-policing. A newcomer may feel hesitant, afraid to ask for something, unable to just eat whatever she wants or sleep in until noon as she might have done at home. But little by little she "becomes accustomed" and in the process—by quietly comparing what she couldn't do before to what she now feels comfortable doing—family is formed and reinforced. So if a young woman has started to feel as if she belongs in her new house, she knows there is a time that she once didn't, and in reconstructing that time and remembering her feelings about it, she creates a backdrop for her own trajectory toward self-improvement and validated kinship. In this way, larger changes are obscured and can only be recognized through a comparison of historical points.

In contrast to the revelation of accustoming, a child in the Andes is born into an existing household space and grows up surrounded by variously shifting configurations of family members. Relatives, friends, and neighbors visit daily; the child also visits these people, goes to school, and runs errands. The process of getting used to one's own life is one which goes unnoticed and is not remarked upon. This is Bourdieu's notion of *habitus*: "embodied history, internalized as a second nature and so forgotten as history . . . the active presence of the whole past of which it is the product" (1990: 56).

But the radical thing about Bourdieu's habitus is the demonstration that kinship, which is often felt to be and has similarly been theorized as a natural, given object, actually consists of practices that constantly produce and reproduce relatedness (1977: 35–36; also see Medick and Sabean 1984 n9). Habitus contrasts with accustoming, which is also embodied history, but one not so distant as to be forgotten. What distinguishes *acostumbrar* is the young person's memories of origins, self-awareness, and insecurity in the new setting. Because it takes place over time, accustoming lays bare the normally unexamined foundations of habitus and allows a clear view of the different emotional, material, and social variables that converge until a young person feels at home in a new house. The flexible movements of Ayacuchano youth, and the time they take to become accustomed to their new situations, allow an unusually close view of the production of Bourdieu's "structured structures predisposed to function as structuring structures" (1990: 53).

THE ETHICS OF *ACOSTUMBRAR*: DE-KINNING AND THE DANGER OF LOSS

Sarita and I walked through Ayacucho's pretty colonial downtown, passing the statue of Sucre, a hero of Peru's independence, sitting proudly on his horse in the center of the plaza. I invited her to an ice cream cone—it was a hot day—and we kept on walking. Later she apologized to me for not having asked how much she owed me for it, saying ruefully of herself and her siblings, "We've really become accustomed." It was as if her action were bad-mannered because she had come to take my occasional gifts for granted, and—more dangerously—as if getting accustomed to receiving ice cream from a *gringa* would make its absence someday soon sting all the more.

Sarita's words infer an ethical resistance to the dangers of getting accustomed—a tantalizing new life, whether it's represented by a complimentary ice cream cone or the constellations of social betterment that child circulation should unfurl, can be addictive. Young people away from a mother's influence are felt to be vulnerable to the dangers of city life, and they face the risks of losing respect for elders or traditions, drinking, joining a gang, or, for girls, pregnancy. Even when a change is viewed as largely positive, becoming accustomed to it opens up a new risk of loss. Although loss is a danger and fear in most aspects of life, the loss of new habit is that much more vulnerable.[36]

I spent several days up in Margarita's village in August 2002 as her family prepared for the town's annual fiesta, which her nephew (one of her sister Cristina's sons, who now lived in Europe) was sponsoring. Those were long days filled with cooking and conversation—Margarita's kinswomen, those who lived there and those who'd returned for the fiesta preparations, kept dropping by to help. We would sit around a seemingly endless pile of corn that, months earlier, had been harvested from Margarita's fields and spread on her tiled rooftops to dry. Pushing the hard *granos* of corn off their cobs with callused thumbs, we exchanged *adivinanzas* (Quechua riddles filled with double entendres, my mastery of which was always hilarious to new acquaintances) and conversation. One of the visitors, watching how I sat with the others and engaged in the labor of *desgranando*, commented that I was like Margarita's daughter, and I had become *acostumbrada*. Margarita's stepdaughter asked what would happen when I left (a year before that was expected to occur) and I told her I would cry; she replied that so would she, for she is very sentimental. Only now do I connect these comments to friends' constant awareness that I would be leaving one day, and to the poignant pleas to remember them which would only emerge as I was leaving. Ben Orlove has written about such urgent requests at length and with compassion: "As a modern American, I tend to think of forgetting as an unwilled lapse of mental function, as something that happens to one rather than something one does . . . [but] forgetting is a social act rather than an individual one" (2002: 8). The fear of loss, the projection of a new lack, is inextricable from the idea of getting accustomed, especially to treasured social relationships.

It seems the height of banality to underscore that the poor can love—as Margaret Trawick wrote about Tamil families back when she thought it was necessary (1992: 49; see also Bledsoe 1990: 85). What is of interest is *how* Ayacuchanos love—how, as Olivia told me, "Our parents have never said, 'I love you.' We know because of the advice they give us and perhaps their actions toward us—they want the best for us. I don't know if it's from fear or shame, I think it's because no one has ever said it to them." The urban migrants I knew rarely stated their love and affection for each other explicitly, and if they did it was usually after an evening of drinking had uninhibited them.[37] But the expressions of affection that were available for public observation were always couched in the idiom of worry: the tropes of missing loved ones, and of fearing their loss, appeared again and again as expressions of *cariño*. Returning from a trip to Lima to find no toasted corn available to offer guests, Margarita groused, "When I leave everything falls to pieces." I told her that her daughters had missed her and she said, "Sure, but now that I'm here they make me bitter," and Sarita joked, "We missed having someone to make bitter." And yet . . .

Sarita, who had cried for weeks when her mother first left her at her uncle's, eventually didn't want to leave her uncle's house, which was located in a wealthier, cleaner, more central part of town. Germán and his father, living apart for nearly twenty years, "became accustomed" to being apart and actually no longer get along. Reyna made regular visits to her natal family, but when her little sister asked her where her mother was, Reyna pointed to their mother and her sister replied, "No, she's not your mother. Where is your *mamá* Cristina?" While a young companion may miss her parents and siblings, she may also be reluctant to return to their lifestyle. Signe Howell's work on transnational adoption highlights the concept of kinning—how a sense of belonging to the family is transmitted to an incorporated child (Howell 2003). When a young person has accompanied outside her home for long enough, however, she may become so accustomed to the new way of life that she enters into a related, dangerous, and potentially immoral process of de-kinning: becoming unaccustomed to her social origins.[38] De-kinning takes the fear of losing a treasured new relationship one step further into the asocial realm of losing a treasured old relationship.

Yet de-kinning need not always be greeted with fear and resistance. In contrast with a model in which new knowledge or behavioral acquisitions are added to a previous core, Quichua speakers in lowland Ecuador recognized that changes in social relationships or physical locations mean that some aspects of identity must be divested, "dissolved so that new ones can be built up" (Uzendoski 2005: 16). This model bears a close resemblance to George Foster's notion of "limited good" among Latin American peasant societies (1965: 289–99)—the idea that there exists a limit to the number of possible social relations, such that getting accustomed seems to also imply, of necessity, the deliberate tempering, distancing, or breaking of other relations.

CONCLUSIONS

As must happen when parents decide to temporarily place their children in an orphanage, parents like Diana's mother must be motivated to let a child go—whether out of obligation to the requesting adult, desire to strengthen that relationship, or belief that the child is going somewhere with better opportunities available to her. Receiving adults like Cristina must have reasons—the fear of loneliness, the need for household help, a trust in the child's good character and permanence—to make the economic outlay necessary for another's child's subsistence. The idea of orphanhood eluci-dated in the previous chapter has much to do with why children are invited to accompany their elders. Andean lives are unmistakably social, and being alone is perceived as a lack. Child circulation connects households and builds up social relations—a young person's relocation materializes the duty that her natal household may owe to a relative or social patron. Such movements also speak to the value Ayacuchanos place on togetherness, especially coresidence.

A young companion can fill that aching emptiness, but in doing so, she indexes the reasons for that emptiness (a failure to carry out filial duty) and her own vulnerability (why her parents might let her go). The social ground of Andean kinship is the basis for the relations of child circulation as well as for much of domestic service. There's no denying that there is a strong resemblance between these two notions. One of the material mani-festations of those relations is the *propina*, an economic practice, expressed within the social geography of the house, that undergirds relations of inequality. My insistence on representing child circulation as different from servitude comes out of the descriptions of Lupe and others like her, who don't equate the two. Yet the similarities can be seen in descriptions like Reyna's, descriptions that suggest on some level there is little difference.

Circulated children's positioning within a new household must be got-ten used to, through the practice of accustoming that lays bare the founda-tions of kinship and habitus. To say that it must be gotten used to raises two important points. First, moving to a new household is a change, and not always an easy one. It takes social work, the active sharing of social space and conscious adjustment, for the new house to resemble a home and for the new relationships to become second nature. Sometimes this work is difficult or impossible, and *acostumbrar* becomes a resignation, a coming to terms with loneliness. This difficult transition raises a second issue—why, apart from the pressures of duty already mentioned, would a young person do this? The answer can be found in Reyna's story, which opened this chapter. As her father told me, Reyna moved into Cristina's Ayacucho home "to become educated and to accompany." From the young person's perspective, there is another set of reasons, another moral position, which further justifies child circulation. These reasons are the subject of the following chapter.

Five.

SUPERACIÓN: THE STRATEGIC USES OF CHILD CIRCULATION

On a warm summer day in January 2003, I went to the market near my house: an entire city block covered with corrugated tin and blue tarps, its thick adobe walls enclosing hundreds of raucous stalls vending an assortment of meats both living and dead, vegetables, fruits, spices, dry goods, olives, breads, cheese, and cleaning products. I was there to visit the kiosk of my usual seller, who had just turned thirteen. I frequented her stand because she usually had good-quality eggplant, difficult to find in Ayacucho's markets, along with my usual standbys of tomatoes, peppers, limes, celery, carrots, beets, and aromatic fresh herbs. She had two small kids with her, one a boy, and she asked me, "Can you take him home with you, *casera*?" I'd quickly learned to respond in a joking fashion to such offers, and retorted, "What in the world would I do with a little boy? Is he your son?" She said no, he was her brother. I smiled in return, "Sure, come on with me," and the boy giggled and giggled, but stayed put.

As such everyday occurrences demonstrated, I was living in a place where children did not always reside with their natal parents. Gentle jokes like these (see also Van Vleet 1999: 146n18) indicate the ubiquity of this social arrangement, but before I learned to parry them, my best-laid plans to study tourism in Cusco were derailed by several offers of babies that drove a revision of my research question: why was this so prevalent, and what lay beneath?

The perfectly ordinary encounter with my *casera* also demonstrates that I was living in a place where thirteen-year-old girls run market stands. I never saw an adult at this particular kiosk; the young woman was sometimes replaced by her fifteen-year-old male cousin, and both were at times accompanied by small children. Unlike the day-long travails of children working in mines or forming adobe bricks, the labors of these two adolescents allowed them both to contribute to their household income while staying in school. But the fact that they had learned to labor (in the sense of Willis 1981) in this way is intimately connected to the need for and reliance upon child circulation strategies. Poor people must innovate in order to survive, and child transfers take place within the context of an impoverishment that also shapes rural-to-urban migration, child labor, orphanage use, and other survival strategies. Their poverty is both all-consuming and banal—the Ayacuchanos I knew both struggle with it every day and live with it as if it were commonplace, which, of course, it is.

FALTA DE ECONOMÍA: AN ECONOMIC LACK

April 2003: Sarita came over early in the morning. She never calls ahead—a half-hour trek down into the center of town is preferable to the fifty-*céntimo* expense of a public phone. The front door had been left ajar, so she peeked in, saying she would just read her e-mail on my computer and not be a bother. I sighed, set her up, and got myself organized while she took half an hour to type out a message about family conflicts to her cousin in Europe. Afterward, she told me quietly, and eventually with tears running down her cheeks, that she was saddened when her father arrived home to Ayacucho from their village, where he spends most of his days—he looked old, she said. She needs money, actual money, tangible coins and bills softened from overuse, and she just can't ask him for it—he works so hard, and says that he tried to find paid work and couldn't, but at least he can keep his kids *bien alimentados*, well fed,[1] farming his fields back in his village, working so hard. She has told her siblings and friends that she may drop out of university, because she will have to make photocopies and buy two separate uniforms for the requirements of this year's courses. She then complained that for a lab course, because of the university's poverty, the students are required to go out to the cemetery and collect bones (from graves whose inhabitants' relatives' payments have lapsed), and they'll have to go out and hunt down toads to cut open and look at their circulation systems. She said, fervently, that all Peru's problems come down to a *falta de economía*, a simple lack of money.

"I hope you've enjoyed our poverty," Sarita remarked, not unkindly, when clearing away my empty soup plate a few days later. I had gone up to her house for a visit and stayed for lunch, the entirety of which she spent railing against her professors who'd backed down in a recent university strike, and against the United States, which was obliging Peru to pay off external debt, money that Sarita felt should go toward educating her country's citizens.[2] Sarita often referred to the soups she served me on different occasions as "our poverty." Poverty, *pobreza*, is a term that the Ayacuchanos I spoke with often claimed as their own.

The "economic lack" perceived by Sarita and her age-mates suggests that they experience poverty as an incompleteness. To define an impossible choice as caused by a fundamental lack is essentially to identify what is lacking, a step which is necessary before they can seek and create new possibilities for themselves or their children. This framing, the "lack," is not restricted to economic matters; it is a formal calculus that also applies to gendered morality (a "lack of orientation" provokes young women to become sexually active and pregnant too soon) and gendered maturity (Wilmer, a father of five, told me as he critically tasted the unpleasantly dry *puca picante* one of his daughters had prepared for him that *she*, not the meal, was lacking, and should watch her mother more carefully). The emphasis on what one is lacking suggests an orientation of relative deprivation: more and more, the hardness of life is interpreted as a negotiation between local social realities and imagined possibilities (Appadurai 1991: 198).

Thus poverty is also a structural condition, the result of a global process (Farmer 1999: 7). Development in Latin America prioritized urban centers and led to the marginalization of agriculture and, by extension, the Andean region, whose numerous attempts to strengthen its economic standing were doomed to failure (Degregori 1997: 40–41). More than half of Peru's twenty-eight-million souls eke out a living below the poverty line, women, children, and the indigenous foremost among them (Anderson 1993; O'Donnell 2001: 7; UNICEF 2007). This impoverishment is produced from goings-on both distant and near: the efforts of international financial organizations, the privatization policies of a neoliberal government, the social and political remnants of a bloody civil war, and the deeply entrenched and divisive racism and classism that shape relations in Peru and that are partly maintained out of some of the highest levels of economic inequality in the world (Chronic Poverty Research Centre 2004: 29).

In 2002, the chant "Toledo, damn it, where are our jobs?" (*Toledo, carajo, dónde está el trabajo?*) echoed through Ayacucho's streets in weekly protests against the ineffectuality of President Alejandro Toledo Manrique. Toledo, Peru's first modern president to proudly claim indigenous descent, had risen to power not two years previously, successfully negotiating to his own benefit the outpouring of anger against Alberto Fujimori, the president of Japanese ancestry who escaped to his parents' homeland amid allegations of human rights abuse, corruption, and criminal behavior. But Toledo's political honeymoon was brief—he was spectacularly unsuccessful in creating new jobs and improving the Peruvian economy anywhere but on paper, and many Ayacuchanos responded with the wish that Fujimori would return. Yes, I was told, the *"Chino"* (the nickname for anyone with characteristics perceived as Asian) was a crook—but at least he *did things*, installing water and electricity in poor neighborhoods and gifting towns with police trucks or schools. The Ayacuchanos I knew were pointedly critical of local and national politics, viewing their economic lack as part of a larger picture, and not entirely within their control.

Because so much is outside their control, working-class Ayacuchanos must maximize every opportunity and carefully weigh every decision. This struggle to survive leaves no time, resources, or luxury for planning for the long-term or the unpredictable, and so many come up short when an emergency strikes. Sometimes life stories unspin as a series of impossible choices between basic needs. Jim Yong Kim and his colleagues describe a Peruvian woman who could not afford to pay for the medical supplies required before health center staff could diagnose her with tuberculosis and offer her free treatment thereafter (2000: 128, 133). Her priorities came through cleanly and sharply: food for her family (a perceived immediate need and a more obviously social act) over a definitive diagnosis. Thus, in the grip of an unforgiving poverty that forces a difficult choice between two unpleasant prospects, poor Peruvians make that choice using the criteria they know and the resources they have.

Gisela, a new mother at twenty-five, was supported emotionally and economically neither by her child's father nor her own sister (who had disapproved of her pregnancy). She weighed the difficult option of leaving her small, sad toddler with a friend while going to the jungle to work for one month. While this was an acknowledged option among her circle of friends, they criticized it in her absence: "What kind of desperation would make someone leave their baby for a month? My mother always said she would never do that." Just because this is an understandable choice does not mean that it is easy or even widely acceptable. Gisela's friend recognized the possibility of such desperation even as she articulated her firm belief that leaving one's child should be the last of last resorts.

And so, lodging a child at the orphanage or sending a child to live with someone else is one of these complex and context-dependent choices. There are moments of crisis when it can seem better for that child to leave—to provide her with new opportunities, to earn money desperately needed back home, to strengthen a relationship key to the family's day-to-day survival. This conclusion reflects individual decisions, on a case-by-case basis, to maximize opportunity at times of crisis. It also reflects Ayacuchanos' recognition of a global capitalist economy in which they may not be the best positioned to help their children, but where what they can do is strategically transfer their children to someone of higher socioeconomic positioning. If a choice is made to relocate or send a child elsewhere, it was probably preceded by a judgment that a worse alternative existed—and a firm idea that the place the child is going will somehow be better. There is a word for this: *superarse*.[3]

SUPERARSE: AN IDEOLOGY OF BETTERMENT

When I headed to the field, I had never—to my recollection—encountered the idea of *superarse*. I remember having to look it up in a battered old dictionary, as it came up in interview after interview. It's a centuries-old Spanish word (Corominas and Pascual 1980: 278), derived from the Latin verb *superâre* (to be ahead or above), noun *superus* (sky or heavens), and adjective *super* (above), and it translates as to get ahead, or to defeat (Cuervo 1998: 622–24).[4] A Quechua-Spanish dictionary equates *superar* with *llalliy*, also conveying the idea of triumph or defeat (Ladrón de Guevara 1998:

338). The term concretizes a locally meaningful concept of progress and development.

These ideas of overcoming one's own constraints (*superarse*), getting ahead (*salir adelante*), and defeating or triumphing over (*llalliy*) all imply efforts that explicitly refer to a preexisting situation. *Superarse* becomes meaningful for the Ayacuchanos I knew only when set against the background of *falta de economía*. In practice, *superación* looks like young people perceiving and articulating the limits of their socioeconomic positioning, working toward their own self-improvement, and contributing to their family and extended community. Lobo, writing about Andean migrants to Lima, calls it "progress" and defines it as a literal progression from a negative state to the positive connotations of modernity and a physical location within an urban space (1982: 65; see also Allen 2002 [1988]: 213). *Superación* archives local interpretations of betterment and uses them to understand social mobility.[5]

This ideology of upward mobility and betterment masks a social ugliness that becomes visible when conceptualizing what it is that is being overcome. To fully overcome poverty means that one must take on several social qualities—becoming educated, speaking Spanish instead of Quechua, dressing in store-bought "Western" clothing instead of woven skirts or felt hats or rubber-tire sandals, eating noodles instead of potatoes and drinking beer instead of *trago*, living in the city instead of in the *campo*. In other words, to overcome means to become whiter and to shed an Indian way of life (Whitten 1981: 15; see also Colloredo-Mansfeld 1998 and Weismantel 1988).

Specifically, overcoming poverty—*superando*—means sloughing off the markers that might make others define you as indigenous. Like the accustoming and de-accustoming discussed in the previous chapter, to *superarse* means to acquire some traits and shed others. This is an active reframing and a deliberate use of context—race in Peru is situational, a point that has been bolstered by recent scholarship on the location of race in the Andean landscape from the Enlightenment into the present (Poole 1997; de la Cadena 2000; Weismantel 2001). That is, these ethnic efforts are not isolated—all such moves must be ratified by others. Traces of indigenous identifications remain, and even attaining the nation's highest office is no guarantor against being referred to as *indio* and *cholo*, as Alejandro Toledo found.

On the Day of the Dead I saw a cemetery guard come and yell at a family seated on the grass: "Get off the grass! Where do you think you are, your fields?" At a fiesta later, Eduardo, a middle-aged Ayacuchano, kept offering me *trago*, cane alcohol, explaining, "These are our customs and some people say that we are *indios sin gracia* [uncouth Indians, "without grace"], just living in the past with our customs." The overly sensitive anthropologist with whom he drank insisted anxiously that these customs are part of the present, not the past, and he agreed. But later, a drunker Eduardo apologized for his drunkenness and said, "You see, that's what it means to be an *indio sin gracia*." This seeming self-hatred is a painful but necessary tactical move. Like women's bargains with patriarchy, described by Deniz Kandiyoti (1988: 286 n1), disenfranchised Peruvians who buy into racist ideology and hierarchy—cracking up at the televised antics of the cross-dressing "Paisana Jacinta" character, for instance[6]—are implicitly sketching out that which they hope they, or their children, will overcome. If race is mutable and relational, ideologies of ethnicity must be strongly reified and internalized in order to make a transition possible and traceable. And, in the Ayacucho region, the violence of the past two decades has been indelibly associated with the Andeanness that must be surmounted.

The second ugliness behind *superación* is that it perpetuates the us-versus-them of Andean race relations. To overcome, to surmount a condition which everyone in the immediate vicinity possesses as well, is to be assured that there's always someone worse off than you are. Witness Peter Lloyd's synthesis of comments he heard in Medalla Milagrosa, a Lima migrant community:

> Other settlements fully deserved the pejorative epithets customarily bestowed; Medalla Milagrosa, in contrast, was unusual in being so orderly and achievement-oriented. The loyalty of these [young university students] seems significant because, on the verge of entering upon professional careers and thereby the middle classes, they could have so easily denigrated the slum into which, by chance, they had been born. (1980: 89)[7]

Notice how the students of whom Lloyd writes, while remaining true to their kin and their home community, nonetheless insidiously allow all other migrant settlements to bear the weight of the stereotype. "Why yes, there *are* disorderly, lazy migrant communities out there—but we're different," they proudly intimate. It is as if, by vaunting the stereotype and producing an orderly and achievement-oriented community, they are not at all disavowing the negative presumptions about migrants—they are reifying them. They're on their way up—but they certainly aren't bringing anyone from another *barrio* along with them.

CIRCULATION WRIT LARGE: MIGRATIONS AS SOCIAL MOVEMENTS

While back in Socos for a town fiesta, middle-aged Francisco asked me why I thought all his family was in Lima, and I said that I thought they were there to work. Clarifying what he'd meant by "why," he reiterated, "But how do you think we got there?" Leaving no time for me to guess, he went on to explain that his mother, Inés, is the "mother of us all." Years ago, she was the first to go—a bucket of warm apple-flavored water in one hand and a bucket of glasses in the other, ready to sell liquid nostalgia and sustenance on Lima's streets. One by one, six-year-old Francisco and his siblings, cousins, and one unrelated girl (who soon was treated as a daughter) followed, in what Francisco called *una cadena*, "a chain."[8] He added that there was a similar multigenerational, kin-based chain in his family between Peru and Europe. Chains like these make social connections visible and materialize the geographies of relatedness, revising the mythology of a deeply divided coast and Andes.

Francisco continued in his fiesta-morning reminiscences, "When we come back to our town we reflect on what we would be if it weren't for Mama Inés—we would be *chacreros*, farmers." His comment traces the migration chain onto the map of socioeconomic hierarchy: from a peasant to someone who works for cash. In the anthropologist Catherine Allen's second edition of her evocative ethnography *The Hold Life Has*, she suggested that the preference of cash over the multilayered exchanges and reciprocities peasants enter into through the *ayni* system is a relatively recent development, and to her quite a jarring one (2002 [1988]: 213). *Superación*, getting ahead, is traced here in economies of relatedness versus money, and it is a transformation made material through migration.

Migration has a long history in the Andean region, rooted in ecological strategies of trade and cultivation within horizontal and vertical space

(Collins 1988: 27).[9] The population of rural-to-urban migrants has been growing steadily since the 1940s; 65 percent of the Peruvian population qualified as "rural" then, and just under 30 percent do now (INEI 2004; see also Millones 1981: 19).[10] Lima absorbed significant numbers of Afro-Peruvian and Chinese immigrants throughout the latter part of the nineteenth century (Millones 1981: 17–18), before migration from the highlands made the vast coastal capital—which holds one-third of the country's population—into an Andean city (Mendez G. 1993). Meanwhile, in Ayacucho, the sandwich-board sign promoting Socos-Vinchos Lube greets travelers as they leave the city heading west in the direction of both Socos and Vinchos and hints at the numbers of city neighbors who still call those towns home.[11] Labor migration took a back seat to the collective fleeing of the violence in the 1980s but remains the primary motivator today.

At least since the 1970s, anthropologists commenting upon rural-to-urban migration noted that it was perceived as part and parcel of "modernization" (Isbell 1978; Bourque 1971) and *superación* (Smith 1973: 198; see also Millones 1981: 15). The Andean migrants to Lima with whom Susan Lobo worked used the even starker label of *progreso*: "Progress is viewed as moving away from something negative, in this case away from life in the highlands, which is remembered in terms of scarcity of food, illness without relief, severe climate, and tremendously hard and wearing work with very little compensation. Progress is also seen as moving toward the positive ideal embodied in urban living, exemplified by plentiful food, good health, productive work, and adequate pay" (1982: 65). Again, progress is viewed as the surmounting of a lack, whether perceived as strictly economic or more subtly and insidiously racial, ethnic, or class-based.

But is it wholesale or unidirectional "progress" when migrants are always coming home? As one migrant told me, one's town is like one's mother, an *imán*, a magnet, always tugging at you until you return. The pull of this magnet is strengthened by obligations to the state: Peru requires its citizens to vote in their places of origin, so election days fall on long weekends and are preceded by an immense flow of migrants reversing course (and followed by the payment of fines by those who were unable to return). Home is also the place to celebrate the thoroughly enjoyable religious celebrations, especially one's hometown's saint's day (for example, the Virgin of the Assumption, *Mamacha Asunta*, in Socos on August 15).[12]

When visits are deterred by work schedules or tight budgets, the oft-traced pathways of these interprovincial social networks are made material through frequent gifts: of clothing from city (where it is cheaper) to highlands, and of food from highlands to city. My *comadre* occasionally sent large burlap sacks full of fava beans, corn, grains, or potatoes to her grateful Lima relatives. Although the foods had been cultivated on these migrants' land, they did not claim to view this as her obligation but rather as a gift to them, and they nostalgically savored every morsel. There are similar exchanges in international migrations—Cristina's children who migrated to Europe pay for their mother's telephone service so that they can reach her whenever they want. It's a service (in fact, one that is owned by a Spanish multinational) which is much too expensive for most of my interlocutors to purchase, so her daily chores are constantly interrupted when the phone rings with calls for her neighbors.

And how are these images of evolutionary social trajectory complicated by what Ninna Nyberg Sørensen has referred to as "multiple residence practice" (2002)—claiming residency in, physical links between, and social ties to two places at once? The families I knew best often kept one foot in the village and another in the city. Wilmer spent most of his time tending his fields of corn, potatoes, and fava beans and feeding his bulls and pigs; his wife and children spent most of their time in Ayacucho. Flora's family, though residing much more obviously in the city, returned to their village periodically to oversee the harvest on the fields they'd left behind and paid neighbors to tend. Migrations are often temporary and multidirectional, producing a large group of people and products that are in constant movement between their community of origin and the city of their work (Collins 1988; Collins 1985). They are social movements on a massive scale, as migrants are transported daily or weekly by foot, by minivan, or by car back and forth across the city or the country. After the long wait for the bus to fill and leave, interrupted by vendors who approach passengers to sell pop or popcorn, such a perennially transitory rural-to-urban migrant may close her eyes, lulled to sleep by the heat inside the packed minivan or interprovincial bus whose windows are never opened for fear a child may catch cold, and in such a fashion proceed over speed bumps, around precarious curves, and so homeward.

The constant returns of migrants like Francisco to their natal towns, and the multiple residence practices or commuter lifestyles of families like Wilmer's, together argue that "circulation" is a better descriptor for these movements than "migration," which carries more permanent connotations.[13] Such circulations or migrations can then be charted on a continuum from more to less permanent, more frequent to less frequent visits. At one end of this continuum, we might even locate the great distances that urban migrants must often travel to reach their places of work (especially in Lima, where some migrants live two hours, by bus, away from their workplaces), and the draining of the resource of time that this is for the poor (see Farmer 1999: 190).

The notion of *superarse* may have become especially important in Peru about sixty years ago as waves of migration to the cities (Millones 1981: 19) and the concomitant process of urbanization (Parker 1998: 36) commenced. But while the resonance of *superación* may have been ascendant during the massive migrations of the 1940s and beyond, it seems to have acquired further local meaning as Peruvians came to grasp the increasing fragility of their national and individual situations over the past twenty years. *Superarse* makes implicit sense within a context of extreme poverty, of recent violent and divisive conflict, and of a growing frustration with the inadequacy of the Peruvian government to provide basic services. The persistence of stark socioeconomic imbalance between coast and highlands, elite and disenfranchised, essentially requires poor people to claim an ideology in which they must escape poverty in order to succeed, and in which, if they do not overcome, it is their failing alone.

As a response to, and method for dealing with, this reality, migration and child circulation are very similar: just as a potential laborer migrates from countryside to city in search of a better life, so does a child migrate from natal home to receiving home in search of a better life. Elsewhere in the Andes this has been labeled "lending" or "sending" children, and is viewed explicitly as something that is good for the children. Children who are sent to the city from a small town will get to know the city, learn to work for a living, be able to send money home, and come home bearing knowledge, new clothes, and a small amount of money (Swanson 2007: 714–15). The racial and geographic hierarchies negotiated and concretized by rural-to-urban migrants are comparable to the social and economic hierarchies navigated and reinforced by circulated children. And sometimes, child circulation maps onto rural-to-urban migration, when rural children relocate to urban households. The techniques exercised in the name of *superación* overcome, but also reify, the sharp divisions between poor and not-quite-so-poor, peasant and professional, child laborer and student.

GROUNDING CHILD CIRCULATION: *SUPERARSE* AS EDUCATION, AND EDUCATIONAL

Sarita told me that she moved to Ayacucho from her small community "because of my studies, so I could *superarme*, in search of *la superación*."[14] Reyna's father told me that the two reasons she had been sent to Ayacucho were to get educated and to accompany. Olivia told me that if she were to become pregnant, her parents "wouldn't beat me, but they would kick me out, and I would understand them. Your parents sacrifice themselves so that you can study, and for you to repay them like that . . . ?" Pregnancy, for adolescent girls trying to *superarse*, is an especially bitter pill—in this context it represents a failure to seize all the opportunities available in life (figure 10). But Olivia points out that there is one opportunity above all others that must be seized and held fast. For the majority of my informants *superarse* had one primary referent: education.[15]

Education here refers to a superior public-school education. Rural highland schools in Peru are plagued by language differences between teacher and students, a lack of staffing and materials, and the prohibitive distance children must walk to get there. Although public education is nominally free, scraping together the cash for uniforms, school supplies, fees, and fines may mean that a family can afford to send only one of several siblings to school.[16] Education has another cost as well: the loss of a child's labor, whether in or outside the household. Urban children have more educational options, and those who can pay for it may elect to attend private school (whose main benefit, as far as I could tell, was that their teachers do not strike regularly; however, a key drawback is that students do not receive state-sponsored health insurance).

The formal education received in primary and secondary schools in Ayacucho does not automatically lead to life success, however. There is a

10. A billboard outside Ayacucho's hospital cautioning about the woes of teenage pregnancy: "A pregnancy too soon can change your plans."

terrible bottleneck as those young people graduate from high school and aim for acceptance into university. The public University of San Cristobal of Huamanga, said to be the third oldest in the Americas, offers students a sought-after, locally prestigious, and generally affordable route to higher education.[17] But its entrance exam is grueling and competitive—an entire industry has sprung up in Ayacucho to "prepare" high school graduates for the exam, but failure is both common and, because of the symbolic and material meanings of education for students and their families, very serious (see Lloyd 1980: 71 and Lobo 1982: 27 on public university admissions in Lima).

Education has not always nor everywhere been the obvious ticket out of poverty—J. D. Y. Peel underscores that it can only be seen that way when certain kinds of work gain value and when children are not needed for agricultural endeavors (1978: 148). There are broader transformations within which the linkages of *superarse*, education, and other strivings are forged. And as Degregori has convincingly argued, without this local emphasis on education as transformative, Shining Path would not have come to such power in the region: schools are a "cargo cult" of their own, inspiring "superhuman expectations" (1997: 44–53).[18] Poor Peruvians truly believe—because they *must* believe—that education is a way out of poverty.

This belief insidiously obscures the structural forces that keep migrant Ayacuchanos down, placing the onus on the individual to make a go of it.

Several of my interlocutors announced that they were sharing their stories with me so that I could use them in my academic writings and get the degree I sought—aligning my desires with their own, and perhaps also glossing a particular respect for the superior education presumed to be available in the developed world. A university education is widely viewed by the poor and striving as the ticket to self-improvement and, fundamentally, to modernization (Degregori 1997: 53). In Ayacucho, a degree from the public university can lead most directly to a coveted contract as a public employee, which is thought to be the most lucrative and stable job opportunity available without emigrating. Educated people are referred to in Spanish as "professionals," a category that in Peru is explicitly opposed to "peasants." Thus, education has the power to transform peasants into professionals.

In a context where "peasants" is officially code for "Indians," education is a technique for divesting oneself of certain ethnic markers. The peasant / professional continuum is a central part of the Andean racial complex, and provincial peasants and upwardly mobile urban migrants internalize these divisions when they praise education as a tool for overcoming a devalued race and class. It is this shift—one which frequently accompanies a change in the social geography—that has led scholars of race in the Andes to rightly label the emphasis on education as racism in disguise (see de la Cadena 1998: 160; 2000: 16; and Colloredo-Mansfeld 1998). As Maria Elena García has noted, throughout Peru's history education has been "one of the principal mechanisms through which 'Indians' were to be transformed into citizens" (2005: 63). At the same time, my interlocutors would never describe it this way. The shedding of indigenous characteristics through education is instead expressed through terms more closely resembling those of class—as Susan Lobo's informants indicated when they told her that "children, once educated, will be able to move into the middle class and earn enough money to afford some urban pleasures and luxuries" (1982: 27). That movement is both social and geographic.

Sarita remembered, years ago, leaving her uncle's house, located *abajo* or closer to the center of Ayacucho, and returning to her parents' side in the new house they had constructed in Ayacucho's outskirts. Even now, the neighborhoods keep creeping farther and farther up the hills surrounding the city, connected to the city center by a fifty-*céntimo* public bus that hurtles its riders down dirt roads that lose purchase with every rainy season. Sarita's new house was counterposed to her uncle's due to its location *arriba*—up high on the dusty slopes of the city near the highway.

> I didn't want to leave there either, because I had already gotten accustomed, and when I came to my house it wasn't the same as in my uncle's house. It was years that I was there, but whatever, sometimes you come to be accustomed to whatever environment that you go to, and as time passes you keep on getting accustomed.[19]

The house and environment stand in for culturally constructed connections between place and social class. Sarita's physical movement from small town to middle-class Ayacucho household marked a potential shift in social class as well, tempered when she had to effectively retrace these steps, trudging back up the hillside. Moving into the middle class is an education all its own—when a young person begins to *superarse*, she comes to know another lifestyle. Such changes, like the transition a *huamanguina*'s maid may face when she leaves her rural home with its small outhouse and bumps up against an indoor toilet with plumbing, can index an ethnic transformation. These changes produce a social education like Bourdieu's habitus (1990: 56) that can have the effect of making young people want to strive after this new life. *Superación* feeds into itself: children who go to overcome become converted to, and convinced by the superiority of, the new lifestyle. They will already have been well primed by their parents' commitment to this ideology, and by their parents' desire for the children to have greater social and economic opportunities than they themselves had.

The anthropologist Caroline Bledsoe describes fosterage in Sierra Leone as a process in which an adult receives a hard-working young person to help out in the house and market, and will in exchange train and educate the child in life skills. As Bledsoe suggests, "children do not simply learn knowledge: they must earn or 'buy' it [in a model] . . . of fairly straightforward exchange" (1990: 79–81; see also Renne 2003: 98 on Nigeria). Similarly, *superación* ideologically grounds child circulation, promoting decisions that open up new fields of opportunity and possibility for children as they grow. Andean child circulation, leading to both formal and social education for young people, is locally seen as being in what the international field of social work calls "the best interests of the child."[20]

LABOR, EXPLOITATION, TRAFFIC

But not all observers agree that child circulation is a boon for children. In the previous chapter, some of these tensions were explored—the mistreatment and loneliness entailed in companionship, and the inequality bolstered by the *propina*. Social critics, from Spanish-born historian Sebastián Lorente in 1855 to the director of an anti-child-trafficking NGO in 2003, condemn the perils of child circulation. It's a discourse which appears in scholarly works as well—Nara Milanich writes that for poor children in nineteenth-century Chile, being sent out for "education" or in domestic service were "in practice one and the same" (2004: 316), and Karsten Paerregaard remarked, when analyzing rural Arequipeño children who are sent to city relatives to learn Spanish and urban ways, that "it is often hard to tell the difference between adoption and labour exploitation" (1997: 160 n12). In this section, I'll examine this linkage more closely.

In his "Thoughts on Peru," Sebastián Lorente connects the circulation of children with race, poverty, and risk in a stinging critique:

The *cholito* is the Indian who is enslaved almost upon leaving the cradle. Sometimes it's the mother who condemns the child of her loins to servitude, because her poverty makes her believe that he will be happier in the master's home, or because she was obligated to sell him to be able to pay for his father's burial. More often, the cholito was removed from maternal tenderness by someone who wanted to speculate with his brothers' flesh, or make a gift . . . And anyway, isn't the cholito going to a house where he'll have a better life? Doesn't a more pleasing future await? Oh, there are some kind masters who will raise him and treat him like a son, but how few such generous souls exist![21] The best the cholito can hope for is that the daughters of the house will have affection for him, and to occupy in their hearts a place between the monkey and the lapdog; sometimes he suffers like an animal; he is often like a slave; and he also has the disadvantage that since he didn't cost much, he can't be sold at a high price, so he isn't treated with great care . . . And no matter how lucky he may be in his servitude, he will always have grown up without a mother's presence, with an abandoned child's barrenness of heart and affection . . . Most are saved, with time, from this disgrace; transported carelessly to climates that are very dangerous for children of the sierra and with a brusque change in their regimens, they tend to perish not long after being brought to the coast. These are the lucky ones. (1967 [1855]: 29–30)[22]

The social stratifications of capitalism leave a poor Indian mother little choice, Lorente suggests, but to send her child away in the hopes that he, and perhaps she, can benefit. But transferred children are at terrible risk of mistreatment, a warped heart from a lack of maternal affection, and what Lorente paints as a welcome death.

Today, IDEIF, the anti-child-trafficking NGO introduced in chapter 2, suggests that little has changed in the century and a half since Lorente penned his polemic. IDEIF makes a similar argument in a more consumable form, however: the colorful comic book. In 2003, when I first visited the Lima office, four charming pamphlets were available for distribution to elementary schools. One depicts a young boy from the countryside who goes to live with a wealthy godmother and is made to work instead of study, as he was promised (figure 11). Sandra Soria, the IDEIF's director, told me that the cartoon child's relocation would only be acceptable if he were studying and performing age-appropriate tasks. For IDEIF, the combination of failing to comply with a promise to educate a child (the ethic of *superarse*) and labor exploitation of that child constitutes traffic.

The strength of IDEIF's condemnation comes from their good intentions, the inclusion of the caveats that there are acceptable ways to move children, and the emphasis on education as a culturally logical end for child circulation. But from an anthropological perspective, the danger of their stance is that it carves into the amorphous complex of child circulation practices, marking some as tenuously appropriate and others as harmful.[23] To protect every child's rights, an explicit discussion of the exact terms of the transfer would be required. But because this is socially impossible among the vertical threads of race and class within which child circulation takes place, such a requirement would limit, in a very real way, both child givers' and child receivers' abilities to use this strategy. It isn't pretty, but it makes sense. Leaving for another household means believing that it could

11. A page from IDEIF's comic book: Juanito laments his poor treatment and asks his godmother to let him go to school. Terre des Hommes.

go well, and that schooling is involved. It means downplaying or ignoring the possibility of exploitation. In the unspoken understanding maintained by my interlocutors in Peru, there are degrees of mistreatment, and in many cases these risks or problems are deliberately overlooked or tacitly accepted because the desire to *superarse* is so powerful.[24]

I tried to articulate these thoughts to Soría, but it didn't come out very well. I said that I hoped that policies and laws against trafficking avoid *atentar contra cultura*, "attacking culture," or preventing poor people from using a legitimate and necessary strategy. Her smile vanished and I tried to beat a hasty retreat, while insisting (apologetically) that such projects, widely interpreted, might close doors that people use all the time. She replied:

In the countryside there is a lot more ease in letting go of children. I don't want to criticize, but . . . in the 1970s there was an economic crisis and an earthquake at the same time, and in the Arequipa market the mothers sat there and people would pass by saying "I'll take your child," and they'd respond, "How much?" I think they think the kids will be better off somewhere else than with them, or the reality, they have so many children . . . There are mothers, and then there are mothers, right?[25]

In a later conversation, her former boss at IDEIF, José Alvarado de la Fuente (who was, at the time of our interview, MIMDES's [Ministerio de la Mujer y Desarrollo Social] General Director of the Boy, Girl, and Adolescent), disagreed that this was, as I had framed it, an issue of "culture." "I don't think *any* culture considers turning over children to be a valid option," he stated. "Turning a child over to improve himself, fine, if he keeps being your child . . . Traffic is when you seek to get rid of a child so that you can get something out of it. It's a temporary loosening when the child goes to an aunt. Of course it helps you, because you don't have the responsibility of the child, the aunt does. But the mother continues to relate to the child, it's not as if she has nothing to do with him." From both Soría and Alvarado, then, we are given a veiled criticism of the poor women who let their children go. This differentiates their discourse from Lorente's, who explicitly acknowledges the poverty and inequality that framed movements of children in the nineteenth century. Then, Indian children were taken from their mothers— and even when poor mothers were complicit in this removal, they clearly had little choice in the matter. The gendered criticism of poor and indigenous mothers that colors the IDEIF position, however, echoes some of the criticisms found in the abandonment files. It's easier, and fits better within Peru's historical trajectory of racism, to criticize than to address (and take responsibility for) the conditions that lead to these women's poverty. Such critics do mean well, but they are speaking from a position of incomprehension. Like the police officer I spoke to in 2006 who refused to admit the possibility that "material abandonment" could be unrelated to "moral abandonment" (described in chapter 2), they imagine that the poor have awareness of and access to the same resources that their critics do.

Child circulation looks like a fairly unvarnished exploitation to these social critics, speaking from their comfortable but sincere location in Lima's professional classes. In Ayacucho, the working migrant families who engage in it have a more complex view. Child circulation can lead to loneliness, sadness, anxiety, or what Sebastián Lorente called "barrenness of heart and affection." But child circulation allows young people to *superarse*, and it provides companionship and household chores for an older, lonely person. This more complicated view shapes why, under the contested conditions described here, child circulation is heavily skewed toward girls.

THE GENDERED DYNAMICS OF CHILD CIRCULATION

Olivia's contrasting of unplanned pregnancy with education, described above, resonates with her mother's statements to me about parenting adolescent girls. Olivia's mother, my *comadre*, described to me what she thought was important to impart to her children: respect first of all, and then to be good, kind, orderly, and industrious. Parents must convey to their children a respectful orientation to the social environment around them. In Marie Arana's bicultural memoir, she points out that for her father—a recent immigrant from Peru to the United States—"the notion of building a life around children was alien, bizarre, inexplicable. In Peru, it had been the other way around: children built lives around their parents. The elders defined the world" (2001: 259). Children must respect adults, above all, and this attitude is admonished, swatted, and even beaten into them. For Olivia, becoming pregnant would have been an embodied statement of disrespect, and her parents and male relatives would be within their rights to whip her for that. In many of the migrant households I visited, next to framed Catholic images and prominently displayed on a nail in the peeling plaster wall, rested a foot-long, three-tailed whip made of braided plant fibers.[26] Social relations between parents and children are constituted, and framed hierarchically, through such violence: the legitimate and accepted disciplinary aspect of the larger context of Andean parenting (Harvey 1994: 69–70).[27]

Ayacucho is Peru's handicraft capital, and one of the beautiful products of the region is a painted wooden decoration called *tabla de Sarhua*, depicting locally and socially relevant events or conditions. In this one (figure 12), a single mother is spurned and disrespected by her child's father. In life as in art, pregnancy is emblematic of the many risks young women face, and

12. *Tabla de Sarhua* (painted wooden artwork from the southern part of the department of Ayacucho) by an anonymous artist, from the collection of the author. "The single mother wants to give her son to his father and the father doesn't want him, so he is escaping."

it's unsurprising that it is the referent of much parental education. This discipline can take verbal form, referred to locally as *control* (intervention) or *orientación* (instruction and guidance), a moral direction aimed at teaching a young person respectful and social behavior. But girls are the primary focus of this—young women are weaker and need male relatives to protect them, because their falls from grace threaten their kinship networks and social positions.[28] The placement of a moral compass in young adult bodies is a gendered act, designed partly to prolong a girl's unmarried and childless state for as long as possible so that she has a better chance of achieving professionalization and *superación*.[29] Girls understood and internalized this; one young woman told me, "If I made the mistake of getting pregnant, with pain in my soul I would try to abort and, I don't know, that would cut off my future, I wouldn't have the economic means to take care of it. I am still in school."[30] But the Ayacuchanos I spoke to often blamed *parents* when children went astray, for it is a parent's responsibility to help the child avoid risk.

If young women are in greater danger than young men, it seems incongruous that they, over men, would be more likely to be circulated, sent away from the sphere of moral influence their parents command. But the cases of young women in my notes far outnumber those of young men; in part this is due to the gender divisions that characterize the Andean region and inform fieldwork there, and in part it is because girls are simply more likely to be in these situations. There are no official statistics on child circulation since it is completely unregulated, but Alvarado suggested in our interview that the young people who are circulated in this way are about 15 percent boys. One author working in Cuzco wrote that high rates of rural-to-urban migration in that department include "a significant proportion of girls, especially from age ten onward" (Barrenechea Lercari 1988: 83; see also Lloyd 1980: 62).[31]

This gender imbalance is the ironic result of Andean gender ideologies and practices that divide the working world into two complementary halves,[32] and the result of the implications of the rural-urban divisions that thread through this book. Because of the nature of women's work, as teenaged Luís told me, women "have more possibilities of work." His sister Olivia elaborated: "They know how to do more things, they get involved more easily."[33] Even though their mother believes that "sons and daughters should know everything—to work like a man, to cook," her daughters bore the responsibility for more household tasks than did her son. (In 2006, both Olivia and Luís were living and working in Lima, and Olivia told me that their mother had instructed Olivia to go to Luís's and make his bed for him!) Similarly, Andean women tend to bear the majority of the burden of housework: slow cooking over fires, hand-washing clothes, caring for small children. For the same reasons that older boys were preferred in nineteenth-century North American adoptions as farm laborers (Zelizer 1985: 194), young women's labor is a valued commodity within the political economy of the urban Peruvian household, lying at a distance now from its fields.[34] Alvarado summed up this view by stating that girls are more frequently transferred "because families look for girls to help cook, wash, iron, and often care for children—it's a *machista* vision."

Alvarado used the word *ayuda*, "help." It's not an accidental word choice —recall the work/help distinction noted by the anthropologist Ben Orlove in the work diaries of Bolivian peasants described in the previous chapter. Orlove's data indicate the power of gender in shaping the definition of the domestic sphere. And circulated children enter into and are typically positioned in relation to the household and domestic economy, not the fields.

To follow Orlove's line of thinking, children who are transferred into another person's house and who do household chores or care for children or animals are therefore "helping." Help is contrasted to work and is something kin and neighbors do for one another. It's a transitive verb, implicating at least one other person, the one who is being helped. "Help" implies a relationship, connotes the idea of companionship that is woven through articulations of child circulation. But "help" is also a kind of labor that implicates gender. Young women, of a lower class than the families that take them in, receiving affection but also helping with household chores—from the *criadas* of colonial Peru to circulated Ayacuchanas today, they are mobile and gendered laborers.[35]

Relocating girls on the basis of their gendered skills results in advantageous opportunities for them insofar as it enacts the concept of *superación*. While some of these circulated girls are exploited, and they all have to work (Green 1998), they also have more access to the advantages that can accrue from transferring into a socially and economically wealthier home. These circulations become implicit exchanges (Barrenechea Lercari 1988: 74): room, board, perhaps a *propina*, and the hope of *superación* in return for the gendered performance of household labor, gratefulness, and humility. This apparent advantage for young women is comparable to the kinds of opportunities that have historically been available only to young Andean males: military service and forms of hard labor such as mining or construction.[36] In a country where education is a highly valued goal for many, and where rural girls are often denied schooling ("Voces que buscan" 2001; García 2005: 102), having the opportunity to move to the city and go to school because of one's feminine gender becomes an interesting advantage, for girls and, ultimately, their families.

THE RELATIONAL CONTEXT OF *SUPERACIÓN*: UNHAPPILY STRIVING

Claiming the ideology of *superarse* defines borders—in Peter Lloyd's example cited earlier, between a home community like Medalla Milagrosa and other neighborhoods. Most of the Ayacuchanos I spoke with also framed *superación* as something they carried out not only for themselves but for a specific social group.[37] *Superación* defines the limits of relatedness, expressing desirable associations into the future. This individual effort—overcoming one's own conditions—is a moral act: it occurs within a social web of relations who will, ideally, benefit as well. To *superarse* is an imperative of self-improvement where self includes close kith and kin.

Sarita's father Wilmer told me that his children would probably hire *peones* to work the land he would leave them. He seemed content with the idea that they would move beyond the limitations of their parents, attain professional status, and no longer work the land out of need. As his daughter said to me on a separate occasion, her father shows that he loves them by "worrying about us, and wanting the best for us." The best, it seems, would be to be better than him—as can be seen in Wilmer's grown nephew's tearful assertion, over a couple of fiesta-morning bottles of beer, that "my boys *will* be better than their father."[38]

The moral aspect of *superación* is clear in Wilmer's imagination of his children's *peones*. He told me that there will always be people available to work the fields, because rural parents don't emphasize education for their children (as had, in fact, been his own history).[39] Wilmer felt meaningfully different from rural parents who, he believed, did not consistently value education for their children. His choice to send his daughter Sarita to live with her aunt and uncle (who, along with their children, are "professionals") in the city at a young age underscored for him his own moral and social competence above other parents.

These messages from parents to children are taken seriously and internalized by young people like Sarita:

> I perhaps also grew up with this desire, with this goal practically, and once I returned to live with my parents this was growing more and more, because I saw my mother sometimes suffering, crying over money, arguing just over money. I always had the mentality that I was going to study and I was going to *salir adelante*, which I told them sometimes when they argued about money. I told them, "I'm going to work and then no one will humiliate you, no one will tell you that because of money."[40]

Instructed in this project of overcoming, the children of urban migrants then come to internalize the same goal of wanting something more than what their parents had been able to attain. (And once again, money is the axis around which these tensions revolve. Sarita distills the set of discriminations she and her parents face into class-related ones, but money whitens, and poverty is closely connected to racism and oppression.) As Sarita's statement makes clear, the goal of overcoming is thoroughly enmeshed with a desire to help her family. Ultimately, Sarita and other politically engaged university students link and extend *superarse* to their self-proclaimed socialism: they want Peru to become a better place for everyone.

Superarse is a technical device urging poor Peruvians to get ahead, survive, scrape by, but there is something more at stake. The greater end of *superación* is found squarely within the family, neighborhood, and community: it is not a wholly self-centered act, but one which draws on and reinforces generational relationships within social context. *Superarse*, though worded in terms of self, is clearly a family project, and it is this valence that makes the concept so poignant and meaningful for youth who come to realize that their own potential is often the only possibility through which their entire family can *superarse*. This realization shapes their life experience. The children being circulated in the practice I describe here are not isolated from their families—their efforts in and around circulation and household labor speak directly to their families' hopes and possibilities.

The generational implications of *superación* are also visible in the migrations or imagined journeys of women I knew in Ayacucho.[41] Both Tania— who migrated to Europe during the period of my fieldwork—and Lupe discussed migration in terms of *superación* as an embodied and relational ideology. For Tania's tightly knit sibling group, migration was a necessary condition for overcoming the poverty and impossible challenges of everyday life in Peru. She told me, "I don't want a big house, I just want a slightly better life, and more than anything I want to be able to help people." Tania's *superación* is not explicitly material—it is a small and intangible improvement in her life, her children's lives, her siblings' lives, and in her own ability to help others. Similarly, Lupe, who one day may be able to migrate to Europe through family connections, told me that she would only do it after her son is old enough to "see that I am going to leave so that we can all *superar*."[42] Lupe positions *superarse* as an engagement on behalf of, and with the full comprehension of, her entire family.[43] Overcoming is not just an enclosed, individual process: it is the province of an entire family and their future descendants.

Still, there remains a deep ambivalence about moving children, for everyone involved. Over and over, when I asked interlocutors if they would have their future children live in such situations, they said they would not, finding it difficult to imagine circumstances that would force them to do so, even though every day they saw families in similar circumstances. Young people's investment in the family project of *superación* will lead them to accept humiliation and exploitation in light of the benefits thought to be accorded. Possible loneliness or sadness is treated as an unpleasant but necessary side effect of the choice to self-improve. The kinds of discomforts and degradations that emerged in my interviews often related to the social differences between circulated child and receiving household; because the movements are vertical, inequalities and class differences shape the kind of treatment that is possible and expected. Entering into a household and family of higher socioeconomic position than the giving family lays the groundwork for a child to *superarse*, but it also highlights those inequalities between family members or acquaintances.

Juana, the eldest of four siblings who have each (at one point or another) been circulated out of their natal home, recalled how one of her first meals in the new household was fried ham, a meal completely foreign to her but presumably one that she should have viewed as a special treat from her new patrons. The intense abdominal discomfort she felt afterward sent her to the emergency room. This experience became a metaphor for the mistreatment she perceived at the hands of her patrons, who became her godparents after she had moved in with them. As she reeled off examples—like how the family criticized her when their coiffed and beloved dog choked on a bone she had failed to remove from its supper—she was producing a moral evaluation of *acompañar*. Child circulation can entail instruction in the lifeways of a higher social class, but it can also lead to a provocative critique of relations of inequality when young women like Juana evaluate the motivation of *superación* against the treatment they receive, and define certain humiliations as too much to bear.[44] During the period of my fieldwork, Juana rejected the sting of frequent scoldings and moved alone into her mother's house.

Sonia and Alberto are two of four siblings born to a couple from Socos who "did not know how to work," meaning that they were agricultural rather than professional laborers and had difficulty in making ends meet. Margarita, their relative in a way that I never was able to reliably chart (they call her aunt, with great respect and affection), was a blanket seller who made frequent gifts of fruit and supplies to the family of six. Now, the siblings are successful Lima-based migrants and are in a position to help Margarita, sending her clothes and food on her birthday and Mother's Day. They also receive Margarita's children, Sarita, Olivia, and Luís, as laborers (they cook and clean) during the summer, exchanging the labor for much-needed *propinas* and school supplies. Margarita's children are not treated like guests—they are there to help in the household, and they receive sometimes humiliating treatment. This is perceived as the four siblings helping Margarita's family, not the other way around. What especially galls these young people is, not only do they have to put up with humiliations and the potential of labor exploitation, but they are expected to be grateful for it![45]

Because of the tight links between *acompañar* and *superación*, however, many of them are. Sarita's words are especially poignant as she described, in painstaking detail, her suffering as a monolingual Quechua-speaking six-year-old who went to Ayacucho to live with her upwardly mobile aunt and uncle:

> The punishment they gave me, I thank them for it, but it's that if I didn't stop or didn't want to stop speaking my Quechua, because I was simply ashamed of speaking Spanish, I don't know what happened but I didn't want to. And what my aunt and uncle and cousins did is that simply if I kept speaking in Quechua, and I spoke to them in Quechua, they didn't answer me . . . They almost forced me to learn, obligating me, but I thank them. Of course, for me this time was—for many reasons I felt hatred for them and the only thing I did was cry, cry, but now I realize it was for my own good, because my classmates didn't speak Quechua.[46]

Sarita remembers how she suffered, but she realizes that it was for her own good: "I always understood that it had to be this way, for my own good, always."[47] Acknowledging the sadness underscoring her movement permits a glimpse of children's agency. Even though she did not make the choice to relocate (as children sometimes do), she retrospectively decided that it was for her own good. Similarly, Lupe, who said she would have liked to grow up with her grandmother, added the caveat "but it would have been impossible, because my grandmother lives in the countryside and I don't think I would want to be a person who doesn't even know how to read, because it would always have been that way."[48]

CONCLUSIONS: PROGRESS AND RELATEDNESS

Valentina, an unmarried teacher approaching thirty years of age, is the only child of Blanca, a single mother. She told me that she had presented a university paper about terrorism, which had been received well in Spain, and she'd been offered a scholarship to study there, but her mother became sick. Blanca cried until Valentina decided not to go; as Valentina explained, from the time she was a child she'd learned to love and care for her mother, and she couldn't leave if Blanca didn't want her to go. Valentina recounted to me her kinship theory: that in Peru, families are much closer than they are in Europe or North America, where she believes people are much more individualistic. She said this is both good and bad: "because we are so tied to our families, we aren't able to progress." Valentina's reflection on her relationship with Blanca situates *superación* as thoroughly enmeshed with relatedness.

Child circulation is a gendered practice, providing for interesting ways in which girls, desired by receiving households for their labor skills, can have real opportunities. Remember that, in a region where boys just barely outnumber girls (INEI 1993), there are slightly more girls than boys in Ayacucho's orphanages (a 55–45 ratio), yet a few more boys than girls are placed for adoption (a 53–47 ratio).[49] Revisiting these numbers in light of the gender claims made here, it's clear that girls are more likely to be temporarily placed in the orphanage, but they are also more likely to be retrieved by poor parents. The same beliefs and practices about gender difference that cause girls to be circulated as useful companions and household helpers mean that boys are slightly more likely to be permanently abandoned at an orphanage, and subsequently adopted.

Superarse is a material, social, and moral process that resonates among urban migrants in the Andean countries, and among circulated children who have become cognizant of the effects of poverty. By leaving home and putting up with loneliness, mistreatment, and humiliation, young people feel they can contribute to the betterment of their families. The linkages between *superarse*, education, and racial whitening underscore the movements of children as social mobility. It is especially ironic that assumptions about what constitutes appropriate labor for girls actually contribute to girls' ability to improve their own (and ultimately, their families') social positions through education and circulation. And it's deeply troubling that buying into the meaningful ethic of *superación* both perpetuates racism and deflects attention from the structural reasons that *superarse* is even perceived to be necessary: *falta de economía* and the persistent divisions between races, classes, and genders.

Child circulation sometimes gives way to out-and-out exploitation, an uncomfortable possibility that troubles the IDEIF, motivating their important efforts. More often, however, the sadness of child circulation lies in the humiliation of mistreatment, and in the separation from loved ones.[50] When young people are not living with the people they have been born to, it is usually not the first choice. Most young people told me how much they missed their parents and siblings and that they would prefer to be with their parents but recognized that this was unrealistic. *Superación* is an ideology that helps young people deal with the pain of missing home: they know that it's in the best interests of the child. But they articulate their sadness in terms that speak of nothing so much as kinship, emotion, and belonging—topics to which I now turn.

Six.

PERTENECER: KNOWLEDGE AND KINSHIP

 Sarita, whom I met when she was in university, had lived with her aunt and uncle for a few years as a child so that she could attend primary school in Ayacucho. Sarita eventually got accustomed to living in the new household, but she added:

> I didn't love my aunt and uncle—that is, I appreciated them very much and thank them very much, because they had me for so long in their house, they supported me in different ways, but they never earned my affection, they are maybe too reserved, too . . . Their children were all they cared about, I was like just another person who lived there, and not a niece—that is, they never showed me affection, and neither did my cousins. Sometimes they did, but there was always the difference that I was just a cousin.[1]

Sarita is speaking a central theme of young people's narratives of circulation: the knowledge of one's true nature, bolstered by affection and emotional response. Not only did Sarita fail to feel love, the emotion she most tightly associated with kinship—she also knew that she was qualitatively different from that of a child of the household, describing herself as "just another person who lived there."

Ayacuchanos negotiate the social world around them through wielding the notion of *pertenecer*, or belonging—a belonging documented by papers, words, and sentiments. In the integration of circulated children and in their conversion into particular kinds of kin, observers can witness, along with the origins of Bourdieu's habitus, a kind of identity work. Belonging is produced through emotions (which, as Barth 2002: 1 suggests, in turn produce knowledge), or "what Max Weber called a *Zusammengehörigkeits-gefühl*, a feeling of belonging together" (Brubaker and Cooper 2000: 20). It is also produced through documentation and legitimacy, archival tools by which Ayacuchanos come to know themselves and others.

TOGETHERNESS, AND BLOOD: THE PRODUCTION OF *CARIÑO*

Olivia explained that Micaela loves her half-sister Karina in the same way that "we and [our half-sister] Lupe esteem each other very much because we have lived together." Micaela's uncle told me that he and his siblings were closer to Margarita and Cristina than to other (genealogically closer) relatives, because they had grown up right next door to one another in Socos, where Margarita played with them when they were small. Margarita's niece commented that because she was raised by her grandmother in Socos and grew up right next door to Margarita, Margarita "suffers for me when I am suffering." And in Margarita's words, "I have a lot of affection for my niece, because I grew up together with her."

The Ayacuchanos I knew inevitably presented having lived together, over time, as a justification for the emotional connections they experienced. Present-day *cariño*, affection, is a direct result of past cohabitation. Conversely, remember Lupe's discovery that simply moving in with her father and half-siblings was not enough to make a relationship—that "it's hard when you don't grow up with a person from childhood." Similarly, Micaela barely knew her birth father. She had met him once, "in the cemetery when he was 'escaping' from his wife," but she never came to know him (*llegar a conocer*). *Because* she never lived with him, she didn't cry much when he died; *because* she never lived with her half-siblings, borne of another wife, she doesn't care much about them.

Living together implies tending to one another and sharing chores, spaces, and secrets. Andean days are measured out through shared meals—when no one else is home one doesn't feel like eating, as Reyna told me (see chapter 4)—and Mary Weismantel's work has shown the tight associations between eating, affection, and kinship (1988). Preparing, offering, receiving, and consuming food materially produce relatedness and community. Serving someone heaps of food (more food than an uninitiated North American belly can comfortably stomach) is defined as affection (cariño); a plate without much food on it means one is uncared for. When the sun descends behind the surrounding brown peaks, cohabitation grades into co-sleeping, which also produces cariño and connectivity. Bedrooms, rarely used for daytime activities, delineate a family's relationships. For rural-to-urban migrants, sharing a bed with a child or sibling is the norm.[2] Once I spent a night with Sarita, sharing her firm new double mattress, which rested on the floor because it was too big for her sagging wooden bed frame. We slept with heavy woven wool blankets to our skin, without sheets. In the adjacent room, Sarita's mother and younger sister shared one narrow bed and her younger brother slept in the other.[3] Several times as we were falling asleep, Sarita asked me if I was comfortable, and when she fell asleep she talked aloud, saying "My anger! My anger!"

Sarita's sister, Olivia, viewed the time spent with (and money spent on) cohabitating family members as essential to the production of cariño. Sounding like the anthropologist Nancy Scheper-Hughes, whose work has explored why poor and marginalized mothers in Brazil did not grieve their infant children's deaths in a context of high infant mortality (1992), Olivia commented that yes, it was sad that six of Cristina's twelve children had died, but at the same time, madrinita linda, "when the child is born, and is still a baby, you don't feel so much affection." Sadness at an infant's death is far eclipsed, she suggested, by the death of a teenaged child, because at that age "you're going to put everything into him, you're going to invest your money."[4] Olivia's words imply a social, economic, and emotional investment in younger household members by elder ones that is key to the emergence of family affection.

But Olivia also told me that, for a child, there is one kind of cariño that needs no cohabitation to be realized. She proposed that maternal affections are innate, natural, unlike paternal affections, which like any others are produced through cohabitation:

Fathers do feel affection for their children, but not as much as does the mother who brought them into the world. There are fathers like mine, who live together with their children and come to love us as much as a mother. But the father who doesn't live with his children doesn't—he loves them in a certain way because they are of his blood, but he doesn't know what their character or their personality is like. For me, the father that doesn't live with his children is not a father.

I thought this was rather ironic, since in my view Olivia's father spent most of his time physically elsewhere, in their village farming and taking the animals to pasture. Unfazed by my suggestion, she answered, "Yes, he travels, but he always comes back to see how we are doing."

Olivia mentioned blood, which she positioned as a metaphor for the knowledge of relatedness. (A father who did not know his children were "of his blood" would not love them.) Taking up the blood metaphor is often an unpleasant exercise for kinship scholars—from the one-drop rule used to produce race and racism in the United States to the "blood quantum" of Native American identity and belonging, "[t]ies through blood," as Donna Haraway testifies, "have been bloody enough already" (1995: 366). Anthropologists, sensitized to the ethnocentric and historic predominance of blood and genealogy in our own kinship theories (Schneider 1980), are particularly loathe to address connections interpreted as blood relations.

But in the Ayacuchano migrant case study, blood represents—as it does in much of Europe and North America—relatedness. (This differs from other approaches to family throughout the Andean region; for example, the Zumbaguans with whom Mary Weismantel lived viewed all the adults referred to as "parents" as equal and did not privilege the genitor or genitrix (1995: 691).) Ayacuchanos can have more than one mother, but they also know how to distinguish between the women filling that role. My interlocutors perceived an underlying truth about one's social origins, identity, and relationships with others. *Cariño* may be forged through coresidence, sharing meals or beds, but it takes root and thrives in the fertile, if bloody, ground of genealogy. But genealogy is a way of knowing—"blood relations" are not actualized if they are not known.

This is a crucial point at which the beliefs about identity and nature held by Ayacuchano migrants dovetail with those held by adoption office staff.[5] In adoption policy, an underlying identity is presumed to exist apart from the new family's nurturing and incorporation.[6] Adoption office staff believed Peruvian adoptive parents should tell their adopted children the "truth" of their adoption but asserted that such parents often withheld that information out of fear or shame (according to the Lima office's public relations representative, Peruvian couples tend to view adoption as an embodiment of their own failure to reproduce). The method for addressing the "truth" is different, but the belief in its relevance is the same. Blood, however, is not the only or even the most common metaphor for knowing a connection to another human. Ayacuchano families also produce and circulate knowledge of relatedness with the aid of kin terms, another old anthropological standby.

"LIKE A DAUGHTER"

During the first several months of fieldwork, my partner and I typically refused requests to godparent; we felt that we didn't know anyone well enough yet to take on that responsibility. But we had met Cecilia on a summer trip in 2000, through a fellow Inca Trail hiker who introduced me to her because she ran an orphanage. When we visited her again in the fall of 2001, she said she was very glad we'd come, and—when her promptings of shy, twelve-year-old Paulina went unheeded—asked us herself if we would become Paulina's godparents for her graduation from middle school. We agreed and set a date for me to take the two of them shopping.

Cecilia had a dress that Paulina would wear on the December occasion, but small white shoes were still required, and this was the object of our market trolling. After canvassing the market, Paulina finally settled on a pair from the first stall we'd entered, and I paid for them. The vendor disappeared into the depths of the market to break the large bill, and Cecilia turned to Paulina and told her: "Now you are her goddaughter, and you have to call her *madrina* with all respect." The timing of this fascinated me—as soon as the money had changed hands, Paulina was my goddaughter, although I hadn't gone through any ceremony. I replied to Cecilia (stupidly, as I should have waited to see what she said), "We are *comadres* now." She agreed and we all hugged happily until the man came back with my change.

The reason I should have waited to see whether Cecilia called me her *comadre* or not—apart from just being good anthropological practice of not leading my interlocutor—was that she had "taken in" Paulina at age six, six years ago. Their relationship on the surface looks like a mother and child; Paulina calls Cecilia as many different forms of *mamá* as she can think of. Cecilia also calls Paulina "daughter" occasionally, and tells her five-year-old birth daughter to "go ask your sister" for something. But to me, when describing the relationship, Cecilia says Paulina is "like a daughter; she's been with us since she was very small." Her explanation underscores the importance of cohabitation over time but still positions Paulina as not a daughter . . . but like one.

"Like a daughter," in Cecilia's home, encompasses a range of behavior. She feeds and clothes Paulina, treats her with affection and warmth, and makes sure her path through life is smooth—from supplying her with extra tutoring when her grades dropped, to acquiring a pair of *gringo* godparents for her middle-school graduation. But Cecilia, her husband, and their five-year-old daughter sleep in a double bed with a mustard-colored satin cover, adjacent to their infant son's single bed, while Paulina's room—small and a few doors away—holds a bed and little else.[7] Paulina is separate from the other family members in other ways too; for example, Cecilia told me that Paulina doesn't like the sun in the countryside and prefers to stay home and watch TV instead of joining the family in weekend outings. The everyday performances and enactments, the conscious use of kin terms, are what create and reinforce the borders of their relationship.

In her *Cholas and Pishtacos*, Mary Weismantel frames the "passports, letters of introduction, or business cards, as well as other, less tangible verbal forms—such as professional titles" (2001: 196)—as documents that give weight to racialized privilege and affiliation with the state. These respectful titles that underlings use for their superiors (Engineer, Doctor) are echoed in other preferential terms of respectful address: from the Brother and Sister of evangelical Peruvians to a range of Mister or Ma'am (*Señor/Señora*) for strangers, Neighbor (*Vecina*) for nearby acquaintances, and Mother and Father (*Mamita/Papito*, or in Quechua, *Mamacha/Taytacha*)[8] for warm, close elders including grandparents, in-laws, godparents, and even God or the Virgin Mary.[9] Like these titles, kin terms are oral documents that Ayacuchanos use incessantly, spurning given names, to produce and gauge their relatedness to others.

I was always left wondering: when a man speaks of "my daughter," to which daughter is he referring? When my *comadre* talked to me about "your *compadre*," which of my many *compadres* did she mean? (This was a particularly frustrating example, as it eventually turned out that she was talking about her own husband!) Once I shared a meal with a woman who, every single time she addressed the hostess, started her sentences with "*Tía.*" Aunt / uncle was the classificatory category that most frequently perplexed me. I could not figure out how people decided when, and for whom, to use those terms. Finally, I turned to my teenaged goddaughter Olivia, who told me that *tío* means "your mother's brother" but acknowledged that she and most people she knew included many others with that label.[10]

Thoroughly curious now, I gave Olivia a *trabajo*, a "homework assignment": to write down for me a list of all the people she calls "*tío / tía*" and the reasons that she used that term. We discussed one example before she set to her task:

Tío / Tía Details

Carla N. An elderly woman who has always treated Olivia like a niece. She has supported Olivia's family. There is *cariño*. They are neighbors.

A few days later, Olivia came over with a carefully penned list of about 215 *tíos*, confessing to me that in several cases she had not known the person's full name or specific connection to her, so she had asked her mother for assistance.

As I learned from Olivia's exhaustive list, the naming of family is broadly inclusive, encompassing both what is felt and what is known. The classificatory category of aunt / uncle extends widely to include numerous respected older people. She counted beloved kinspeople, fellow villagers (*paisanos*), people with whom she shared no last names but still recognized a connection, and kin with whom, although she did not want to call them *tío* because of the lack of both support and *cariño*, she was socially obligated to use the term. Finally, she added that all the people she listed are still alive; if she were to include the dead the list would have been far longer. The dead are lovingly remembered years after their passing (annual masses for the *Difunto* outnumber all other services in church records, as they are often celebrated more than twenty years after a death), but the shallow, broad tendencies in Olivia's *trabajo* provide still more support for the Andes-wide

findings that Enrique Mayer and Ralph Bolton collected to wean anthropologists of the Americas from a reliance on African models of kinship (1977).[11]

Tomás, a young man who, during the latter portion of my fieldwork,
lived in the spare room of Olivia's family's house so that he could attend
technical school in Ayacucho, is the son of one of these *tíos*. Olivia explained
that Tomás is trustworthy, familiar, and friendly—if someone were to ask
her "Who's the boy who lives there?" she would reply, "He's my cousin."
Cousin, then, is a classificatory kin term along the same lines as *tío*, but for
one's own generation. Olivia's naming Tomás as her cousin is both produced by and productive of their behavior toward one another. But, as with
the kin terms used in many cases of circulation, it is also strategic. For
Tomás to be able to live in a house in Ayacucho, far away from his parents'
home, it would be prudent both from his point of view and from Olivia's
family's for him to be seen as kin. If he were not explicitly, daily described as
a cousin, the presence of this young single man in a household with two
adolescent girls might be troubling.

Moving children, for social and economic betterment, is a tactic that
requires kinship in order to function (compare Ossio 1984, who makes this
observation about *compadrazgo*). When a poor woman calls the patron who
will be taking in her child *comadre*, she is requesting that the patron structure her relationship with the child in the terms of *compadrazgo*: material
support, kindness. If a domestic servant calls her employer *tía* or *madrina*,
she is attempting to force a kinship claim. To phrase these ambiguous
relationships in the terms of kinship is a strategy which can, on one hand,
permit labor exploitation without significant guilt or remuneration—but,
on the other, encourage better treatment. The use of kinship terms in gray
areas can be transformative—as the anthropologist Greg Urban has argued,
they contain "discourse expectations" (1996: 131), or assumptions about
proper social behavior. Accordingly, children are consciously taught how to
address their relatives properly, and bundled into these instructions are
definitions of what each relative is and how they should behave.[12]

But this analysis can be extended into social realms that are, on the
surface, not thought to be so ambiguous. I saw this most powerfully in the
tensions around how an unmarried musician friend addressed his new baby,
still nameless at ten days old. Attending a birthday party for a member of
Ayacucho's middle class (a singular event involving everyone sitting quietly

in a circle around the room, drinking small amounts brought out cere-
moniously in tiny glasses), I reacted with disbelief when the man introduced the baby—I'd not known he was expecting one, and by that point I
had been indoctrinated in the kind of joking interactions I figured this
probably was. His mother, leaning over, informed me that she, too, hadn't
known about the baby until just days before. When a hired cameraman
arrived to film the party's more festive musical phase, the musician told him
to film "the little one." Immediately, his father admonished him: "Say 'my
baby.'" The use of a possessive kinship term would work to transform this
infant, though related by "blood," into the man's true son.

If the use of kin terms can foster relatedness, the deliberate disuse of
those terms can reflect or hasten the breaking of relations. A playful self-
defense tactic I heard among small Ayacuchano friends in Lima, when
being bothered by a cousin or sister, was "You're not my little cousin / little
sister any more." More seriously, Rocío, who was raised by her grandparents, calls her birth mother and aunts and uncles by their first names.
Her birth mother also names Rocío rather than using "daughter," the
common form of address for daughters throughout Latin America. As
Rocío put it, "I call my mamá by her name. It doesn't feel natural to me to
call her 'mamá' [No me nace mucho; literally, it's not really inborn]. It feels
weird, I can't say it. We are like siblings, almost." Kin terms can be revoked,
playfully or more seriously, on a permanent or contingent basis, should the
relationship fail to live up to expectations. Yet the basis of the relationship is
still recognized: the practitioners of kinship, the parents, children, affines,
and siblings of the world, perceive relatedness as a naturally occurring thing
that can be fortified, or challenged, by people's actions.

In this world with its strong ties to kinship and relatedness, there was of
course a variety of attempts to fit me in. I thought of these as strategic uses
of kin terms to promote particular behaviors, or as attempts to reconcile
my oddly "familiar" behavior with my as-yet-unkinned status. I would variously be labeled as Cristina's or Margarita's daughter (with the accompanying jokes about how my father had been a tourist or a gringo), Cristina's
daughter-in-law (implying I had married one of her sons),[13] and Sarita's
friend. Finally, everything was vastly simplified when I became a godmother to a few children in this family. Margarita, mother of my godchildren, explained on that occasion that "in the past we have treated each

other like *familia* and with lots of *confianza*, but now it will be even more." She added that if I ever needed help hand-washing my laundry, I could ask my goddaughter to do it.

After being friends for so many months, it seemed strange both to me and my godchildren to switch to the formal terms of address. They consulted with me during this period of adjustment, feeling that a switch from "Yesica" to *"madrina"* would be strange. I agreed, but this was nixed by their mother, who told us as we giggled, "This shouldn't be mocked," and told her son when he called me Yesica, "It's '*madrina*,' *malcriado*" (literally, badly brought-up: bad-mannered). And when my partner and I baptized five-year-old Pámela in Lima, her aunt Sonia instructed her that she couldn't just be saying *"madrina"* one minute and "Yesica" the next, whenever she felt like it. Although the sudden switch from first names to kin terms seemed strange to me, it was easily engaged in by my new Peruvian *compadres* moments after this baptism, and such momentous changes in status are always accompanied by frequent naming. As we drove back to the house, Sonia's husband sounded out the new relationship with occasional, earnest inanities like *"Comadre*, out your window is Lima's bullring, the Plaza de Acho."[14]

DOCUMENTS: LAST NAMES AND OTHER ARCHIVES OF IDENTITY

As an atheist born and bred, I smile to think that stashed somewhere in a handsome old church in downtown Lima is a document recording my promise to be godmother to Pámela and her cousin Karina. Certificates inscribing birth, baptism, or marriage are touchstones of identity, charting legitimacy and belonging. The posters plastered on the adoption office walls, described in chapter 2—"I exist, I want a name"—reference the state's campaign to get all Peruvians officially registered, a status that equates to civil existence. A person's last names, set down in pen and ink for prosperity, are meaningful documents of identity because they're backed up by a paper. Last names do the work of situating their bearers in a social world by indicating connections to relatives; "a family name locates a person both in the social hierarchy and in a network of kin relations" (Kertzer 1993: 119). Names and social genealogies are of great importance in Huamanga,

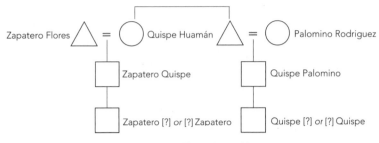

13. Illustration of hypothetical last names.

whose elite society—like the highland world described by the memoirist Marie Arana—"nurtured family histories as if they were precious instruments, radar nimble, eggshell fragile, unfailing in their power to triangulate the truth about a man" (2001: 51).

To the consternation of North American adoptive parents who have definitively settled on the perfect name for their child, there is little flexibility in the Latin American system of last names. A child will receive two last names,[15] the first being the paternal (her father's paternal last name) and the second the maternal (her mother's paternal last name).

In figure 13, Mr. Zapatero Flores and Ms. Quispe Huamán have a child, whose last names are Zapatero Quispe.[16] (Note that women do not change their last names to their husbands' at marriage, although some elite women add "de X" at the end of their last names, that is, "[wife] of X.") Ms. Q's brother, Mr. Quispe Huamán, and his wife, Ms. Palomino Rodriguez, have a child, whose last names are Quispe Palomino. Those two children—first cousins, in conventional kinship terms—have one last name, Quispe, in common, underscoring their relationship. But when each of them grows up, perhaps marries, and has a child, that next generation (second cousins in conventional terminology) would no longer share last names. It takes two generations for the visible named connection to disappear—but Zapatero Quispe's child, though not a Quispe herself, still knows that Quispe is a family name. Forced by an inquisitive anthropologist to spell out in irrelevant exactness how she is related to another Quispe, she may respond that, well, perhaps they aren't related after all,[17] or perhaps his mother was her father's great-aunt, or . . .

This is, in old-school kinship terms, a bilateral system with patrilineal skewing. It's bilateral because relatives on both sides are named with the same terminology. That is, both one's mother's brother and one's father's brother are referred to as "uncle." Also, because a child bears one last name from each parent, connections with relatives on both sides are spelled out. Bilateral systems like this can be useful in agricultural, peasant societies, when periods of intensive work require a farmer to call on as many kin as possible (Bourque and Warren 1981: 38). Last names index connections to others; infants abandoned at birth have no such connections. (Such children receive the judicial appellation "N.N.," which, joked the adoption office lawyer, means *"No tiene Nada de Nombre!"* [No-Name]. Orphanage staff provide the children with first names only, so a typical name might be "Juan Andrés N.N.").[18] The naming system is skewed patrilineally, however, because the names that are passed down are ultimately the men's last names. Ayacuchanos felt strongly, however, that to omit the maternal last name, as most North Americans do, is an insult to one's mother.

Before leaving Ms. Quispe Huamán for good, one more iteration: what if Mr. Zapatero Flores, instead of marrying her, got her pregnant then disappeared for parts unknown? Without a man to sign the birth register, and later the baptismal certificate, she would be left with little alternative but to put down her own two last names. Her illegitimate child would go through life as a Quispe Huamán, two names which identify him as a younger sibling to his "progenitrix." If Mr. Zapatero Flores came back one day and decided to make things right, both the state and the Church would accept this "recognition," and I saw several such recognitions of "natural children" penned into the margins of church baptismal records:[19]

José, natural son of Francisca Quispe Huamán and of Santiago Zapatero Flores, born 2 December 1958, baptized 5 April 1959, recognized on February 19 1968 by Santiago Zapatero Flores; *or*

José, natural son of Francisca Quispe Huamán and of Santiago Zapatero Flores, born 2 December 1958, legitimated by his parents' subsequent marriage on June 3, 1959; *or*

José, natural son of Francisca Quispe Huamán and of Santiago Zapatero Flores, recognized by Adilberto Zapatero Flores as "son of my deceased brother Santiago Zapatero Flores" . . .

Legitimacy in the baptismal records is key for a later marriage record, which can read "José Zapatero Quispe, *legitimate son of* . . ." The transmission of last names ensures the continuity of a house and family (Lévi-Strauss 1983, cited in Carsten and Hugh-Jones 1995: 7).

Without a man willing to sign the birth registry or baptismal record, an unmarried mother may nonetheless strategically inscribe her child with the presumed father's last name—leaving the door open for him to one day recognize her or for her to assay child support claims, but essentially not altering the child's illegitimate status. I might not have known about this option were it not for a political scandal that unfolded during my fieldwork. President Alejandro Toledo had for years denied Lucrecia Orozco's claims that he had fathered her child. In 1987, Orozco registered her daughter in Piura's birth records with the name Zaraí Toledo Orozco, but Toledo did not sign the registry. A 1995 court filing by Toledo, irreverently referencing important political figures from the nation's recent history, pronounces: "If the claimant's minor daughter uses the last name Toledo, Romero, or Fujimori, it doesn't make the claimant's daughter into my daughter, nor the banker's daughter, nor the daughter of the current President of the Republic . . . I don't know if the claimant's minor daughter has used the last name Toledo, García, Belaunde, Fujimori, or Pérez de Cuellar since she was born or whether she changes it depending on the circumstances" (Muñoz Nájar 2002: 20).[20] Faced with mounting evidence of his paternity, however, the president eventually made an about-face and recognized his daughter in 2002.

Toledo's filing makes clear that simply using a last name is not enough—without a man who agrees that the child is his, and without an official document legalizing the child's legitimacy, the use of his last name is relatively meaningless. However, using a set of last names is an extant strategy that surfaces in narratives of both child circulation and adoption. Jesús, a gentle, talented harpist, told my partner and me one night that he had been raised by "a couple without children," a kind of adoptive parents, whom he now called his *abuelos*, or grandparents, but whom he also described as *una familia ajena*, a family other than his own. Jesús explained, "I discovered this when I started school and I was signed up with my last names, and my *abuelo*'s last name is P— and my *abuela*'s is N— [his last names did not coincide with theirs], and it was *muy chocante*, a real shock." When the reality of documents countered the social reality Jesús had known, he privileged the documentary accounting of his origins, discovering that his genitrix had been his grandparents' maid, and that when she gave birth to an illegitimate son the couple invited her to leave him with them when she went to work elsewhere.[21]

Paulina, the young woman taken in by Cecilia several years ago, is perfectly aware that her last names differ from those borne by her new parents. But she is comfortable using Cecilia's and her husband's last names with acquaintances, revealing the "truth" of her relations and her identity only to close friends or representatives of the state like schoolmasters. She negotiates legitimacy and belonging, choosing which last names to use when, a social act that does important identity work. But the route of legally changing a child's last names—transforming that child into your own, on paper and in the eyes of the state—is one that requires *trámites*, paperwork. Those involved with adoption position paperwork as the very heart of the process—as Gloria Atúncar, the public relations face of adoption in Lima, explained, "for it to be called adoption, there must be paperwork." "Paperwork" represents the time-consuming and costly interactions with the state necessary to bring home a child. It also exposes families to the risk that their parenting credentials, when examined, will be found wanting. But most powerfully of all, it materializes security: an adoption must be inscribed so that it's never contested, for (as one young woman hypothesized) "if not, what will I defend myself with? It has to be legalized with a paper."[22]

And so we come around again to the legalities of adoption. The existence and new awareness of this legal act ironically may set up a greater distance between circulated children and their new families than was, historically, the norm. The adoption file of one Peruvian couple in their thirties—he's Cuzqueño, she's Limeña—contained the intriguing statement, "It's worth pointing out that with this couple lives a nineteen-year-old nephew, whom they consider as their son."[23] The couple is responsible for this young man, who helps with the household chores and provides *compañía*. But despite the long coresidence, they desire a child they can call their own and went through infertility treatment before deciding upon adoption. Intentionality and documentation are key in distinguishing between the young man whom "they consider as their son" and the baby, whom they deliberately sought out and are connected to with documents. Cohabitation is not enough to produce relatedness—it only produces affection, a sentiment that can also come out of other kinds of relations. The "Empathy Report" that caps the adoption file informs us that upon meeting, the new baby received the parental *cariño* very naturally, *con toda naturalidad*. This file reveals how adoption produces difference between children, in the sense that without the option of adopting a baby, the young man might have been—by the principles of both coresidence and blood—considered more truly a son.

Abandoned or circulated children, of course, can also become "own children" through adoption. In one of the surprisingly complicated files I found in Ayacucho's adoption office, I read about a childless couple who engaged in some fairly "irregular" conduct. They located an illiterate, poor, abandoned pregnant woman who, they discovered, planned to *regalar* or "gift" her baby upon its birth. In exchange for economic support during her pregnancy, she voluntarily gave them infant Gustavo, and ever since, "the boy is their son; that's how they feel and that's how they treat him." "Irregular" adoptions like Gustavo's remove the state from the equation, lowering certain kinds of risk (expense, hassle, and the dangers of state interference) while increasing others (the permanence of the placement). Raising Gustavo from birth, the couple never told him of his origins, but after several years they decided to "regularize" his adoption, slowly providing the required paperwork to the adoption office. In Gustavo's case, an extralegal transfer was ultimately brought within the state's purview and received its blessing.

The Salasacas of highland Ecuador, in Peter Wogan's careful account, understand the official documents produced by church and state as powerful ratifiers of existence, mediating between indigenous people and outsiders (2004).[24] Indigenous Toba and Wichí peoples in the Argentinean Chaco surprised the anthropologist Gastón Gordillo by unexpectedly showing him *documentos* or identity papers—"mundane symbols of state power" that materialized a relationship between individual and state against the memory of its recent deprivation (Gordillo 2006: 162).[25] And similarly, it was against the context of Ayacucho's recent anguish that Margarita went about getting a document for her stepdaughter, Laura. Margarita explained to me that Laura "can't be just the way she is," an undocumented young woman with a mild developmental disability. During the violent *movimientos*, she told me, police and military would often ask people for their documents and would easily *aprovechar*, taking advantage of their position to abuse or exploit the undocumented. Even after the violence, the justice system still has not recovered from its decimation during Fujimori's presidency, and many Peruvians are, quite reasonably, distrustful of the state and its personnel.

When Margarita married Wilmer, a widower, she took on his two daughters as her own. Laura lives at times with Wilmer's mother Basilia in a small village above Socos, and at times in Wilmer and Margarita's house in Ayacucho. When I first met Laura, who was in her twenties at the time, she didn't have a National Identity Document, the card that is proof of citizenship, and of existence. It is a status of "civil death" she shared with one and a half million Peruvians ("Documentos, por favor . . ." 2006). In practical terms, the *documento* is necessary for voting, employment, and interaction with the state. Proof of parentage is required to obtain this document, and rather than incurring the expense of traveling to the municipality of Laura's far-flung hometown to locate a copy of her birth certificate, Margarita took advantage of a priest's appearance in Socos to baptize Laura.[26] (Wilmer was out working in the fields at the time and only learned about all this after it had transpired.) The certificate she obtained proclaimed Laura's birthplace as Socos, her mother as Margarita, her maternal last name as Margarita's last name, and her name as Basilia—which Laura (that is, Basilia) herself chose, after her paternal grandmother. (Margarita did worry that Lupe, Laura's only full sister, would resent this name change—but I never learned how she felt about it.)

> **Huamán Palomino, Basilia.** Baptized 15 August 2002. Born in Socos, 14 July 1976, to Wilmer Huamán Vargas and Margarita Palomino Zavaleta.

With a baptismal certificate and two witnesses, including a municipal employee, Margarita had Laura inscribed in Socos's Book of Records, proof of which was used to issue Laura's government identity document.

Margarita's story amazed me when she recounted it the next day over the bubbling pot of soup she was preparing on her hearth in her Socos house. (I had just read an essay by José Alvarado about child trafficking in Peru [IDEIF 2001] and was particularly impressionable.) Could anyone just stroll into the municipality, claim to be a child's mother, and get officially registered as such? Margarita retorted that the two witnesses at the municipality knew very well that Margarita was the stepmother who had had Laura "at her side" ever since her mother died. The two men had asked her if anyone would ever come to complain about this, and she had said no, using the same justification found in legal declarations of abandonment: none of Laura's relatives had even come to inquire about her in more than twenty years. Margarita was no child trafficker: everyone knew she had raised Laura and was married to Laura's father, and as long as the city employees could be reasonably assured that no one would ever complain, they saw no problem in proceeding. And in fact, altering names and identities is a fairly unremarkable practice in much of Latin America (compare Fonseca 2002a: 412), although it is technically a crime.

What is particularly striking about this whole affair is the power imbued in documents like Laura / Basilia's baptismal certificate. Such documents can literally rewrite one's life history and identity, an instability in an otherwise impermeable wall of documentation. With the help of the priest, the cooperative godmother, and the two witnesses, Margarita recognized Laura: in other words, she claimed maternity. Laura is Margarita's daughter, not born but made, through coresidence, affection, documents, and a feeling of responsibility. What Margarita did was provide for the protection of her stepdaughter, circumventing the letter of the law, rewriting the past with the aid of the Church, all in the name of Laura's identity and citizenship.

WHO'S WHO: A CONCLUDING STORY

In 2006 I bought tea and cakes at a restaurant on Ayacucho's plaza, treating three sisters I'd known during my fieldwork to a fancy little dessert. While we ate, I told them about my beautiful new niece back in the United States, and they each expressed delight and anticipation. Implementing the next stage of my small social experiment, only after describing her as my niece did I tell them she had been adopted. As I anticipated, this elicited a somewhat confused response—"*entonces . . . no es de ellos*," that is, she's not "of them."

I think that many Peruvians do not understand how someone could expect to love a child who is not "of them." This deep-seated belief threads through this chapter: *cariño* may not find purchase when there is not already a base, a fertile ground, of relatedness or commonality. Yet these same interlocutors would deliberately omit an opposed possibility well known to each of them, that one might *not* love someone who *was* family. Considering that land disputes mar even the closest-knit families, and that everyone I asked could cleanly state a preference for one relative over another, it's fascinating that love and relatedness are equated. The contours of these two phenomena do not line up identically, but there is nonetheless a compelling link between them.

Child circulation, as a strategy, fits well into this particular social context with its emphasis on cohabitation and the kin ties that often underlie children's movements. But it's a strategy that is complicated by discourses of legitimacy, of belonging, and of documentation. Documents are incredibly important in Peru as fetishized, almost sacred proofs of identity, legitimacy, and kinship: the bureaucratic hurdles they inspire can affect possibilities for inheritance, coresidence, and interactions with the state.

Furthermore, in affective terms, it is clear that parent-child relationships are prized far above many other possible arrangements. This means that child circulation, though an essential and often beneficial strategy, is often overlaid with a wash of sadness. For example, Micaela, who lived with her grandparents for four years of her young life, is now "untrusting" because of it, in her mother's words. On many occasions when I asked Ayacuchano interlocutors about child circulation practices, I was told that "it just isn't the same" (*no es igual*), with clearly negative connotations, to not live with one's parents. This often reiterated claim reminds me not to indiscriminately equate every experience of circulation—domestic service, apprenticeship, and extra-institutional adoption overlap, but they differ in important ways.

Rocío grew up with her parents and two older sisters in the city of Ayacucho, in a neighborhood that lies along the hill up toward the highway to Peru's capital. Every few years, when the money allowed, another sister, Fernandina, would come to visit from Lima where she worked as a maid. When Rocío was eight years old, her sisters told her that Fernandina was actually her mother. In the sisters' tale, Fernandina had given birth to Rocío as a teenager, and Rocío's father had been killed by soldiers (who, as Rocío put it, "confused him with a terrorist") a year after her birth. Brutally, immediately, the listener can situate Rocío's tale in the wartime Ayacucho described in chapter 1. Although multilayered families like Rocío's can be located across the Andean countries and throughout much of the world, her particular tale is founded on the violence of soldiers and insurgents that devastated her homeland. Emerging from the sadness of her loss, according to Rocío's sisters, Fernandina had gone to Lima to work and left Rocío with her parents—seeking economic and social opportunities for herself and for her daughter.

Rocío said that when her aunts told her who her birth mother was, she thought they were joking; it was *chocante, muy duro*, shocking and difficult. She instantly felt rejected by her mother: "In ten minutes my life changed. I felt a little hate or resentment, feeling that she had abandoned me, because they never told me. I was angry with her one or two years and then . . . if I had a child at that age I wouldn't know what to do. Maybe she had her reasons." The aftermath of her genealogical and spatial movement deeply affected her. Rocío felt angry and resentful for nearly two years and euphemistically described the results as "I became rebellious." The unwelcome and painful surprise of her origins forced Rocío to renegotiate the rocky terrain of relatedness, redefining kin and reevaluating emotion.

After discovering that her parents were genealogically her grandparents, Rocío immediately began reconsidering her life. The intersections of knowledge and emotion just discussed were the tools she used to interpret her own sense of belonging, and ultimately, her identity. Where, before, she would say that she never questioned her position or her family's love for her, now she could say that "my grandparents gave me enough *cariño*," gauging the connections between affection and genealogy, deeming them acceptable. She also observed that Fernandina sent money from Lima both to support Rocío (to buy her clothing and school supplies) and her own parents (in Rocío's retelling, Fernandina had explained to her, "It's partly to thank them but it's also my responsibility because they are my parents. It's to thank them for not saying, 'She's your child, you had her, now you take care of her.'"). As with the *propinas* discussed in chapter 4, Rocío calculated the affective meaning of economics in interpreting her own, and her mother's, social positions.

Ultimately, she told me, she came to feel more understanding of Fernandina's decision; in fact, to my surprise, she said she wished she had found out "at the age I am now, [so that] I could understand better and I wouldn't have been angry. At age thirteen or fourteen, one is more reasonable." But when I asked her what made her finally cease resenting Fernandina, she explained that she had gone to Lima and, for the first time, lived with her birth mother for two full months. I also took careful note of Rocío's desires for her own future and family: "To have children, one must have some material comforts. I don't want my child to suffer neediness. I would want to have a child when I can give what's needed, so that my child wouldn't suffer economically or psychologically." Like Rocío, the young people I knew who had been circulated drew effectively on their own interpretations of their poverty, their *falta de economía*, to express their own social reproductive hopes and desires.

Rocío told me that she did not regret not having grown up with her birth parents; her father drank, so "it would have been an uglier life than I lead now." For her, living with her grandparents is akin to what living with one's parents would be like; there is trust. The one difference she expressed was this: "When I lack something or need something, I can't ask them for it; I don't feel comfortable doing that." Rocío is thoroughly accustomed, having grown up with her grandparents as her parents, but the new knowledge of the relationship meant that this one particular aspect grated. Yet the fascinating twist is that *other* children feel the same way with their *natal* families—remember Sarita, who felt she could not ask her hard-working father for the money she needed for university requirements. For Sarita, the inability to ask for something necessary does not mean she is unaccustomed; it means she does not want her father to have to suffer the pain of either denying her or of giving up some other necessity. But Rocío interpreted an identical reluctance as a question of identity, of belonging, not of poverty and caring.

Seven.

CIRCULATING CHILDREN, AT HOME AND ABROAD

For decades if not centuries, Andean *ayllus,* families, and social networks have mobilized to take in related children. The responsibilities of parenting—affection, economic support, and guidance, among others—can be divided between those persons who have the capabilities to shoulder each responsibility. The joys of parenting—the companionship, loyal affection, and household assistance a child can offer—are similarly redistributed. And the paths along which these children travel help to delineate social groups, establish or strengthen ties between houses, and chart out local ideas of moral betterment.

The preceding pages have built up a descriptive interpretation of child circulation—the familiar and reasoned movement of children. In a context of rural-to-urban migration, scrambling for work during high unemployment, the globalization of Peru's economy and the tensions of debt service, and the horrific violence of the final two decades of the twentieth century—child circulation should now make sense to a reader unfamiliar with its premises. Each case is different—Rocío's case, described in the previous chapter, that involved Fernandina's single motherhood and her felt need to migrate to Lima for work, draws on different tropes and tensions than does, for example, Reyna's case, told in chapter 4, in which she knew her place within kin networks and had an acute sense of the reasons for her relocation to her father's widowed godmother's city home. But taken together, the examples of child circulation recounted here reveal common themes about kinship, mobility, and morality in the Andean region.

In child circulation, risks and benefits are weighed. The practice is glossed with the terms that evoke the movement's strengths. *Acompañando* is highly desired by the recipient of a child; the fear of loneliness is a foundational and motivational piece of Andean kinship, its raison d'être. Understanding this central component of kinship reveals children's social worth: they can provide company for adults, as well as the gendered and companionable work known as "helping." Young people's relocation, their reconfiguration as particularly mobile, is made meaningful through its stated purpose: to accompany another. *Superarse* is a morality craved by the child and her sending family, a local expression of socioeconomic self-improvement whose effects are felt far beyond the striving child. And *acostumbrando* mediates between these two principles, quietly arguing that a transferred child can get used to her new setting, that she can become familiar to the receiving family, and that she and her sending family can acceptably drift apart—the making and breaking of kinship relations. But pain is evoked in the loss of the sending family, coupled with the discomfort and ambivalence a transferred child may feel, and the tensions of class and race that linger in the transaction.

Child circulation is such a key process in the elaboration of Andean social worlds because it draws on and produces two central connections constitutive of life in the region: relatedness and inequality. Like the analogous relations of *compadrazgo*, child circulation is based in understandings of relatedness—children who are relocated are usually moving to the home of others understood as genealogical kin, and if not, then the receiving adults are made into kin as soon as possible, through entering into relations of *compadrazgo* or through the deliberate use of kin terms as "discourse expectations." Yet child circulation is also understood to produce relatedness, through companionship over time.

And like (vertical) *compadrazgo*, the Ayacuchano child circulations I witnessed were largely rooted in the inequalities that permeate the region. Economic, social, and class hierarchies are both contested and ultimately reified through child circulation. Young people may improve their social position, or *superarse*, through education, but their movement does not erase the radical social skewing between indigenous and white—it reinscribes those categories, whether by keeping the circulated child in a subordinate position within the new house, or by assuring (as did the young people in Peter Lloyd's Medalla Milagrosa) that others fail to *superarse.*

It's this bare inequality that makes child circulation an ambivalent and often unhappy project. Young people (more often young women) who may be working class, indigenous, poor, with peasant parents, relocate to a more *noble* home inhabited by their upwardly mobile and less indigenous kin: a recipe for hierarchical intersectionality. Children must interact with others according to the logic of their society: they cannot disregard manners and respect. So the hierarchies of age interact with and cross-cut status inequalities, ensuring that the young and mobile are not always acting of their own accord. A child may claim to want to relocate, but the claim may derive from the sense that her parents want her to have a better life, although she may be perfectly happy in the fields at her parents' side. Or a child may wish to relocate but feel obliged to stay home so that an aging parent will not suffer the pain of loneliness. Taking into account these complex ambiguities, children who are circulated often have an identifiable say in the matter, manifest more than simply a reflection of what adults encourage and direct. And sometimes this say reveals itself in sadness, loneliness, and conflict.

But child circulation—the thoughtful movement of the young—is social reproduction, in a setting where international laws and conventions on adoption encounter a kind of local, historicized, and flexible kinship that sometimes stymies representatives of the state. The incorporation of Juana into the receiving home (her employers' home, in unvarnished terms) through *compadrazgo* was a deliberate effort to improve her treatment and regularize her position. Sarita's migration into her aunt and uncle's home was clearly expressed in terms of *superar,* of social betterment. The "abandoned" little girl's relocation, in the introduction, may have been strategically designed to emphasize her paternity—lodging her with a relative of the man who had failed to recognize her would have made a powerful statement. Like other reproductive technologies both old and new, then, child circulation produces kinship by strengthening ties, drawing on culturally relevant symbols of relatedness, all within its contemporary and local social framework.

CIVIL WAR, TRANSNATIONAL
ADOPTION, AND THE INSTITUTIONALIZATION
OF ABANDONMENT

That social framework is shot through with the devastation of discrimination, inequality, and death. The violence unbound in Ayacucho in the 1980s and early 1990s was a particularly bloody expression of the conflicts and tensions that have animated indigenous peoples' relationships with the state—their citizenship—for a much longer period. When I first arrived in Ayacucho in 2000, and during the years that would follow, the most overt forms of this violence had ended, but the people I knew continued to distrust the motives of the state and its representatives. Yet, far from being isolated from the interventions of government, rural-to-urban migrants living in the city of Ayacucho engaged with official presence when accessing the state-sponsored family planning program (Leinaweaver 2005c), by temporarily lodging children in orphanages (Leinaweaver 2007b) and by entering children into the civil registry and obtaining the little laminated *documento* necessary for recognized existence.

Looking inward, nationwide, this was a war that deeply affected indigenous people, who, overwhelmingly, were killed, disappeared, orphaned, and dislocated. By narrowing the possibilities available to families of all classes and social locations, the war also made it more difficult for kin to take in related children—the basis of child circulation. During a time when it was both more difficult and more necessary to avail themselves of child circulation strategies, the poor often turned either to orphanages or, in similar moments of desperation, to—borrowing an idea from João Biehl— "social abortion," the abandonment of children.

Looking outward, thinking transnationally, war—as it so often is—is intimately connected to the rise of international adoptions (Briggs n.d.). During the devastation of the Peruvian state, sending children overseas in adoption was seen as a humanitarian response, and it also reduced any burden that those children would have placed on the government agencies responsible for their welfare. With lower- and working-class families in crisis, and indigenous people more than any other group reeling from the repercussions of the violence (CVR 2003), "traditional" or "extra-institutional" methods of incorporating children became, in many cases, unfeasible. The meaning of "orphan" crystallized and international adoptions soared in the wake of the violence. Those adoptions were only tempered by the introduction of a new law in 1992, the same year that Shining Path's leader was captured.

In the 1990s, as the violence persisted and political and legal changes continued to transform the nation, poverty intensified as neoliberal policies took hold, and revisions in family and adoption law—based proudly in international treaties, legislating Peru as a modern and internationally aware nation—reshaped poor and indigenous Peruvian families. Adoptions are now one of the clearest sites at which families are constituted—both formed and broken—by global discourses and local bureaucracies. By making adoptions dependent on a legal declaration of "abandonment," and by legally disengaging the condition of abandonment from the condition of poverty, the civil code introduced a new justification for the surveillance of poor and indigenous families. Poor children with living kin could now be refashioned as "abandoned" based on a conscientious critique of adobe homes, emotional states, and low protein consumption.

The effects of these changes, carried out in a moment where postwar Peru was trying to recover from the civil war and define itself as modern through adopting international protocols, were felt strongly by poor and indigenous Peruvians as they, too, struggled to get by. The state's performance of modernity constructs a child as an individual—a disconnected being whose care is paramount. Abandonment proceedings produce children who are unlinked from their surroundings, and this single-minded focus on the *child*'s best interests paints a picture of children as passive beings in need of protection (Oviedo 1999). In sharp contrast, the practice of child circulation is built around the notion of a child as not only thoroughly connected but as an active connector, a valuable resource. Children's agency is part of the equation: kids "consent" to their own circulation, whether overtly at the time or in retrospect via their own interpretations, even when there is little or no possibility for an unequivocally happy resolution.

It's worth asking why the neoliberal state would want to take on the burden of additional children to care for. Why do the courts go to such great lengths to secure decrees of abandonment, thus producing more wards of the state? The answer, I suggest, lies partly in a co-optation of the "best interest of the child" standpoint so widely accepted in the international sphere. To follow globally agreed-upon guidelines for child protection is one step the Peruvian government may take to perform itself as modern. Further, the responsibility for legally abandoned children is not borne by the state alone; numerous private organizations, along with the Catholic Church, play a major role in supporting these children. Finally, there is a narrative floating just beneath the surface of court documents, occasionally showing itself when criticisms of "adobe houses" and the like bubble over. Echoing North American approaches to the rearing of Native American and First Nations children during the mid-twentieth century (Finn 1991; Strong 2001), those who hold that Peru suffers from its "Indian problem" might very well posit that the removal of indigenous, poor children from their natal homes is, in the long run, good for the country. In this sense, it links the contemporary *puericultorio* where children are contained to the scientific puericulture of early-twentieth-century eugenicists: professional child raising can improve the health of the nation's population (Stepan 1991: 77). This interpretation suggests that the state's involvement in children's welfare is both a performance of modernity and a refusal of indigenous identities.

Significantly, the circulation of children—historically and today, a strategy used by working-class Peruvians not only to eke out a living on the economic margins but also to strengthen social relationships and give their children more opportunity—is also one of the features of the life of the poor and indigenous that is criticized by well-meaning government employees. In other words, the "modernity" being performed through state representatives' upholding of international norms is at odds with the lifeways of many lower-class, indigenous citizens. The case with which this book opened makes this point clearly.

A RETURN TO THE ARCHIVE

In the opening story, reconstructed from adoption files, a lawyer articulated the Peruvian state's resistance to alternative forms of kinship and produced, from his critique, an abandoned child. The narrative found in the files is one of an older woman, living a peasant's life, who believed she had a traceable genealogical relationship to a little girl and who was willing to care for the girl and her mentally disabled mother. A social worker colleague of Nelly Alanya duly carried out an investigation to support the lawyer's claims, and, following the procedures outlined in chapter 2, the little girl was declared "abandoned." But now, with a better sense of why child circulation happens so widely in Ayacucho and in places around the world where kinship matters and poverty threatens, we can reread this file with a more nuanced interpretation.

First, the state's lawyer disapproved in writing of the undocumented relationship between the caretaker and her great-niece. Chapter 6 explored this documentation of relatedness: the failure of the progenitor to recognize his daughter effectively halved the number of relatives legally empowered to become her guardian. Although some of the baptismal records I reviewed showed individuals claiming paternity on behalf of their vanished or irresponsible relations, this didn't happen in the case considered here. Did church representatives never travel to their town; was the great-aunt unaware of this option; did she deliberately choose not to recognize the girl?

The records of the abandonment proceedings raise more questions than they answer—the reasons why the girl's father abandoned her mother and went to Lima are muddy. Migration, even when it separates partners or spouses, has been and continues to be a defining feature of the Peruvian landscape. A move from the countryside to Lima hints of labor migration and of a social mobility expressed in geographical terms. But back in Ayacucho's courts, the man's movement could be interpreted by the lawyer as evidence of his claims that the father's identity isn't really known, the mother's memories are faulty, and the man she identifies is married with children and denies having fathered the little girl whose future is under discussion. Such a woman—who can't hold onto a man, or who doesn't know who the baby's father is, or who doesn't take the responsible step of insisting that the progenitor recognize his daughter . . . is a woman like this really deserving of her parental rights?

But the woman has other flaws as well. By order of the family court, the girl's mother—a woman in her mid-twenties—was examined and found to be suffering from a series of mental complications. Such disorders—described as "light" or barely present in the files—are often ascribed to emotional shock, like the shock of being abandoned by a loved one. Within a broader analysis of medicalization (see Oths 1999), mild disorders such as these can be linked to the gendered impact of poverty. The examining psychologist, working within the paradigms of his own field, recommended that she undergo psychotherapy and receive emotional support and counseling. We can't know what happened next, but it's difficult to imagine that she received this care. Care like this is barely accessible in highland cities, and certainly not available in small towns or villages. It is not too great a stretch to interpret this as another trickle-down effect of neoliberal policies—locating individual blame in an emotionally traumatized woman, conscientiously recommending medical care, while eliding the question of whose responsibility it should be to seek it out and pay for it.

Finally, another failing: the double relocation of the child. First, her mother allowed the girl's paternal great-aunt to care for her. This, combined with the aunt's unsuitable adobe house, proves in the lawyer's eyes that the mother is uninterested in her child's future success. Second, the child was lodged at the orphanage. Her great-aunt asked the orphanage to retain her until age two, then promised to care for her. This action situates the case in its historical moment, as the orphanage, the relative newcomer to the Ayacuchano social landscape analyzed in chapter 3, can now be seen as one logical site to leave an infant so that she can receive good care. It's not hard to fathom that the great-aunt may have decided that the orphanage was better equipped than she to care for an infant and a toddler. Or, perhaps she had no intention of reclaiming the child and wished only to avoid the girl's ultimate disappearance into an adoptive family. Another possibility—she was thinking of the little girl as someone who would contribute to the household and who would accompany her. A two-year-old is better able to participate in the emotional relations of kinship and has begun to show the potential of contributing to her household.

Although we can't know all the hidden motivations and explanations for why the little girl ended up in the orphanage and, like her sister before her, was adopted into a new and loving family, this book has made clear that child circulations like hers are a valued and essential feature of the social landscape in postwar, poor but upwardly mobile Ayacucho. But, in contrast, it is only the documented circulations that make sense within the files and courtrooms of official Peru. This little girl's relocation into her paternal great-aunt's home shares foundational principles with six-year-old Sarita's movement into her aunt and uncle's home in Ayacucho, or teenaged Juana's acceptance of a structurally diminished maid position in the home of a woman who became her godmother. Her subsequent circulation into the orphanage is also a familiar tale, underlain with a cultural logic in which particular forms of state or NGO assistance are accepted, cautiously, and in part because they fit into the narrative child circulation tells. And her eventual adoption happened within a framework where the Peruvian state, its enactors shaken by the memory of recent bloodshed, articulates with the globally modern through the conscious assumption of international discourses of children's rights, acceptable forms of population control, and good adoptive practices.

Glossary

Note: All terms are in Spanish unless identified as Quechua with a Q.

acoger   to take in (enfolding, incorporating)

acompañar   to accompany another person

acostumbrar   to get accustomed

adopción   adoption, referring to the legal and documented transfer of a
    child

ahijado / ahijada   godchild, godson or goddaughter

andino   "Andean"—when used in an analytic sense, a term referring to
    regional and diachronic similarities

ayllu (Q.)   a defined social group of some kind, especially family or com-
    munity (Allen 2002 [1988]; Weismantel 2006)

campesino   peasant, in the sense of someone who works the land—also,
    the politically correct term for Indian ever since Belaunde's pronounce-
    ments on the matter

cariño   affection, love, tenderness, warmth

chacra (Q.)   field

cholo, cholito   uncomplicatedly, city-dwelling Indian; can be derogatory

compadrazgo   coparenthood (see introduction)

compadre / comadre   cofather or comother—refers to the godparent of
    one's child, or the parent of one's godchild (and, in blanketing form

[Davila 1971], can be used to refer to other relatives of the primary title-holder)

compañia   company, companion; one who accompanies

criada / criar   maid (literally, raised, fostered) / to raise

falta de economía   economic lack; i.e., poverty

huamanguino   a person from Huamanga (the colonial-era name for the city of Ayacucho); the term has elite connotations

huérfano / huérfana   orphan boy or girl

indio   Indian, indigenous person—opposed to *mestizo*

machismo   sexism (literally, favoring the masculine)

madrina   godmother

mestizo   literally, mixed-race—refers more generally to a racial and class position viewed as hierarchically superior to indigenous

muchacha   maid (literally, girl)

padrino   godfather or godparent

paisano / paisana   countryman or countrywoman; often refers to a village-mate

pertenecer   to belong

propina   tip, allowance

puericultorio   orphanage, place of child rearing and good upbringing

recoger   to take in (in the sense of a stray)

ronda   peasant self-defense groups instituted during the violence

sapalla (Q.)   all alone

Sendero Luminoso   Shining Path, the Maoist insurgent movement

señor / señora   Mr. / Mrs.

solo / sola   alone

superarse   to overcome, to self-improve

tío / tía   uncle or aunt

trago   cane alcohol

wakcha (Q.)   poor, "orphan," without support or social ties

Notes

INTRODUCTION

1 "Lo que evidencia la carencia de cualidades morales y mentales por la falta de cuidado en la crianza y de su futura educación."

2 This introductory framing device and some of this book's central arguments are recapitulated in an article in *American Ethnologist* (Leinaweaver 2007a).

3 Of this semantic pairing, *recoger* conveys a sense of picking up something that has been discarded. In early colonial Peru, *recogidas* (literally, taken-ins) referred to women given shelter by the Catholic Church; definitions of *recoger* in that period included "a covered shelter extending from a wall . . . for beggars or mendicants" and "to provide asylum" (van Deusen 2001: 1). *Acoger* is viewed as having a more neutral or positive incorporation.

4 By "social work," I don't mean the formalized occupation of social worker, or the tasks she or he performs. When I use it here (and, from now on, without the quotes) I mean that some sort of social action, meaning, or practice has been achieved.

5 Weismantel (1995) has written the only full-length article on Andean fostering, based on fieldwork in rural Ecuador.

6 See Fischer (1999: 474) on "cultural logic."

7 In Gelles's elucidation of the debate within Andean studies over *lo andino*, he points out that the notion has been rightly criticized (see especially Starn 1992) as productive of an essentializing image. However, he counters that such a dismissal shores up Peruvian elites' rejection of the "Andean," and ignores an important source of potential community-building in indigenous rights movements (Gelles 2000: 12). By raising the specter of *lo andino* here, I do not mean

to imply that practices such as child circulation persist, unchanged, from a preconquest past. Instead, I am following Gelles in identifying an analytic (and potentially political) utility to the concept.

8   This is a familiar colonial practice, also documented by Ann Stoler for other European colonies (1991: 80).

9   Milanich makes an attempt to quantify this practice, establishing that the figure of 17 percent of households (containing children that are being raised by people other than their parents) is perfectly documentable and likely a significant underestimation, as it omits those whose status went unmentioned in censuses and those whose caretakers left them nothing in wills (2004: 313–14).

10   A few stalwart studies of *compadrazgo* (Christinat 1989; Davila 1971; Foster 1953; Mintz and Wolf 1950; Ossio 1984) are supplemented by its mention in every Andean ethnography (see, for example, Allen 2002 [1988]: 88; Miles 2004: 28; Ossio 1992: 260; Stein 1961: 129; Weismantel 1988: 82).

11   This and other charts follow the conventions of traditional anthropological kinship charting. Males are shown as triangles and females are symbolized by circles; a square stands for a person whose gender is unknown or not relevant to the diagram. Vertical lines indicate offspring, horizontal lines designate siblings, and an equals sign represents marriage. While Schneider (1984) and others have rightly criticized the genealogical bias of such charts, I include them here to illustrate the relations I am describing, because kinship scholars have yet to develop a better system.

12   Kathryn Burns provides a fascinating analogue in colonial Cuzco. Where in *compadrazgo*, a child mediates between two kin groups, a single daughter placed in a convent could mediate between a family and the spiritual world. As Burns puts it, elite families "married" convents, forming advantageous alliances with key convents by sending a daughter there (1999: 148).

13   Although it was common in the city of Ayacucho for relatives to become godparents, the Peruvian anthropologist Juan Ossio disagreed with my comparison of *compadrazgo* and fosterage. He said that children are circulated to family members, but (at least in the community in southern Ayacucho where he worked) family members could not be tapped to serve as *compadres*. Thus, this analogy should be viewed in context.

14   Becoming a godparent demands both a social commitment and a material expense. Although we asked many people what our role was and what we ought to pay for, this was apparently too awkward to discuss outright. Completely guessing, we ultimately paid approximately $300 for a band, $100 for two sets of white dresses, tights, turtlenecks (it was winter), and shoes, and $50 for invitations and souvenir pins. The children's parents paid for the mass, dinner for all the guests, two prepared whole turkeys as our gifts, and decorations and candy for the home. They also purchased beer to sell to the guests. We still have no idea whether we did this correctly.

15 However, Stein, who worked in the Peruvian highlands in the 1950s, described a fascinating counterpart ceremony to mark child circulation: "If the actual parents of the adopted child are alive, they are in this way made *compadres* with the foster parents. If the parents are dead, other relatives may act as sponsors for the adopted child, and they become *compadres* with the foster parents. In adoption, there is no religious rite. The fiesta for both sets of families involved is given by the foster parents" (1961: 286).

16 "Kinship" has now been well studied as a historical, analytical concept. Early and foundational critiques include Needham 1971 and Schneider 1984. Brief histories of kinship studies include Carsten 2000; Franklin and McKinnon 2001; Holy 1996; and Strathern 1991. On kinship's basis in the nineteenth-century United States, see Bouquet 1996; Feeley-Harnik 1999; and Trautmann 1987. For some examples of new kinship studies, see Gailey 2000; Ginsburg and Rapp 1995; Inhorn 2003; Kligman 1998; Ragone 1994; Schweitzer 2000; Simpson 2001; Strathern 2005; and Weston 1991.

17 In North America, the topic of adoption has been usefully addressed by a variety of disciplines, ranging from applied social work (Kirk 1981; Kirton 2000; Simon and Altstein 2000) to psychology (Fravel et al. 2000). Anthropological literature leans heavily toward depictions of the extralegal fostering practices found cross-culturally (Bledsoe 1990; Brady 1976; Carsten 1997; Carroll 1970; Donner 1999; Goody 1969 and 1982; Kottak 1986; Renne 2003; Rousseau 1970; Schildkrout 1973; Schrauwers 1999; Stack 1974; and Trawick 1992; but see Modell 1994 and 2002 for important work on adoption in the United States which has been foundational in this field).

18 Marisol de la Cadena has described ways that upwardly mobile youth in Cuzco can perform certain sanitized aspects of indigeneity without laying claim to its poverty (2000). Few such outlets exist in Ayacucho, however.

19 Some of my friends referred jokingly to the president as "Cholo Choledo." In Peru, "cholo" is a pejorative term used to dismiss the unwarranted self-congratulatory airs of an indigenous person who has failed to fully acculturate to the urban environment.

20 Michel-Rolph Trouillot, writing of Haiti, has called this "social direction," that is, "the measure of the social distance between what is thought to be known of an individual's origin and what is thought to be known of his or her future" (1990: 121). I thank Joshua Tucker for this reference. I am also indebted to Mary Weismantel for persisting in her position that I could engage more directly with these issues, and for her collection of published work on the subject.

ONE. **AYACUCHO**

1   "Todavía no había terminado mi tía su colegio y empezó a estudiar colegio mi tía, pero por la noche, de noche, a veces yo iba con mi tía, a veces me quedaba sola en la casa, esas fechas yo lloraba pe, como quedaba sola en la casa, oscuro no, daba miedo, me daba miedo esos tiempos, era tiempo de peligro, había apagones, no había luz, todo eso, yo me quedaba llorando solita, me encerraba en mi cuarto y ahí lloraba solita llorando de mi mamá."

2   "Share" is the operative word here: stories and recollections are directed, with the express desire of making others understand or remember. There is a kind of give-and-take to storytelling in the Andes, a sociolinguistic strategy referred to as dialogicity. Dialogicity is the joint construction of stories by two or more interlocutors, imagined or real, in such a way that the actual sharing of the story is what gives it life (Mannheim and Van Vleet 1998). In these tales, laughter relieves the tension as often as do tears. For every story that ends with a fellow villager's death, another story ends with the joke on the clumsy insurgent or soldier.

3   Historians have done excellent work exploring the roots of the War of the Pacific (Bonilla 1974; Flores Galindo 1988; Mallon 1995; Thurner 1997). Andean oral historians can be included in this list: the narrative of the Cuzqueño strapper Gregorio Condori Mamani collapses the War of the Pacific, the battle of independence, and the European discovery and conquest of Peru as one historical event under the broad theme of "us / them" (Valderrama and Escalante 1996: 39, 154–55n5).

4   "Este lugar está condenado a bañarse en sangre y fuego para siempre."

5   Guzmán had traveled to Mao's China in 1967, thoroughly inspired by that brand of communism (Degregori 1997: 46). The movement is also based in the writings of the Peruvian Marxist José Carlos Mariátegui.

6   The appearance of Sendero Luminoso, as Carlos Iván Degregori has argued (1997: 51–53), supports the claim that race and poverty can be overcome through education (see also de la Cadena 2000); without a strong local ideology of education as central to improving one's life-path, Shining Path might have had a far smaller impact.

7   Previous estimates included the police's suggestion of 22,854 victims (CVR 2003: Annex 2, 22n16). The new, and surprisingly high, number made the North American headlines. The Truth Commission's researchers broke down the proportions as follows: Shining Path was responsible for 46 percent of the dead and disappeared, agents of the state for 30 percent, and others (including self-defense committees and another insurgent group, the Movimiento Revolucionario Tupac Amaru [MRTA]) for 24 percent. The period of violence is commonly held to have ended in 2000, because although Guzmán was cap-

tured in 1992, ex-president Fujimori's violent human rights abuses continued through the end of the decade.

8 In 2001 the figure of 43,000 was offered (Programa de Apoyo al Repoblamiento 2001), based on a census reporting that 35,000 had died or disappeared during the war. The number was not recalculated after the Truth Commission's surprisingly high figure of 70,000 dead was released. The Truth Commission's report states: "It has not yet been possible to determine the exact number of widows and widowers, nor of orphaned children" (CVR 2003: 303). Meanwhile, UNICEF reports that approximately 720,000 Peruvian children (aged 0–17) are orphaned (2004). This very high figure would include many orphans whose condition is unrelated to the war and would exclude those "war orphans" who are adults, as a great many of them are. See chapter 3 for further discussion.

9 On the relationship of the Peruvian state to the communities at its margins, see Deborah Poole's work (2004); and see Das and Poole 2004 on the state and its margins more generally.

10 Gerardo Ludeña, lawyer, hotelier, and onetime mayor of Ayacucho, recently published a book on adoption in Peru. He selected Ayacucho for his case study for the same reasons I did: "it contains a high number of displaced persons, due to the socio-political situation, and therefore a high number of abandoned children" (Ludeña Gonzalez 2000: 33, 35).

11 "transmite la sensación viva de cómo lo hispánico imprimió su sello en la cultura de los indios . . . con una capacidad de conversión mucho mayor que en otras ciudades serranas del Perú."

12 The laundry list of possible causes of gang violence also includes material poverty (including significant migration from poor rural areas and subsequent inability to find work); the disintegration of the family (abandoned or orphaned children, unwanted pregnancies, experiencing or seeing sexual or physical abuse at home, and lacking support and guidance at home); and the disenfranchisement of poor, marginal youths (lack of public participation or active citizenship, exclusion from political power, powerlessness at home, school, and society, and the resultant bad attitudes, disrespect for the law, and lack of mental health). The nonprofit and governmental community has proposed several solutions to gang violence, including the construction of youth centers in outlying neighborhoods; a renaissance of the *ronda* or local self-defense committee; and efforts to occupy young people's days with instruction in something that truly interests them, like cosmetology.

13 A town in northern Ayacucho, where eight journalists were brutally killed in 1983 in an event which highlighted both the severity of the war and the deliberate ignorance on the part of coastal scholars who came to "investigate" the events and produced a politically charged and anthropologically indefen-

sible report (see Degregori 2000: 47–48) suggesting that peasants living in the past killed the journalists out of confusion (Vargas Llosa 1983). It has also been suggested that military killed the reporters, then disguised the scene to blame the peasants.

14 Techniques of memory in the Andes include remembering as well as structured forgetting (see Abercrombie 1998: 117; Flores Galindo 1988: 20).

15 This echoes Julia Paley's description of Chile's National Commission of Truth and Reconciliation (whose report was delivered in March 1991). Over 2,000 deaths or disappearances were documented by Chile's commission. At the time President Aylwin "used the occasion to send a seemingly contradictory message. Ironically, he framed the presentation of the Rettig Report as a moment to end the preoccupation with the history of human rights abuses . . . [H]e urged Chileans to move on," emphasizing reconciliation, in sharp contrast with commissions in Argentina, Brazil, and Uruguay which had emphasized "Never Again" (Paley 2001: 127). Peru's Truth Commission also has "reconciliation" in the title; nevertheless, the commission was pushing for memory, while many Ayacuchanos seemed to emulate Aylwin's stance that forgetting was preferable.

TWO. **INTERNATIONAL ADOPTION**

1 And of late it is becoming a well-studied topic by anthropologists, although most studies emphasize reception of children and formation of families in the First World countries to which children move rather than the conditions in sending countries that facilitate adoption (Jaffe 1995: 9). See, for example, Chantal Collard's studies of Haiti (2005), Barbara Yngvesson's work on Swedish adoption from Chile (2003), Sara Dorow's research on North American adoption from China (2006), Signe Howell's investigations of transnational adoptions to Norway (2006), and two recent edited collections on transnational adoption (Bowie 2004; Volkman 2005).

2 Peruvian adoption law determines who may legally adopt, giving a preference to married couples. Thus, I have chosen to refer to "parents" throughout, although single women are also legally allowed to adopt. Single men, gay and lesbian couples, and unmarried straight couples currently may not adopt from Peru.

3 There are important legal differences between Peruvian and international applicants. Foreign adopters must engage in the process through agencies in their home countries, certain of which are approved by the Peruvian state. Only ten countries have approved agencies: Canada, the United States, Spain, Denmark, Luxembourg, Italy, Norway, Germany, France, and the Netherlands. (Article 4 of the adoption law allows for adoptions from other countries to be considered in special cases.) Peruvian couples are favored legally over

foreign parents because of strongly held beliefs about cultural and natural identity (compare Fonseca 2002b: 32, on Brazil). This legal privilege also derives from the United Nations Convention on the Rights of the Child, which insists that international adoption be considered only if a child cannot be raised in her or his country of origin (United Nations 1995: 337, 344). However, while international adopters are guided through the process by approved agencies in their home countries, no agencies in Peru support domestic adopters—thus, it becomes more challenging to meet the same standards in Peru (I am grateful to Kris Freeark for sharing this point with me).

4 Note that these pages describe the administrative process of adoption— "stranger adoptions." There is a separate, direct judicial process for family adoptions (e.g., the adoption of a child by his or her grandparent) or adoptions that formalize the relationship between an adult and a child who have been coresident for over three years. Similar documents are required, but the process is overall faster and simpler.

5 The shadowy presence of inadequate and thus undeserving caretakers implied by the humanitarian overtones in adoption is a discourse that circulates elsewhere. In 2000 I attended an exhibit called "Adopt a Painting" in an Ayacucho gallery, where the term "adopt" evoked not only the way the sponsors of each colonial painting chose to enter into a relationship with the work but also an implicit criticism of the paintings' previous caretakers, who "ought to have cared for them" but failed to do so (Leinaweaver 2001: 18).

6 Sara Dorow complicates the discourse of "choice" so common in adoptive language by noting not only that "adoption is not usually a first choice" but also that "given the discursive power of the 'chosen child,' especially as a response to the specter of adoption as a second-best form of kinship, it becomes all the more difficult for adoptive mothers' narratives to accommodate what looks like birth mothers' 'unchoosing' of motherhood" (2006: 181).

7 The guide goes on to state, "Valid motivations do not include using the child as a pretext to keep the spouse, turning the child into a servant, wanting a child to keep oneself from being lonely, or to hide one's infertility, or to take refuge in the child after a breakup or divorce and show the other person s / he wasn't necessary and has been replaced by a child, or to replace a child who has died" (Se considera motivaciones válidas cuando la persona o pareja desea adoptar a un menor de edad *por amor*. . . . No se puede presentar como una motivación válida para adoptar el usar al niño como pretexto para retener al esposo, o para convertirla en doméstica, o como escudo frente a la soltería, o para ocultar que se es estéril, o para refugiarse en el niño tras la ruptura de una relación sentimental o divorcio—para demostrar a la persona que se fue que ya no es necesaria y que fue reemplazada por un niño—, o para reemplazar al hijo fallecido) (PROMUDEH 2001: 8). Compare Marcia Inhorn's condensation of cross-cultural statements on the primary reasons people have children:

social security (labor contributions and caring for aged relatives), social power (specifically, as a source of power for women in patriarchy), and social perpetuity (as a contribution to the world) (2003: 78).

8 A formal *denuncia*, leading to a guardianship investigation, may also be triggered if the orphanage reports the presence of a newly interned child. Not all children enter the orphanage via being placed there by the courts for their own protection. As I will explore in the following chapter, some children enter orphanages "via the administrative process," where a relative drops off the child at the orphanage, and the orphanage informs the courts.

9 The meaning of documenting paternity is explored in chapter 6.

10 Similar strategies occurred during Peru's civil war, when a participant in a feud of long standing could inform, for example, government counterinsurgency forces that his or her foe was a member of Shining Path.

11 "debido a que son de una economía precaria y les es imposible mantenerla a dicha menor."

12 "pues la madre de dicha menor se encuentra con deficencia mental y posiblemente se hayan burlado, y que por referencias de la propia madre dice ser el padre de la criatura la persona de nombre P——."

13 See Article 248 of Law 27337, "Ley que aprueba el Nuevo Código de los Niños y Adolescentes," which was passed in 2000 (this version of the code was current during my fieldwork).

14 Like most of the officials I spoke to in Ayacucho, the police officers I consulted recognized a distinction between overt exploitation and certain forms of child labor, namely, working alongside a parent, that are understandable and acceptable under Ayacucho's conditions of poverty. This is a complex model of child labor, combining an abolitionist perspective with strains of protectionism (White 1994).

15 A Peruvian legal scholar has recently commented that the refusal of judicial personnel to learn and conduct proceedings in any of Peru's indigenous tongues prevents justice in the courts (Ardito Vega 2004); this linguistic barrier rings true for many of the abandonment proceedings.

16 This is a story repeated throughout history and around the world, in the name of the "best interests of the child." For instance, in the 1950s Native American children were removed from their homes to "rescue" them from the uncivilized conditions of their lives on the reservation (Finn 1991: 125, 133–34). These "interventions" asserted that Indian parenting could *never* be in the "best interests of the child" (Strong 2001). The 1978 Indian Child Welfare Act established certain collective rights for Native American tribes, the result being that conflicts now arise over what political entity or legal system has the right to determine native children's best interests, as relationships between tribes, states, and the federal government are contested in the space of chil-

dren's bodies (Brown and Morrow 2001). For a related conflict, see Judith Modell on "the intersection of an American child welfare system with Hawaiian cultural interpretations of moving children from household to household" (Modell 1998: 156).

17 I was granted access to all the files and observational opportunities for every stage of the adoption except the Council meetings, where the couples are paired with their children. Though I was not able to obtain prior consent from each family individually, the University of Michigan's Institutional Review Board approved my examination of the files under specific conditions of confidentiality. I protected the anonymity of the families through several means, including using only initials for the notes I took on the files, as well as reviewing the previous year's files while accompanying adoptive parents in the current year, thus deliberately not overlapping written information with visual and observed information.

18 "yo existo, quiero un nombre," "MANA SUTIYUQ, IMATAQ KANCHIK," and "¿Ciudadan@s o sombras?"

19 This is, of course, not the first incarnation of adoption law in Peru. Adoptions have been legislated since the time of Spanish governance, and Peru's first civil code dealt with them in 1852.

20 This principle has been part of international declarations since at least 1959 with the Declaration of the Rights of the Child (Alston 1994: 3). With regard to the appearance of "best interests" in the CRC, Alston suggests that "its meaning seems either to have been taken for granted or to have been considered unimportant . . . the drafters of Article 3(1) appear to have been sufficiently familiar with the phrase 'the best interests of the child' from its extensive usage in the domestic law of many countries" (11), suggesting that the diffusion of this principle long predates the CRC.

21 A number of anthropologists have documented the state's interest in reproducing families, for example, Das (1995), Fonseca (2002a), Ginsburg and Rapp (1995), Inhorn (2003), Kahn (2000), Kligman (1992 and 1995), and Rugh (1981).

22 Nancy Scheper-Hughes (1990) has written sensitively about organ trafficking. In Peru, organ-trafficking rumors map closely onto a legendary creature of long standing in the Andes: the *pishtaco* or *ñakaq* (Mannheim and Van Vleet 1998; Oliver-Smith 1969; Weismantel 2001; see Weismantel 1997: 29 for an explicit link to international adoptions). The *ñakaq*, whose name means "butcher" in Quechua, is a significantly white being who sucks the fat from native Andeans, killing them in the process, and uses the fat toward historically relevant ends (the current iteration is for sale on the international market). When Andeans speak of *ñakaqs* they may be invoking post-colonial political critiques (Weismantel 1997: 11). Mary Weismantel has also drawn out the links between child trafficking, organ theft, and the *sacaojos*, a creature that removes body parts instead of fat, and that similarly comes disguised as a *gringo* (2001: 225).

23 The anthropologist Claudia Fonseca makes a compelling argument for the link between organ trafficking and adoption across the continent in Brazil. She suggests that the Brazilian national psyche is damaged when foreigners who take in disabled or black children are labeled "generous," and that "the organ transplant scare serves as an unconscious defense mechanism. If we do not want these children, the logic goes, then nobody could want them" (Fonseca 2002b: 38; see also Dorow 2006: 78–79 for China).

24 The political scientist Alison Brysk observed that an international NGO's "adopt-a-child" sponsorship program (cf. Bornstein 2001) failed in highland Ecuador until it was renamed to invoke traditional notions of godparenting (2000: 200).

25 "[El] niño es expuesto en vitrina para que lo ven y lo venden . . . Etiquetado: niño para ser adoptado . . . En tiempo record ya está designado para una pareja."

26 Law 28251, passed in 2004 after I left the field, began to broaden the definition of trafficking to include that for sexual purposes. As I was finalizing the revisions to this chapter in January 2007, I received notification from the IDEIF that Law 28950 "against the trade in persons and the illicit trafficking of migrants" ("Ley contra la Trata de Personas y el Tráfico Ilícito de Migrantes") was passed by Congress on January 16, 2007. This bill includes language that allows a much broader picture to be drawn of what "trade in persons" might consist of, and states, "The kidnapping, transportation, relocation, taking in, receiving, or retaining of a child or adolescent with the purpose of exploitation will be considered part of the trade in persons, even when it does not involve any of the mediums indicated above."

27 The IDEIF's position at the time was that Peru's legal definition should be based on that of the United Nations: " 'Trafficking in persons' shall mean the recruitment, transportation, transfer, harbouring or receipt of persons, by means of the threat or use of force or other forms of coercion, of abduction, of fraud, of deception, of the abuse of power or of a position of vulnerability or of the giving or receiving of payments or benefits to achieve the consent of a person having control over another person, for the purpose of exploitation. Exploitation shall include, at a minimum, the exploitation of the prostitution of others or other forms of sexual exploitation, forced labour or services, slavery or practices similar to slavery, servitude or the removal of organs" (United Nations 2000).

28 I have generally tried to avoid using words that may be hurtful to adoptive families; here, while the term "surrender" may be problematic, it is meant to indicate that most of these children are not "placed for" adoption.

THREE. **PUERICULTURE AND ANDEAN ORPHANHOOD**

1 Each of these terms also has its own carefully constructed definition; in brief, "disappearance of both parents" means that parents have disappeared, with no explanation, no hope of return, and no success in efforts to locate them; "abandonment by both parents" means the intentional surrender, to no one in particular, of parental rights and claims; "desertion by both parents" references the willful refusal to parent; "separation from both parents," means involuntary but legal separation for good cause; and "loss from both parents" refers to the permanent and involuntary separation caused by a major and verifiable event such as war (United States 2006: 8 CFR 204.3(b), 90–91).

2 Much of this information comes from the recollections of my friends who were orphans and grew up in this new institution (see also Ludeña Gonzalez 2000: 210 for more JAVA history). Foreign volunteers teach English at the orphanage, resulting in orphans who are comfortable with outsiders, unlike many of their peers who saw no tourists at all during the years of violence. This background gave a context to my own conversations with them.

3 Although Ayacucho had no orphanages prior to the onset of the violence, there have been orphanages elsewhere in Peru since the early days of the Spanish colonial government. The roots of these institutions are found in Spain, where an official "father of orphans" position was first created in 1407, and institutions for housing orphans and abandoned children were founded throughout the fifteenth and sixteenth centuries (Jimenez Salas 1958: 142n47, 205; see also Kertzer 1993: 12 for the invention of the abandonment system in Italy). In the 1550s, a Lima attorney "was appointed official 'father of orphans' " (Lockhart 1968: 187) following the Spanish model. Peru's first orphanage was founded in Lima in 1603 and "provided refuge to Spanish boys and girls, many abandoned on church doorsteps, in the streets, corrals, or irrigation canals of the city . . . by the 1620s, the orphanage housed more than 120 foundlings and nearly 50 other children" (van Deusen 2001: 109). Philanthropists in Cuzco and Lima would later establish orphanages to house abandoned *mestizos* (Lockhart 1968: 190). Meanwhile, though, as Milanich has noted, "poor, abandoned, and illegitimate minors in Latin American and Caribbean societies, from the colonial period into the twentieth century, have often been informally reared in *casas ajenas*—other peoples' homes" (2004: 311)—in other words, as circulated children.

4 Juan Ossio, personal communication. See chapter 1, note 13, on Uchurraccary.

5 "Ellas no tiene ningún interés por medio. Un trabajador secular siempre ve por su casa, pero las madres no; es como una mamá." This is a tension also addressed by secular children's homes, such as the Aldeas Infantiles SOS organization, which requires children's caretakers to be single, divorced, or wid-

owed women between ages twenty-five and forty with no dependent children (www.aisosperu.org.pe). That is, caretakers should be women without kin and affines who will divert their affections.

6 The orphanage school is staffed by teachers who have, as one of them described it to me, "accepted the challenge of understanding" the children. Note that some of the children who receive education at the orphanage are "externals" (*externos*) who, in contrast with the confined orphans of the 1980s and 1990s, come for classes and lunch, then return home, leaving "internals" (*internos*) to their music lessons, a video, or the library.

7 I'm grateful to her for permitting me to use her words here. While I have been a member of this listserv for many years, identifying myself as a researcher in my first posting to the community, I have only posted occasionally and I do not use any of the statements made on the listserv without express permission. I have learned a great deal from the generous, well-informed adoptive parents on this listserv.

8 Orphans who did not grow up in the orphanage also subscribe to the idea that their unique positionality within the social landscape of Ayacucho gives them an affinity with one another. Salvador, a paternal orphan who left his mother in their small town and apprenticed himself to an Ayacucho weaver when he was only eight, told me that he and his wife, Raquel, a maternal orphan, were "compatible" because they had both experienced the loss of a parent. Sometimes in Ayacucho, he said, people who have both parents look down on those who don't.

9 I'm grateful to Liz Roberts for introducing me to this reference.

10 Stepan explains that "the Latin American countries shared with France several political characteristics that gave support to the notion of puericulture: an emphasis on agriculture and the resonance of agricultural metaphors of cultivation, a pronatalism based on high maternal and infant mortality rates and the consequent worry about inadequate population growth, and an essentially conservative profamily outlook" (1991: 78).

11 The young residents are discouraged from leaving except under proper supervision (on excursions to mass or the countryside) or via print or electronic media (appearing in studies of nutrition or psyche, human interest stories, or photo essays).

12 For an adolescent, the foster care system means that he or she will receive housing, food, and education. Just as importantly, influential families acquire household help. In the past, the nuns arranged these situations privately, leading to perceptions that money was paid them in exchange for the free labor of an adolescent orphan. Now, the same process continues but is regulated by the adoption office and court system. Ideally, the young man or woman placed through this foster care system would live like a member of the family (eating with them at their table, doing a few chores) but is not a house-

hold employee. However, in a formal interview, Ayacucho's family judge explained to me that foster care could easily be misinterpreted because "in Peru, it is understood that to take in [*recoger*] a child of a lower class, cultural level, and educational level, is only for serving the patron, reaching pots and so on."

13 In Peru, between 8,000 and 12,000 children are believed to actually live on the streets; UNICEF often severely overestimates (by millions) the number of street children (Green 1998: 61), as does the public. In Ayacucho, a Dutch aid worker who established a home for young street children estimated that thirty-six children live on the streets of Ayacucho, but locals thought this figure was absurdly low, seeing as they do dozens of children begging in the streets each day. What seems to be occurring here is a public blurring of notions of orphans, homeless children, and beggars or other kinds of working children (see Swanson 2007 on begging in Ecuador). Within the orphanage, however, staff keep "orphans" and "street children" carefully separate, as they view the two groups to be inherently different.

14 During the violence, these characteristics were ascribed not to their orphanage training but to the fact that victims were often town authorities from upstanding rural families, and their children were felt to be well brought-up.

15 Bilingual Andeans will freely use the Spanish word *huérfano* with similarly doubled connotations. My *comadre*, when running for political office in her community, told me she was going to work on behalf of *huérfanos*, proving to me that she meant poor children when she elaborated that she'd appeal to nongovernmental organizations for donations and defend the free breakfasts presently offered in schools. On another occasion, she referred to a young neighbor (who lived with her grandmother and her siblings but whose parents were both alive) as *huérfana* when trying to get her attended at the health post. The Spanish word can take on Quechua meaning when used in this bilingual context.

16 It is curious that while a child whose parent has died is an orphan, a parent whose child has died has no equivalent title, in English, Spanish, or Quechua. Unlike widow(er)s and orphans, bereaved parents do not have a distinctive title. This probably simply reflects the regularity of losing children due to high infant mortality rates, although it may also suggest the differing importance of certain kin ties from the point of view of parent and child.

17 The Quechua term *wachuy* refers to the agricultural procedure of cutting a furrow, but—like many Quechua words—this bears an obvious double entendre (Bruce Mannheim, personal communication).

18 The idea of a *wakcha* receiving a newborn animal interestingly recalls the use of the term "to refer to the animal that has been separated from its flock" (Montecino 1996: 43n11). On a related note, Catherine Allen's second edition of *The Hold Life Has* comments that in recent years, working for *ayni* (recipro-

cal labor obligations) was characterized by the Sonqueños she lived with as the lowest possible form of survival, whereas in 1975, working for money had been similarly criticized (Allen 2002 [1988]: 213). This evaluative reversal of reciprocal relations and cash suggests that if similar changes have occurred in Huasicancha, obtaining animals through payment may no longer be so despised.

19 Or even only one—government census categories include maternal orphan (*huérfano de madre*), and people also use the term "paternal orphan" (*huérfano de padre*), phrases which accurately reflect a reality felt in much of the Spanish-speaking world: a person with only one living parent is still an orphan.

20 "Ayacuchano huerfano pajarillo / ¿Porque has ido a tierras extrañas? / Alza tu vuelo vamos a Ayacucho / Donde tus padres lloran tu ausencia. / ¿En tu pobre casa que te habra faltado? / Caricias, delicias demás has tenido / Solo la pobreza con su ironia / Entre sus garras quiso oprimirte." (Ayacuchano, little orphan bird / Why have you gone to faraway lands? / Let's fly away to Ayacucho / Where your parents mourn your absence. / What did you lack in your poor house? / You had caresses, delights, and more. / Only poverty with its irony / Wished to oppress you between its claws.)

21 "Maymi mamayki / Maymi taytayki / Wakchaschay . . . / Mamaysi wikch'uwan / Taytaysi saqiwan / Runaq wasimpi . . . / Hina saqiwachun / Hina wikch'uwachun / Pasallasaqsi." (Where is your mother / Where is your father / My poor little orphan? . . . / They say my mother threw me out / They say my father abandoned me / In the house of a stranger . . . / In that way may I be abandoned / In that way may I be thrown out / As they say, I'll just move on.)

22 Interestingly, Rivera's friend Alonso Lara, a native of Ayacucho city, chimed in at this point to reveal to me that "Fermín has no town." Lara and Rivera told the story together: Rivera was born in a mining town at 5,000 meters in the *puna*. In the 1950s, the mine closed and the town was abandoned. Rivera returned on foot (the train no longer went there) in the 1970s and found an empty town, the houses boarded up, with "not even a dog to bark at you." He concluded, "So now I have no town. But it's better that way—Alonso, what has your town ever done for you?" "Oh," said Alonso, in apparent agreement, "Huamanga pains me."

23 There is historical precedent for this sort of use of an orphanage among highland migrants to Lima, documented by Peter Lloyd thirty years ago. For example, "one woman, thirty years of age, and married to her second husband who is several years younger than herself, has two very young children by him; two older boys of her first marriage are in the orphanage and stay with her only at weekends" (Lloyd 1980: 74).

24 "La mamá tiene que comprometer en visitar semanalmente, sabados o domingos, para que no se pierde el enlace familiar. Y lo que pasa es que al

principio esas mamás vienen tres veces a la semana. Pasa el mes y ya vienen una vez a la semana. Pasa la mes y vienen quinceanalmente. Llega un momento en que ya no viene. Al final la mamá se desaparece—y el niño tiene un año y medio y se va en adopción."

25 I did witness one adoption of an adolescent, something so unusual that Limeño journalists crossed the Andes with cameras and tape recorders to capture the event. A couple from the United States adopted a fifteen-year-old girl whom the husband had met while volunteering at the orphanage. Just shy of the age where the U.S. government would prohibit adoptions, the young woman seemed happy to be entering a family where she would be the oldest of three children, something not usually seen since Peruvian adoptions follow birth order fairly strictly. In other words, they follow an ideology of producing adoption as natural—new arrivals to the family should be younger than their siblings. In general, though, infants and very young children are preferred by adopters, in part "because their kinship and cultural attachments are seen as not fully formed" (Dorow 2006: 59) but also because of widely held understandings of the import of nutrition and medical care at a young age. Older youths, somewhat surprisingly, are categorized along with physically or mentally disabled children in the adoption office's "awareness program," Ángeles que aguardan (Angels that wait), and they will be more quickly assigned to any pre-adopters willing to take on this challenge. Rules about birth order may also be waived (as they were in the young woman's case) to facilitate adoptions of older kids.

26 These statistics were taken prior to the establishment of Casa Luz (the Argentine-run Protestant home) and Los Cachorros (the home for street children, begun by a Dutch woman adopted from Peru).

27 This slight gender disparity may make more sense by the end of the book. For now, compare to Kertzer's finding, in his history of infant abandonment in Italy, that "more girls than boys were left at the foundling homes" as daughters were expensive to maintain and would ultimately be lost by the family through marriage (1993: 111; see also Sargent and Harris 1998 on gendered abandonment in Jamaica).

FOUR. COMPANIONSHIP AND CUSTOM

1 The importance to this equation of calculating relatedness, and of last names, is discussed in chapter 6.

2 Anne Line Dalsgaard recorded a similar statement in Brazil: "The desire of all women is to have a child, because they feel alone . . . being alone in the house is too bad. One has to have something to do, somebody to play and to talk with" (2004: 181).

3 The cultural specificities of childhood have become a respected topic of an-

thropological study in the last twenty-five years (DeLoache and Gottlieb 2000; Reynolds 1996; Scheper-Hughes and Sargent 1998; Schildkrout 1980; Stephens 1995a); for larger, framing studies of childhood, see Ariès 1962; Zelizer 1985.

4 Susan Lobo has written vividly of how her own desire for privacy was not comprehensible to her Peruvian informants: "as soon as I took my typewriter into an empty room or corner, an adult would follow me or more commonly would send a young child to sit with me so I 'would not feel lonely all alone' " (1982: 73).

5 As discussed in chapter 2, the Peruvian government's population control policies took a well-publicized and sinister turn during the Fujimori years (1990–2001), when forced sterilizations were carried out using a quota system. This made front-page headlines while I was in the field (see Leinaweaver 2005c).

6 The notion of reproduction within the heterosexual couple is promoted here.

7 Adults who take in others' children are rarely doing so to fill the gap of never having borne children. More common is an adult who takes in a child because her children have grown and left, or who takes in a child to accompany her similarly aged children, or who takes in a child to do chores and physical labors so that her own kids don't have to.

8 Strategies for resolving infertility include in vitro fertilization, or IVF (financially out of reach for the income bracket I was working with; but see the Ecuadorian case [Roberts 2006]), adoption, and "irregular adoption," or what adoption scholars like Claudia Fonseca call "Brazilian-style" (2002a: 412), which encompasses a variety of strategies such as taking a stranger's baby and registering it as your own.

9 Within Peru, domestic adoption contrasts with child circulation, as it is thought to be primarily for those who are infertile (and can afford and choose to negotiate the complexities of the adoption system).

10 "Yo no má hago todo, ahí también se viene, se regresa tarde ya, ahí a veces yo sola estoy y no tengo ni ganas de comer también, yo sola, solita me siento."

11 Compare to Brazil, where women want to "board out children as long as possible without giving up their mother-right in the children's moral conscience" (Fonseca 1986: 25).

12 "Una vez año pasado como estaba mal, grave me he enfermado. Siquiera no me he dado cuenta, entonces esa vez me ha ayudado la señora, la señora me ha ayudado, tanto de curandero, hacerme curar. Entonces de esa manera mi Diana habrá pensado, 'Sabes que mamá te ha salvado tu vida, la señora también está mal,' me dijo, 'lo ayudo, entonces como modo de acompañar no más estoy, voy a estar ahí,' me dijo. Entonces 'pero Diana, cuando voy a estar aquí, tienes que estar aquí.' 'Ya mami.' Así no más está ahí, la señora también, 'que me acompañe no más, que me extraña yo solita, aquí está extrañando, no hay nadie en mi casa' me dijo."

13 "Sus hijos es como si para ella es como si no existiera, algo así . . . dice ni
siquiera le hablan, a la señora, sino que a veces lo dejan a ella, y se encierran en
su cuarto, están mirando televisión o bien están durmiendo, . . . a causa de eso
también toma, entonces cuando le está conversando con Diana, se está dis-
trayendo, ya no está pensando en tomar. . . . A veces se cocinan sus hijas cada
uno a sus cuartos se meten y se lo comen, ni siquiera capaz de darle a su papá,
a su mamá, si pues y los servicios se dejan para que lave su mamá, hasta que
mientras que recoge su mamá están botados, entonces su mamá también que
'mis hijos no es para mi, si es que me acompaña Diana ya no voy a tomar
importancia en ellas.' "

14 "Más o menos ya me acostumbré . . . ya no, cuando iba mi chacra, ya no
lloraba mucho ya, tranquila ya me venía."

15 "Lupe se había dado cuenta porque quería vivir con su papá."

16 As Modell has put it in her studies of adoption in the United States, "Ironically,
only 'years' could make the birthparent as much a parent as the adoptive
parent had become" (1994: 199).

17 "Al lado de mi papá ya era una casa cerrada, así cerrada, cerrada, y no me
acostumbraba a ese ambiente . . . no me acostumbraba, quería irme allá arriba
donde mi tía, nada no me acostumbraba con mis hermanas también, no me
comprendían, es difícil cuando tu no creces con una persona desde tu niñez, o
tu que dices no, para mi es así . . . pero siempre triste extrañaba, o sea, no era
igual . . . ay no como te puedo explicarte, o sea no estaba tan acostumbrado
con mi papá, y con la segunda con mi mamá no, con la otra mi mamá . . . me
gustaba estar arriba, ir donde mi tío por más que se moleste así."

18 Young people's agency in setting up their own transfers has been documented
cross-culturally, from Brazil (Fonseca 2002a: 408) to Melanesia (Keesing 1970:
1008) to Zimbabwe (Reynolds 1996: 29).

19 "Yo le dije 'profesorita dile a mi papá para . . . estar contigo' le dije así, y
también me iba a dar como una propina la profesora, no así gratis tampoco
pues, . . . como era buena persona, no me gustaba decirlo no, 'ya profesorita vamos a estar contigo' yo le dije ya pue, le dijeron a mi papá pue, pero
o sea mi decisión era, no me decía mi papá 'anda, anda donde ella' no, sino
era mi decisión . . . ya pues tenia que pedirlo permiso a mi papá, porque
yo por mi cuenta no podía venir . . . [No fue un trabajo], como era casa
pequeñita . . . lavaba sus ropas, cocinaba como en mi casa hacia, normal
tranquila, siempre de comida nunca he faltado, siempre comíamos todo ig-
uales, salíamos así pues."

20 Almost a quarter of the family income in poor homes is said to be earned by
minors (Vásquez H. and Mendizabal O. 2002: 141; see also Torres Rodríguez
1999).

21 As Viviana Zelizer has documented, struggles over child labor in North America in the previous century discursively separated love and economics, but

allowances may acceptably reward "good" child labor, such as chores. They also set up the conditions for children to be consumers (Zelizer 1985: 56–112).

22 The interpersonal qualities of the *propina* are underscored by a look at its etymology. *Propina* comes from a Latin word referring to drinking. The various forms of the word indicate to drink to someone's health, to drink and then give another person the rest of the liquid, to give someone something to drink, and—simply—to give (Corominas and Pascual 1980: 552). All of these actions require another person's participation.

23 Parry and Bloch comment that *"for us* money signifies a sphere of 'economic' relationships which are inherently impersonal, transitory, amoral and calculating. There is therefore something profoundly awkward about offering it as a gift expressive of relationships which are supposed to be personal, enduring, moral and altruistic . . . Where [the economy] is not seen as a separate and amoral domain, where the economy is 'embedded' in society and subject to its moral laws, monetary relations are rather unlikely to be represented as the antithesis of bonds of kinship and friendship, and there is consequently nothing inappropriate about making gifts of money to cement such bonds" (1989: 9).

24 In the IPROFOTH (Instituto de Promoción y Formación a la Trabajadora del Hogar) manual for *empleadas*, we learn that "there are other cases in which, being 'goddaughters' of the señora, they pay us one part money, another in clothes, school supplies, food, etc. Some of us are more interested in good treatment, good food, and time to study, than in a salary increase" (Loza et al. 1990: 72). The authors also explain, "There are underage girls who are brought from the *sierra* like 'goddaughters,' and in general they receive the worst treatment, more verbal and physical aggression, and are the most submissive and vulnerable against the total control of the employers, and they can't leave for another job—it's even difficult to know how many they are and how they are because they don't leave or go to school" (74).

25 The *propina* is not only given to children or domestic workers—it is, of course, also a tip in a restaurant, the "alms" given to street children, the bribe given to a police officer, and the sum paid to a highway robber. The *propina*, as an indistinctly economic / kin relationship, thus articulates spaces *between* households of different social classes as well as *within* them.

26 "A veces la gente en el Perú, cuando la gente te va dar, por más sean familiares esas cosas, si te va dar su plata es porque quiere que tu hagas las cosas bien hechas, a ellos les gusta, y para recibir un poco de dinero, si no tenemos nada de esto, hay que humillarnos prácticamente y aceptar lo que nos digan, y eso lo triste de la sociedad."

27 Q: Para servicio tambien llevan a los niños? Quieren llevar un niño para servicio también? A: No, no, no, no, no. Se descalifique si es por hacer eso. Porque a veces mucha gente viene [a la oficina de adopciones] de los cin-

cuenta, sesenta años que ya tienen hijos y quieren una compañia, no es para una compañia, . . . , les decimos 'ustedes no quieren un hijo, lo que quieres es un acompañante.' Entonces para eso, hay personas que le pueden servir, rentadas, pero no. Entonces el enfoque es, ¿Es un niño que quiere, un hijo? No una persona que les puede servir, no?

28 "de ahí ya mi papá ya tomó en cuenta de mí, como ya me había acercado ya al lado de mi papá. Ya mi papá me compraba mis cuadernos, me ayuda para despedida de promoción, todo ya era en cuenta de mi papá ya esos gastos."

29 "Mi tío me dice así y yo le dije a mi papá, dice le voy a acompañar diciendo, mi papá también tú decídete me dice y yo le he dicho a mi tío, ya tío le he dicho ya."

30 These examples are not unlike Catherine Allen's description of politics in the Andean community of Sonqo, where decisions are made behind the scenes long before they are actualized at public meetings (2002 [1988]).

31 "No, trabajé ahí, era como una empleada . . . cama adentro vivía, salía los domingos, donde mi tía me iba . . . y ya pue así empecé a trabajar allí y hacía todo, pero la gente te, ahí te tratan pues como una empleada, allá no te puede tratar como una familia, así cuando trabajas en otra casa, . . . Me gustó, la señora era bien buena, de comida nunca me faltó, era casa pequeña, a mí me gustaba hacer rápido mis cosas, y bien limpia."

32 "No parece familia, se aleja, no debe ser."

33 "De ahí poco a poco he estado, como que entre ustedes eran muy amigables, comprensivas y entonces, ya por eso poco a poco estaba acercando ya, hemos ido acostumbrando, fuimos acostumbrando y entonces . . . el dia que fuimos a tu cumpleaños . . . de ahí poco a poco ya hemos estado acostumbrando, y yo creo que hasta ahora ¿no?"

34 Compare to how North American women who suffer miscarriages and want to be seen as bereaved mothers draw curious looks, because the social buildup of a relationship is not seen as present in a miscarried pregnancy (Layne 2003: 156). The actions of such women and of other expectant parents who interact regularly with their fetuses (talking, playing music, deliberately nourishing) are beginning to support the notion of the social commitment to the desired fetus (see Han 2006). For these expectant parents, time and activity are crucial components in their labors.

35 "En las primeras semanas . . . todo los sábados me iba [mi pueblo] para regresar domingos, y era bien difícil acostumbrarme . . . uno, dos años habré sentido así con irme, cada fin de semana llegaba ya me moría por irme, donde mis papás, donde mi mamá y donde mi abuelita . . . Y ya después de esos dos, tres años ya me había acostumbrado, con mis tíos, a la casa de mis tíos, ya no era tanto el apuro de regresarme a [mi pueblo] nada, a veces no más iba, a veces me quedaba osea, ya había acostumbrado a estar con mis tíos."

36 By way of comparison, in Morocco, "to adopt a child is always to risk losing

the child. Fear of such loss encourages adopting parents to keep the adoption a secret" (Gershon 2003: 442).

37 Neither love nor affection should be read here as "universally constant" (Carsten 2000: 17): both are categories that anthropologists use to carve out spheres of social action, but their parameters need to be verified empirically rather than assumed to be given.

38 Yanagisako has called this "the sloughing off of relatives" (2002: 139; see also Franklin and McKinnon 2001: 18; Carsten 1995). Attachment theorists in psychology might call this grieving, or decathecting; I am grateful to Irv Leon for alerting me to this terminology.

FIVE. *SUPERACIÓN*

1 William Stein has argued that food anxiety, linked to the insecurities of agricultural production, is drummed into highland Peruvians at an early age (1961: 77). Food anxiety appears in the abandonment files as well.

2 In 1996 this expense amounted to almost one-quarter of Peru's fiscal spending (Kim et al. 2000: 151).

3 A portion of this material on *superación*, including the case study of Sarita, appears in *Latin American Perspectives* (Leinaweaver 2008); see also Leinaweaver 2005a.

4 I am grateful to an anonymous reviewer for the press, who gently reminded me that *superar*, "to overcome" in English, doesn't properly express the underlying tenor of this deeply reflexive notion. That is, *superarse*—to overcome *one's own* constraints—is the commonly used form. Throughout this chapter, I also use the term *superación*—overcoming—and I conjugate the reflexive verb as well, to indicate *superarme* (overcoming *my* constraints), etc.

5 In this, *superarse* resembles the Yoruba term *Ọlaju* (Peel 1978: 141). Peel's fascinating interpretation of *Ọlaju*, to which Gillian Feeley-Harnik kindly alerted me, has inspired me to think more deeply about how *superarse* connects to larger socioeconomic and historical patterns. Peel translated *Ọlaju* as "to open one's eyes," referring to a metaphorical enlightenment which grounds his speculation that the word and concept were probably first introduced to refer to cultural knowledge brought by missionaries and intended to be spread through conversion (144–49).

6 Tucker (2005: 9) describes the appeal and revulsion evoked by *la paisana Jacinta* (a toothless, smelly caricature of an Andean migrant woman played by a cross-dressing male comedian in the series "Paisana Jacinta").

7 This is far from an isolated example. In another typical instance, this one caught on tape by ethnographic filmmakers, transnational migrants from

Cabanaconde who have moved to the United States explain that people from this town "like to get ahead" and set a good example for others (Martinez and Gelles 1992).

8 Indeed, this phenomenon has been labeled "chain migration" by scholars.

9 There is a proud tradition of scholarship on Andean migration (see, for example, Paerregaard 1997; Skar 1994; Collins 1988), which builds upon earlier work that elaborated upon ecological and labor migration while emphasizing community integrity (see, for example, Brush 1977; Isbell 1978: 179–95). Andean women were historically less likely to migrate to the cities and were thus disadvantaged for lacking Spanish language abilities as well as cash (Andreas 1985: 55; see also Ardener 1981, quoted in Skar 1994: 159). Labor migration is often interpreted as a direct consequence of globalization and resulting increases in perceived needs (Vincent 2000).

10 There is also some return migration—those who adapted but didn't like the new conditions, like pollution and the faster tempo of life, and those who are supported by the Peruvian government's postwar Project in Support of Repopulation (Sørensen 2002; Stepputat 2002). But the migration is largely rural-to-urban. Still, new urbanites retain ties with their natal regions for important reasons: land and farming above all, a place to fall back on if things don't work out in the city, and a lack of opportunities elsewhere.

11 The residential neighborhoods of Ayacucho echo regional geography (see map 2)—the northern *barrios* like Covadonga are populated with people from the city of Huanta and the jungles beyond, while the eastern neighborhoods like Conchopata are home to people from southern provinces like Vilcashuamán. Similarly, in Lima, Ayacuchanos can be found most readily in the southern neighborhood of Manchay or the northern clusters of Huanta and Huanta II in San Juan de Lurigancho. In both cities, newly arriving migrants would settle near their *paisanos* if possible or join in one of the mass land invasions that were generally ignored by officials.

12 Gwen Kennedy Neville's work on Southern Protestant pilgrimage gives an instructive frame for the annual return of Peruvian migrants for religious celebrations and to enjoy the company of family (1987: 63): "In a society where mobility is the rule and individuals find themselves propelled away from their families into personal lives aimed at fulfillment and achievement, it is not surprising that one of the objects of nostalgia is the permanent fixed place, the location to which one might return 'home' for a time in order to become refreshed" (79).

13 I discuss migration separately from child circulation here for reasons both analytical and historical. Regarding the latter, migration studies do not usually focus on the child's role in helping the family get established (but see, for example, Valenzuela Jr. 1999, focusing on Mexicans in the United States).

However, it should be clear that the two kinds of movements are related, down to their moral roots of *superación*.

14 Compare to the notion of the "school migrant" so common in Madagascar (Sharp 2002).

15 Education is well studied in the Andes (e.g., Arnold 2000; García 2005; León Zamora and Staeheli 2001), and its importance among the working class has been conclusively established.

16 In these cases, according to Ayacucho's Network for the Education of Rural Girls (RENIRA), boys are often favored. This difference is exacerbated in the rural highlands, where 41 percent of poor girls do not attend school, as compared to the urban highlands, where only 7.8 percent do not (Vásquez H. and Mendizabal O. 2002: 109).

17 There also exist private institutes of higher education, both in Ayacucho and elsewhere in the country, but these require tuition payments and the purchase of uniforms and are typically not nearly as prestigious when one is seeking employment.

18 Throughout Latin America, nineteenth-century modernization projects relied on the education of citizens for full participation in democracy, integration into the state, and foundation of social development (see Muñoz Cabrejo 2000: 226; Torres 2003: 27–28).

19 "Ya no quería irme de abajo tampoco, porque ya me había acostumbrado, y cuando yo vine a mi casa, ya no era igual como en la casa de mi tío, ya todo eran años que estaba ahí, pero ya pues, a veces tu te llegas acostumbrarte a cada ambiente que tu vas, y el tiempo va pasando y tu vas agarrando costumbre."

20 Esther Goody has depicted a similar evaluation of fosterage transactions in West Africa (1984: 275).

21 Speaking of circulated children, IDEIF director Sandra Soria echoed Lorente's words: "Some have very good luck but others are exploited: the agreeable *cholo*, there to do your household chores."

22 "El *cholito* es el indio esclavizado casi al salir de la cuna. A veces es la madre quien condena a la servidumbre al hijo de sus entrañas, porque su miseria le hace creer sera más feliz en casa del amo, o porque se vió obligada a venderle por el precio que exigieron para enterrar a su padre. Más, por lo común, el cholito ha sido sustraído a la ternura maternal por alguno que quisiere especular con la carne de sus hermanos, o hacer algún regalo . . . Y además, ¿no va el cholito a una casa donde lo pasará major? ¿No le espera un porvenir más lisonjero? Ah! Hay algunos amos bondadosos que le crían y le tratan como un hijo; pero ¡cuán corto es el número de estas almas generosas! A lo más que puede aspirar el cholito es a ser bien mirada por las niñas de la casa, y a ocupar en el corazón de ellas un lugar entre el mono y el perrito de faldas; a veces es el animal de sufrimiento; por lo común su condición es la del esclavo;

y como tiene sobre éste la desventaja de que como no ha costado mucho no puede venderse en alto precio, no se le cuida con tanta solicitud . . . Y por afortunado que sea en la servidumbre, siempre habrá crecido sin la sombra de una madre, con esa sequedad de corazón y esterilidad de afectos que hacen la desgracia del expósito . . . El mayor número se preserve con tiempo de esta desgracia; transportado sin cuidado a climas peligrosísimos para los hijos de la sierra y cambiado bruscamente todo su regimen, suelen perecer a poco de ser traídos a la costa. Son los más dichosos."

23 Catherine Allen makes a related point about U.S. policies that affect the everyday, ritualized use of coca in Andean communities—"These restrictive measures are not deliberately aimed by policymakers at traditional users of coca. The 'war' has been declared on drug traffickers, not on coca chewers, but traditional chewers are affected nonetheless" (Allen 2002 [1988]: 193). That is, IDEIF's starkest condemnation is reserved for "actual" child traffickers—yet the child circulation practices engaged in predominantly by indigenous and impoverished Andeans are included in the definitions of trafficking they push. Allen suggested that, because coca-chewing is an indigenous practice, it is difficult to separate criticisms of coca from disdain for Indians (Allen 2002 [1988]: 192)—a similar argument could be made for child circulation.

24 This can be instructively compared to Maria Elena García's discussion of why Quechua-speaking parents eschew bilingual education and prefer that their children learn Spanish (2005: 105); certain "cultural losses" or dangers are accepted in view of the benefits that children are expected to receive when their instruction is Spanish-only.

25 A related critique of the poor, indigenous mothers who let their children go ties it to maternal sexuality. When a woman marries or remarries, she may not trust her new husband to love or even put up with another man's children. In this case, she will take them to the orphanage or distribute them among relatives. Women who do this are described critically as prioritizing their womanly nature over their motherhood (see also Fonseca 1986: 18–20).

26 Respect and the whip were associated in broader kinds of relations as well; I was told that "in the old days," anyone who did not remove his hat and properly greet another would be whipped by the authorities.

27 The parental instruction required to discipline and shape a child into a morally and socially mature being is tempered by strategies of migration and child circulation, both of which can require the separation of parent and child.

28 I haven't lingered long on these risks, but should point out that the specter of rape is central in critiques of child circulation. José Alvarado de la Fuente told me that "with the hope they will educate the children, parents send children to the cities, and a masked exploitation results that can lead to the extremes of permanent sexual violation of the girls, who are even used to initiate the sons of the family." Alvarado and Soría have also published a recent book on

prostitution in Ayacucho, underscoring their commitment to discover and condemn sexual exploitation (n.d.). An International Labor Organization (ILO) study in Ecuador found that young, indigenous domestic servants are sexually assaulted with alarming frequency, a state of affairs which their employers validated as *mejorando la raza*, improving the race (Castelnuovo y Asociados 2002, cited in Swanson 2007).

29 This is a fear that my *comadre* associated with contemporary times, saying that when she was young they didn't have adolescence (Mead 1961 [1928]) and marriage and childbearing took place at a "more reasonable age."

30 Abortion, though officially highly restricted, is practiced widely. In the early 1990s, annual rates of clandestine abortion in Peru were estimated to fall between 65,466 to 207,060 (Paxman et al. 1993). One friend informed me that adolescents can also obtain the morning-after pill at the local hospital's private area for treating teenagers.

31 Kathryn Burns gives some fascinating historical context for the circulation of young women in colonial Cuzco, merging gender and race in a thoughtful analysis. Because *mestiza* girls (as is typical for colonialism, these would be the children of colonized women and colonist men) were at greater risk for potentially confounding lineage and heritage transmission, they, not boys, were to be protected by the nuns at Santa Clara (Burns 1999: 16).

32 Gender and the division of labor are well studied in the region (see, for example, Babb 1989; Bourque and Warren 1981; Bunster and Chaney 1989; de la Cadena 1996; Harris 1980; Harvey 1997; Platt 1986; Valderrama and Escalante 1997; Van Vleet 2008; Weismantel 1988; on gender and work more broadly, see Durkheim 1977: 17–18; see also Ariès 1962: 393).

33 In child circulation in Madagascar as well, "because of the daily demands placed on them when they are young, girls may in fact receive more comprehensive training than boys" (Sharp 2002: 263).

34 Similarly, someone working in rural Peru might find that boys are more commonly circulated, or more likely to be laboring; in 1997, 57 percent of working children were male, which was attributed to the fact that "the majority of work in rural areas is agricultural and pastoral; males are more apt for field work than women" (Vásquez H. and Mendizabal O. 2002: 144).

35 In colonial Peru, upper-class Spanish families took in *mestiza* (of both native and Spanish descent) girls, whom they raised and who were treated with affection but seen as servants. The name for these girls is *criada*, which in Spanish means "raised" or "fostered." Tellingly, in contemporary Peru, the term *criada* means household servant.

36 I thank Florence Babb for pointing out this important contrast.

37 Although the word *ayllu* was not used in this context, it is relevant here; as Allen has argued, the Quechua word refers to a collection of individuals distinct from and opposed to another group (2002 [1988]: 87; see also Weismantel 2006).

38 Maria Elena García quotes a similar statement from a Quechua-speaker: "What I want most for my son is that he is not a campesino, like me" (2005: 98). Compare this to the Cuban parents who sent their children north in Operation Pedro Pan, enacting their fears about how communism would influence their children's education; as Torres writes, "The decision parents made to send their children abroad was closely tied to what they wanted for themselves" (2003: 252).

39 The ethic of applying *superarse* to one's children, contained in Wilmer's farming-centered account, is echoed in the narratives of women who work as domestic servants and who set correspondingly high goals for their children (Smith 1973: 200; Loza et al. 1990: 36).

40 "Quizás yo también crecí con ese anhelo, con esa meta prácticamente y una vez que me vine a vivir con mis papás eso iba creciendo más y más, porque yo veía a mi mamá a veces sufrir, llorar por plata así y discutía así tan solo por dinero, siempre tenía esa mentalidad de que yo iba estudiar e iba salir adelante para, yo le decía a veces cuando discutían así con mi papá, por dinero yo le decía yo voy a trabajar y ya nadie te va humillar, nadie te va decir eso por dinero."

41 A great deal of interesting research on transnational families has been published in the last several years (see, for example, Hirsch 2003; Levitt 2001; Miles 2004; Parreñas 2005) and has guided my own approach to these women's explanations of their choices and deliberations around migration.

42 "Cuando comprenda ya, cuando entienda ya, puedo dejarlo a mi hijo decirle no, porque me voy a irme allá, por podernos superar."

43 Since Lupe is not yet in a position to migrate, she goes about *superación* in other ways. This meant that she often became indebted to others. During the period of my fieldwork, she moved to Lima and started living with her stepsister's *tíos*, "helping" in her aunt's house while her husband drove one of the buses that the *tíos* own. (He worked from 6 a.m. to 10 p.m. and earned approximately fifteen dollars per day; she received a "tip.") The *tíos* had given Lupe a room on the roof, itself roofed by corrugated tin, and bit by bit she was making it a home. Lupe pleaded with the family's teenaged son to bring her cardboard boxes so she could cover the windows and holes in the ceiling of the room on the roof and also use them in place of sheepskins (*pellejos*, which are stacked atop one another to make a soft bed in the highlands) since there are none in Lima. In Lima, Lupe seemed quiet; on the weekends she would go with her son to the opposite end of the city to visit her husband's family, who gave her a blanket on one occasion to make the room a bit warmer. When her son would misbehave, she glared at him and gestured frantically for him to stop—I got the impression that his misbehaving reflected badly on her in a way that a child of the household's might not, because it wasn't her house. Ultimately, Lupe hopes to return to Huamanga, have her son educated, and open a store, thereby becoming self-sufficient. She said dreamily to me that when I come back to Peru, I will come to her store and she will invite me in, saying, "This is my store," and treat me to a beer or two.

44 These critiques resemble what Albert Schrauwers has found in Sulawesi, Indonesia. There, children deliberately interpret their exploitative fosterage situations in the historical light of slavery—unable to actively leave a situation, they nonetheless critique it in a culturally relevant way (1999).

45 In Brazil, Claudia Fonseca has documented disagreement over who is the beneficiary of these movements—"Birth mothers will claim they have made a gift to another household, blessing it with the gracious presence of a child. Foster parents, for their part, often broadcast a different sort of discourse— insisting that they have accepted the caretaking 'burden' in order to help out and implying that, in reward, they deserve to keep the child permanently" (Fonseca 2002a: 405; compare Milanich 2004: 317–18).

46 "El castigo que ellos me ponían, les agradezco, pero es que si yo no dejaba o no quería dejar de hablar mi quechua, porque simplemente me avergonzaba de hablar el castellano, no sé que pasaba pero no quería, y lo que mis tíos, mis primos hicieron es que simplemente si yo seguía hablando quechua y les hablaba en quechua no me contestaban . . . y casi a la fuerza pues me hicieron aprender, obligándome ya, pero les agradezco, claro que para mí ese rato era, porque por muchas cosa y yo sentía odiarlos y lo único que hacía era llorar, llorar, pero ahora me dí cuenta que era por mi bien, porque en mi salón mis compañeritas no hablaban quechua." See García (2005: 87) on the painful progress embodied in the "school myth."

47 "Siempre entendía que tenía que ser así, por mi bien, siempre."

48 "Pero sería imposible, porque mi abuelita estaba en la chacra. Yo no creo que sería una persona que no conozco siquiera letras, porque siempre hubiera sido así digo, me entiendes?"

49 Mann's work on refugees includes her speculation that more boys are separated from their families than are girls because boys can look after themselves and girls are needed at home for domestic work. However, she adds the caveat that the gender imbalance in this case may actually reflect the fact that research on separated children has occurred in the public sphere rather than the domestic sphere (Mann 2004: 5).

50 This also appears in stories of *superación* via migration; when Tania emigrated to Europe, her husband visited us almost daily to lament her absence (and to borrow money in order to phone her; when I lent him this money, he promised me he would carry my coffin when I died, no matter where I was). He said his heart was breaking, and that sometimes he thinks he shouldn't have

let Tania go, but he knows that they made that decision together and they now have to carry through and *superarse*.

SIX. *PERTENECER*

1 "Pero no les quería a mis tíos, o sea les tenía un gran aprecio, yo les agradezco bastante, porque me han tenido tanto tiempo en su casa, me han apoyado de una y otra manera, pero nunca se han ganado ese cariño mío, son tal vez demasiado reservados, demasiado este . . . para ellos sólo eran sus hijos, para mí era como una persona más que vivía, y no una sobrina, o sea nunca me han mostrado un afecto, y mis primos igual, había a veces que, si, pero, igual, pero siempre la diferencia en que yo simplemente era una prima."

2 This is in stark contrast to the ideology expressed by Gloria Atúncar, a Lima adoption office spokesperson. She said that adoption legally protects children —for instance, she went on, "the social worker has to verify that he has a bedroom. If I give him to my aunt, maybe he'll sleep in her room and that's not right."

3 Let me put in a plug for Maxis's *The Sims* as an intriguing new ethnographic tool. Playing this computer game with Sarita's brother, I was surprised to see that despite the constraints of a program designed to reflect North American suburbs, he built a house for his family's avatars in which he shared a room with his parents.

4 "Cuando el niñito nace, todavia bebito, no sientes tanto cariño . . . vas a poner todo en él, vas a invertir tu plata."

5 These ideas circulate among migrants, both educated and not, but a clear association of genealogy with education is visible both in Ayacucho's university entrance exam and in the materials that students study to prepare for that exam. The exam usually asks one or two challenging kinship questions (e.g., What is the term for your mother's sister's husband's brother's son's wife?), and the preparation courses define the family as "a group of persons linked by consanguinity, filiation, adoption or marriage who live under the same roof with similar interests, rights, and duties. The family, according to the constitution, is the basic cell of society." The lecture notes also described purposes (both biological, i.e., procreative, and formative, i.e., training and social education) and functions (reproduction, production, affection, recreation, socialization, education, and protection) of the family. Reading these course descriptions is like rereading the anthropological forefather Bronislaw Malinowski, who viewed the institution of the family and its function (nurturing the young) as mutually dependent (Collier et al. 1997: 73).

6 This is apparent in adoption laws that privilege kin, as long as they are not destitute, over wealthy foreigners—as Fonseca has put it, "biology compensates for poverty" (2002a: 418). It is also apparent in the predilection to keep

siblings together, i.e., to ensure that biological siblings are adopted into the same family.

7 The ages of the children probably have some impact on the sleeping arrangements; I will follow up in a few years to see where everyone is sleeping as the children age.

8 Weismantel aligns these titles along a racial axis, with *Mama / Tayta* as names for Indians, and *Señor / a* as appropriate for whites (2001: 286n30). This interpretation did not accord perfectly with the Ayacuchano rural-to-urban migrants I worked with, although there is significant overlap. In Ayacucho, the difference appeared to be one of familiarity, and of course, familiarity within racial or class constellations is more likely.

9 Curiously, little boys are *often* referred to as *"papito"* (see Lobo 1982: 88). Salvador, for instance, continually addresses his young son as *"papá"*; conversely, he also calls his wife Raquel *"hija"* (daughter).

10 The use of the word *tio / a* to describe any older relative seems to be a class indicator, because Olivia also revealed that her cousins, upwardly mobile professionals who disdain their parents' hometowns, use the term with its narrowest genealogical meaning: only for their mother's and father's siblings (see Weismantel 1995: 700n9 on the importance of consanguinity among Andean middle classes).

11 I am grateful to Mary Weismantel for raising this point. Degregori reminds us that the authors in this collection are largely the students of John Murra and as such have tendencies toward economic anthropologies (2000: 47; see also Wogan 2004: 97–102 on contemporary genealogical shallowness).

12 Young people are situated in family history through other kinds of documentation as well. These include family resemblances—one friend is referred to by all her extended family as "Rufina," her grandmother's name, because she is the only one in the family who "takes after her" (*llevó su cara*). They also include keystone events: fourteen-year-old Luis is called "Ingeniero" because his aunt's son, a mining engineer, had suffocated and died in the mine. His aunt was so sad and her relatives told her not to be sad any more, showing her Luís (the only baby boy in the family at that time) and saying: "Look, another engineer!"

13 All these relationships, and particularly the mother-in-law / daughter-in-law relationship (Van Vleet 2002), would of course have differed in practice from the ways in which I was incorporated into the family as an honorary member. I am grateful to Krista Van Vleet for reminding me of this.

14 Relationships of *compadrazgo* also have classificatory uses: Cristina called me *comadre* after I became godmother to her grandchild, and Melquíades calls Wilmer *padrino* because he *wants* him to become his marriage godfather.

15 First names are socially significant as well, though I do not take them up here. These days, urban Peruvian children are often saddled with names that sound

foreign and thus modern: Yesica, Deysi, Willy. But it was once quite common to name a baby with the name of the saint on whose day the child was born, and the use of the word *santo* to denote the birthday celebrant harkens back to this custom. This naming practice was facilitated by ubiquitous wall calendars spelling out the saints pertaining to each date. Calendars like these (bearing one incongruous photo, such as a small blond child in a sailor suit, or a castle in the Alps) are still distributed by local businesses to their customers at the end of the year, and the walls of the houses I visited were plastered with them.

16 Last names are one of the racial markers that usually remain constant throughout a lifetime. Quechua last names like Quispe, Huamán, and Yupanqui have a notably different ring than Spanish last names like Rodríguez, Zapatero, Flores, Vega, and García.

17 This is something that Olivia, a young urban migrant, identified as a behavior pertaining to the countryside; her mother taught her to call people with shared last names "uncle" out of respect, but in the city, she explained, people with the same last name feel no such connection to one another.

18 Historically, abandoned children in Lima were sometimes given the last names Pérez Aranibar, that is, the last names of the orphanage's founder (Roberto Frisancho, personal communication); in 2006, Sainot Gallegos of Aldeas Infantiles SOS told me that the children raised at their network of homes are given the maternal last name of the *madre sustituta* or foster mother who rears them, and the paternal last name of either the home's director or, if he is reluctant, the last name of SOS's founder, Maynard. Latin American orphans in the last century were sometimes given the last name "Expósito," or "Abandoned" (Guy 2002: 146), and European orphans, up until the nineteenth century, were given either the last name of the foundling home or "Espósito" (Kertzer 1993: 120). By comparison, abandoned Chinese infants were sometimes named with a character indicating the place they were found, a practice that ceased in response to discomfort from adoptive parents (Dorow 2006: 93).

19 The Spanish language has long distinguished between the layers of natal, baptismal, social, and civil status pertaining to children (Twinam 1999: 126–28).

20 "Que la menor hija de la actora use el apellido Toledo, Romero o Fujimori, no convierte a la hija de la demandante en hija del recurrente, ni del banquero ni del actual Presidente de la República . . . ignoro si la menor hija de la accionante usa el apellido Toledo, García, Belaunde, Fujimori o Pérez de Cuéllar desde que nació o lo va cambiando de acuerdo a las circunstancias."

21 His father, a teacher in Ayacucho whom he now sees occasionally, hadn't had the money to properly raise him—besides having a wife and children already.

22 Deborah Poole writes perceptively about the meaning of papers and of judicial practices in Ayacucho (2004).

23 "Cabe señalar que junto a la pareja convive un sobrino de 19 años de edad, al cual consideran como su hijo."

24 Salasacas in highland Ecuador believe that God keeps a book, written on lined paper just like government documents and the all-important Civil Registry, which determines when people die (Wogan 2004: 85–87).

25 Documents, as a key point at which individuals participate in state making, have been the focus of several recent works (Caplan and Torpey 2001; Kelly 2006; see also Das and Poole 2004).

26 Small towns in the department of Ayacucho don't have their own priests, so each one has a church in the city itself that corresponds to the village. Ayacucho's San Francisco de Paula parish priest serves Socos and Vinchos as well, visiting during the saint's day to perform mass and occasionally during the rest of the year.

Bibliography

Abercrombie, Thomas A. 1998. *Pathways of memory and power: Ethnography and history among an Andean people*. Madison: University of Wisconsin Press.

Alberti, Giorgio, and Enrique Mayer. 1974. "Reciprocidad andina: Ayer y hoy." In *Reciprocidad e intercambio en los Andes peruanos*, ed. G. Alberti and E. Mayer, 13–37. Lima: Instituto de Estudios Peruanos.

Alexander, Jack. 1978. "The cultural domain of marriage." *American Ethnologist* 5: 5–14.

Allen, Catherine. 2002 [1988]. *The hold life has: Coca and cultural identity in an Andean community*. Washington: Smithsonian Institution.

Alston, Philip. 1994. "The best interests principle: Towards a reconciliation of culture and human rights." *International Journal of Law and the Family* 8(1): 1–25.

Alvarado de la Fuente, José, and Sandra Soría Mendoza. n.d. *Prostitución adolescente volante en Ayacucho, una nueva modalidad de explotación sexual comercial infantil*. Lima: Instituto de Estudios por la Infancia y la Familia.

Anderson, Jeanine. 1993. "Feminización de la pobreza." *Revista Peruana de Ciencias Sociales* 3(3): 109–49.

———. 2004. "The intergenerational contract over time in a Peruvian shantytown." Paper presented at the American Anthropological Association annual meeting, Atlanta, Georgia, December 2004.

Andreas, Carol. 1985. *When women rebel: The rise of popular feminism in Peru*. Brooklyn: Lawrence Hill Books.

Appadurai, Arjun. 1991. "Global ethnoscapes: Notes and queries for a transnational anthropology." In *Recapturing Anthropology*, ed. R. Fox, 191–210. Santa Fe: School of American Research.

Arana, Marie. 2001. *American chica: Two worlds, one childhood.* New York: Delta.

Arce Castro, Gino, ed. n.d. *Pandillas juveniles en Huamanga: Estudio etnográfico.* Ayacucho: PAR (Programa de Apoyo a Repoblamiento y Desarrollo de Zonas de Emergencia).

Ardener, Shirley. 1981. *Women and space: Ground rules and social maps.* University of Oxford, Women's Studies Committee. New York: St. Martin's Press.

Ardito Vega, Wilfredo. 2004. "Cómo vencer la barrera lingüística." In *Justicia Mail, Instituto de Defensa Legal de la Pontificia Universidad Católica del Perú,* vol. 100. Lima.

Arguedas, José María. 1981 [1975]. "Notas elementales sobre el arte popular religioso y la cultura mestiza de Huamanga." In *Formación de una cultura nacional indo-americana,* ed. J. M. Arguedas, 148–72. Mexico City: Siglo Veintiuno Editores.

Ariès, Phillipe. 1962. *Centuries of childhood: A social history of family life.* New York: Alfred A. Knopf.

Arnold, Denise, ed. 1997. *Gente de carne y hueso: Las tramas de parentesco en los Andes.* La Paz: CIASE / ILCA.

Arnold, Denise. 2000. *El rincón de las cabezas: Luchas textuales, educación y tierras en los Andes.* La Paz: UMSA and ILCA.

———. 2002. *Las wawas del inka: Hacia la salud materna intercultural en algunas comu-nidades andinas.* La Paz: ILCA.

Babb, Florence E. 1989. *Between field and cooking pot: The political economy of market-women in Peru.* 1st ed. *Texas Press Sourcebooks in Anthropology,* no. 15. Austin: University of Texas Press.

Barrenechea Lercari, Carlos. 1988. *Los niños del pueblo: Situación nacional y el caso del Cusco.* Lima: TAREA.

Barth, Fredrik. 2002. "Sidney W. Mintz lecture for 2000: An anthropology of knowl-edge" (with comments and response). *Current Anthropology* 43(1): 1–18.

Betanzos, Juan Diez de. 1996 [1551]. *Narrative of the Incas.* Austin: University of Texas Press.

Biehl, João Guilherme. 2005. *Vita: Life in a zone of social abandonment.* Berkeley: University of California Press.

Bledsoe, Caroline H. 1990. " 'No success without struggle': Social mobility and hardship for foster children in Sierra Leone." *Man* 25(1): 70–88.

Bloch, Maurice. 1973. "The long term and the short term: The economic and political significance of the morality of kinship." In *The character of kinship,* ed. J. Goody, 75–87. Cambridge: Cambridge University Press.

Bolton, Ralph, and Enrique Mayer, eds. 1977. *Andean kinship and marriage.* Wash-ington: American Anthropological Association.

Bonilla, Heraclio. 1974. "The War of the Pacific and the national and colonial problem in Peru." *Past and Present* 81.

Bornstein, Erica. 2001. "Child sponsorship, evangelism, and belonging in the work of World Vision Zimbabwe." *American Ethnologist* 28: 595–622.

Boswell, John. 1988. *The kindness of strangers: The abandonment of children in western Europe from late antiquity to the Renaissance.* New York: Pantheon Books.

Bouquet, Mary. 1996. "Family trees and their affinicies: the visual imperative of the genealogical diagram." *Journal of the Royal Anthropological Institute* 2: 43–66.

———. 2001. "Making kinship, with an old reproductive technology." In *Relative values: Reconfiguring kinship studies,* ed. S. Franklin and S. McKinnon, 85–115. Durham, N.C.: Duke University Press.

Bourdieu, Pierre. 1977. *Outline of a theory of practice.* Trans. R. Nice. Cambridge: Cambridge University Press.

———. 1990. "Structures, *habitus,* practices." In *The logic of practice,* 52–65. Cambridge: Polity Press.

Bourque, Susan C. 1971. *Cholification and the campesino: A study of three Peruvian peasant organizations in the process of societal change.* Latin American Studies Program, Dissertation Series, no. 21. Cornell University.

Bourque, Susan C., and Kay Barbara Warren. 1981. *Women of the Andes: Patriarchy and social change in two Peruvian towns.* Ann Arbor: University of Michigan Press.

Bowie, Fiona. Editor. 2004. *Cross-cultural approaches to adoption.* London: Routledge.

Brady, Ivan, ed. 1976. *Transactions in kinship: Adoption and fosterage in Oceania.* Honolulu: University of Hawaii Press.

Briggs, Laura. 2006. "Adopción transnacional: Robo de criaturas, familias homoparentales y neoliberalismo." Trans. Gloria Elena Bernal. *Debate Feminista* 17(33): 46–68.

———. N.d. "Locating adoption in relation to state processes: War, economies, trauma, politics." Paper presented at Reproductive Disruptions: Childlessness, Adoption, and Other Reproductive Complexities, Ann Arbor, Michigan, May 2005.

Brown, Caroline, and Phyllis Morrow. 2001. "'A resource most vital': Legal interventions in native child welfare." *Northern Review* 23.

Brubaker, Rogers, and Frederick Cooper. 2000. "Beyond 'identity.'" *Theory and Society* 29: 1–47.

Brush, Stephen. 1977. *Mountain, field, and family: The economy and human ecology of an Andean valley.* Philadelphia: University of Pennsylvania Press.

Brysk, Alison. 2000. *From tribal village to global village: Indian rights and international relations in Latin America.* Stanford: Stanford University Press.

Bunster, Ximena, and Elsa M. Chaney. 1989. *Sellers and servants: Working women in Lima, Peru.* Granby, Mass.: Bergin and Garvey Publishers.

Burns, Kathryn. 1999. *Colonial habits: Convents and the spiritual economy of Cuzco, Peru.* Durham, N.C.: Duke University Press.

Butler, Judith. 1999 [1990]. *Gender trouble: Feminism and the subversion of identity.* New York: Routledge.

Caplan, Jane, and John Torpey, eds. 2001. *Documenting individual identity: The development of state practices in the modern world.* Princeton: Princeton University Press.

Carroll, Vern, ed. 1970. *Adoption in Eastern Oceania.* Honolulu: University of Hawaii Press.

Carsten, Janet. 1995. "The politics of forgetting: migration, kinship and memory on the periphery of the Southeast Asian State." *Journal of the Royal Anthropological Institute* 1: 317–35.

———. 1997. *The heat of the hearth: The process of kinship in a Malay fishing community.* Oxford: Clarendon Press.

———. 2000. "Introduction: Cultures of relatedness." In *Cultures of relatedness: New approaches to the study of kinship,* ed. J. Carsten, 1–36. Cambridge: Cambridge University Press.

Carsten, Janet, and Stephen Hugh-Jones. 1995. "Introduction: About the house— Lévi-Strauss and beyond." In *About the house: Lévi-Strauss and beyond,* ed. J. Carsten and S. Hugh-Jones, 1–46. New York: Cambridge University Press.

Castelnuovo y Asociados. 2002. *Informe del rapid assessment aplicado a niñas en trabajo agrícola, doméstico, y explotación sexual.* OIT-IPEC Ecuador.

Christinat, Jean Louis. 1989. *Des parrains pour la vie: Parenté rituelle dans une communauté des Andes péruviennes.* Recherches et travaux de l'Institut d'Ethnologie, no. 9. Neuchâtel: Editions de l'Institut d'Ethnologie / Editions de la Maison des Sciences de l'Homme.

Chronic Poverty Research Centre. 2004. *The chronic poverty report, 2004–2005.* Manchester: Chronic Poverty Research Centre.

Colen, Shellee, and Roger Sanjek. 1990. "At work in homes I: Orientation." In *At work in homes: Household workers in world perspective,* ed. S. Colen and R. Sanjek, 1–13. American Ethnological Society Monograph Series. Washington: American Anthropological Association.

Collard, Chantal. 2005. "Triste terrain de jeu: À propos de l'adoption internationale." *Gradhiva* 1: 1–16.

Collier, Jane, Michelle Z. Rosaldo, and Sylvia Yanagisako. 1997. "Is there a family? New anthropological views." In *The gender / sexuality reader: Culture, history, political economy,* ed. Roger N. Lancaster and Micaela di Leonardo, 71–81. New York: Routledge.

Collins, Jane L. 1985. "Migration and the life cycle of households in southern Peru." *Urban Anthropology and Studies of Cultural Systems and World Economic Development* 14: 279–99.

———. 1988. *Unseasonal migrations: The effects of rural labor scarcity in Peru.* Princeton: Princeton University Press.

Colloredo-Mansfeld, Rudi. 1994. "Architectural conspicuous consumption and economic change in the Andes." *American Anthropologist* 96(4): 845–65.

———. 1998. " 'Dirty Indians,' radical indígenas, and the political economy of social difference in modern Ecuador." *Bulletin of Latin American Research* 17(2): 185–205.

Constable, Pamela. 1997. "The family man: Some say James Gagel is an adoption angel. Others, especially in Peru, disagree." *Washington Post,* January 12, F1.

Corominas, Joan, and José A. Pascual. 1980. *Diccionario crítico etimológico castellano e hispánico*. Madrid: Editorial Gredos.

Cuervo, Rufino José. 1998. *Diccionario de construcción y régimen de la lengua castellana*. Barcelona: Herder.

CVR (Comisión de la Verdad y Reconciliación). 2003. *Final report*. www.cverdad .org.pe.

Dalsgaard, Anne Line. 2004. *Matters of life and longing: Female sterilisation in northeast Brazil*. Copenhagen: Museum Tusculanum Press.

Das, Veena. 1995. "National honor and practical kinship: Unwanted women and children." In *Conceiving the new world order*, ed. F. D. Ginsburg and R. Rapp. Berkeley: University of California Press.

Das, Veena, and Deborah Poole, eds. 2004. *Anthropology in the margins of the state*. School of American Research Advanced Seminar series. Santa Fe: School of American Research Press.

Davila, Mario. 1971. "Compadrazgo: Fictive kinship in Latin America." In *Readings in kinship and social structure*, ed. N. Graburn, 396–406. New York: Harper and Row.

de Arona, Juan. 1974 [1884]. *Diccionario de peruanismos*. 2 vols. Lima: Promoción Editorial Inca S.A.

Degregori, Carlos Ivan. 1997. "The maturation of a cosmocrat and the building of a discourse community: The case of Shining Path." In *The legitimization of violence*, ed. D. E. Apter, 33–82. New York: New York University Press.

———. 2000. "Panorama de la antropología en el Perú: del estudio del Otro a la construcción de un Nosotros diverso." In *No hay país más diverso: Compendio de antropología peruana, Perú Problema*, ed. C. I. Degregori, 20–73. Lima: Red para el Desarrollo de las Ciencias Sociales en el Peru.

de la Cadena, Marisol. 1998. "Silent racism and intellectual superiority in Peru." *Bulletin of Latin American Research* 17(2): 143–64.

———. 2000. *Indigenous mestizos: The politics of race and culture in Cuzco, Peru, 1919–1991*. Durham, N.C.: Duke University Press.

Delgado Sumar, Hugo E. 1994. "Compadrinazgo en Ayacucho: ¿Un caso atípico?" *Folklore Americano* 57: 115–34.

DeLoache, Judy S., and Alma Gottlieb, eds. 2000. *A world of babies: Imagined childcare guides for seven societies*. Cambridge: Cambridge University Press.

del Pino H., Ponciano. 1998. "Family, culture, and 'revolution': Everyday life with Sendero Luminoso." In *Shining and other paths: War and society in Peru, 1980–1995*, ed. S. J. Stern, 158–92. Durham, N.C.: Duke University Press.

Díaz Martínez, Antonio. 1969. *Ayacucho: Hambre y esperanza*. Ayacucho: Ediciones "Waman Puma."

"Documentos, por favor . . ." 2006. *El Comercio* (Lima), July 12, 1A.

Donner, William W. 1999. "Sharing and compassion: Fosterage in a Polynesian society." *Journal of Comparative Family Studies* 30: 703–22.

Dorow, Sara K. 2006. *Transnational adoption: A cultural economy of race, gender, and kinship.* New York: New York University Press.

Durkheim, Emile. 1977. *The division of labor in society.* New York: Free Press.

Farmer, Paul. 1999. *Infections and inequalities: The modern plagues.* Berkeley: University of California Press.

Feeley-Harnik, Gillian. 1999. "'Communities of blood': The natural history of kinship in nineteenth-century America." *Comparative Studies in Society and History* 41: 215–62.

Fieweger, Mary Ellen. 1991. "Stolen children and international adoptions." *Child Welfare* 70: 285–92.

Finn, Janet. 1991. "Policies, images and lives: Shaping Native American women's histories." *Michigan Feminist Studies* 6: 119–43.

Fischer, Edward F. 1999. "Cultural logic and Maya identity: Rethinking constructivism and essentialism." *Current Anthropology* 40: 473–99.

Flores Galindo, Alberto. 1988. *Buscando un Inca: Identidad y utopia en los Andes.* Lima: Horizonte.

Fonseca, Claudia. 1986. "Orphanages, foundlings, and foster mothers: The system of child circulation in a Brazilian squatter settlement." *Anthropological Quarterly* 59(1): 15–27.

——. 2002a. "Inequality near and far: Adoption as seen from the Brazilian favelas." *Law and Society Review* 36(2): 397–431.

——. 2002b. "An unexpected reversal: Charting the course of international adoption in Brazil." *Adoption and Fostering* 26(3): 28–39.

Forero, Juan. 2004. "Peru photo exhibit captures pathos of 20 years of war." *New York Times,* June 27, 3.

Foster, George M. 1965. "Peasant society and the image of limited good." *American Anthropologist* 67(2): 293–315.

Foucault, Michel. 1965. *Madness and civilization.* Trans. R. Howard. New York: Vintage Books.

Franklin, Sarah, and Susan McKinnon. 2001. "Introduction. Relative values: Reconfiguring kinship studies." In *Relative values: Reconfiguring kinship studies,* ed. S. Franklin and S. McKinnon, 1–25. Durham, N.C.: Duke University Press.

Fravel, Deborah Lewis, Ruth G. McRoy, and Harold D. Grotevant. 2000. "Birthmother perceptions of the psychologically present adopted child: Adoption openness and boundary ambiguity." *Family Relations* 49(4): 425–33.

Freundlich, Madelyn. 2000. *Adoption and ethics.* Vol. 1: *The role of race, culture, and national origin in adoption.* Washington: Child Welfare League of America Press.

Gailey, Christine Ward. 2000. "Ideologies of motherhood and kinship in U.S. adoption." In *Ideologies and technologies of motherhood: Race, class, sexuality, nationalism,* ed. H. Ragone and F. W. Twine, 11–55. New York: Routledge.

García, María Elena. 2005. *Making indigenous citizens: Identity, development, and multicultural activism in Peru.* Stanford, Calif.: Stanford University Press.

Gelles, Paul H. 2000. *Water and power in highland Peru: The cultural politics of irrigation and development*. New Brunswick, N.J.: Rutgers University Press.

Gershon, Ilana. 2003. "Knowing adoption and adopting knowledge." *American Ethnologist* 30(3): 439–46.

Ginsburg, Faye, and Rayna Rapp. 1995. Introduction. In *Conceiving the new world order: The global politics of reproduction*, ed. F. Ginsburg and R. Rapp, 1–17. Berkeley: University of California Press.

Goffman, Erving. 1963. *Stigma: Notes on the management of spoiled identity*. New York: Touchstone.

Goody, Esther N. 1982. *Parenthood and social reproduction: Fostering and occupational roles in West Africa*. Cambridge: Cambridge University Press.

———. 1984. "Parental strategies: calculation or sentiment?: Fostering practices among West Africans." In *Interest and emotion: Essays on the study of family and kinship*, ed. H. Medick and D. W. Sabean, 266–78. Cambridge: Cambridge University Press.

Goody, Jack. 1969. "Adoption in cross-cultural perspective." *Comparative Studies in Society and History* 2: 55–78.

Gordillo, Gastón. 2006. "The crucible of citizenship: ID-paper fetishism in the Argentinean Chaco." *American Ethnologist* 33(2): 162–76.

Gorriti, Gustavo. 1999 [1990]. *The Shining Path: A history of the millenarian war in Peru*. Trans. R. Kirk. Chapel Hill: University of North Carolina Press.

Green, Duncan. 1998. *Hidden lives: Voices of children in Latin America and the Caribbean*. London: Cassell (Save the Children).

Guy, Donna J. 2002. "The state, the family, and marginal children in Latin America." In *Minor omissions: Children in Latin American history and society*, ed. T. Hecht, 139–64. Madison: University of Wisconsin Press.

Hague Convention on Intercountry Adoption 1993. See U.S. Committee on Foreign Relations.

Han, Sallie. 2006. "The baby in the body: Pregnancy practices as kin and person making experience in the contemporary United States." Ph.D. dissertation, Department of Anthropology, University of Michigan.

Haraway, Donna J. 1995. "Universal donors in a vampire culture: It's all in the family: Biological kinship categories in the twentieth-century United States." In *Uncommon ground: Toward reinventing nature*, ed. W. Cronon, 321–75. New York: W. W. Norton.

Harris, Olivia. 1980. "The power of signs: gender, culture, and the wild in the Bolivian Andes." In *Nature, culture, and gender*, ed. C. MacCormack and M. Strathern, 70–94. Cambridge: Cambridge University Press.

Harvey, Penelope. 1994. "Domestic violence in the Peruvian Andes." In *Sex and violence: Issues in representation and experience*, ed. P. Harvey and P. Gow, 66–89. New York: Routledge.

———. 1997. "Los 'hechos naturales' de parentesco y género en un contexto andino."

In *Gente de carne y hueso: Las tramas de parentesco en los Andes*, ed. D. Arnold, 69–82. La Paz: CIASE / ILCA.

Hirsch, Jennifer S. 2003. *A courtship after marriage: Sexuality and love in Mexican transnational families*. Berkeley: University of California Press.

Holy, Ladislav. 1996. *Anthropological perspectives on kinship*. London: Pluto.

Howell, Signe. 2001. "Self-conscious kinship: Some contested values in Norwegian transnational adoption." In *Relative values: Reconfiguring kinship studies*, ed. S. Franklin and S. McKinnon, 203–23. Durham, N.C.: Duke University Press.

———. 2003. "Kinning: The creation of life trajectories in transnational adoptive families." *Journal of the Royal Anthropological Institute* 9: 465–84.

———. 2006. *The kinning of foreigners: Transnational adoption in a global perspective*. Oxford: Berghahn Books.

IDEIF (Instituto de Infancia y Familia). 2001. "Modalidades de tráfico de niños en el Perú." In *Del abuso al olvido*, comp. Peter Strack and Bernardo Ponce, 99–147. Cochabamba, Bolivia: IDEIF, Infante, and Terre des Hommes Alemania (Oficina Regional Andina).

INEI (Instituto Nacional de Estadística e Informática). 1993. *Censo de población*. Lima: INEI. www.inei.gob.pe.

———. 2004. *Censo de población*. Lima: INEI. www.inei.gob.pe.

Inhorn, Marcia C. 2003. *Local babies, global science: Gender, religion, and in vitro fertilization in Egypt*. New York: Routledge.

Isbell, Billie Jean. 1978. *To defend ourselves: Ecology and ritual in an Andean village*. Austin: Institute of Latin American Studies, University of Texas, Austin.

Jaffe, Eliezer D., ed. 1995. *Intercountry adoptions: Laws and perspectives of 'sending' countries*. Dordrecht: Martinus Nijhoff.

Jimenez Salas, Maria. 1958. *Historia de la asistencia social en España en la edad moderna*. Madrid: Instituto Balmes de Sociologia.

Julien, Catherine J. 2000. *Reading Inca history*. Iowa City: University of Iowa Press.

Kahn, Susan. 2000. *Reproducing Jews: A cultural account of assisted conception in Israel*. Durham, N.C.: Duke University Press.

Kandiyoti, Deniz. 1988. "Bargaining with patriarchy." Special Issue to Honor Jessie Bernard. *Gender and Society* 2(3): 274–90.

Kapstein, Ethan B. 2003. "The baby trade." *Foreign Affairs* 82(6): 115–25.

Karen, Robert. 1998. *Becoming attached: First relationships and how they shape our capacity to love*. New York: Oxford University Press.

Keesing, Roger M. 1970. Kwaio fosterage. *American Anthropologist* 72: 991–1020.

Kelly, Tobias. 2006. "Documented lives: fear and the uncertainties of law during the second Palestinian intifada." *Journal of the Royal Anthropological Institute* 12: 89–107.

Kertzer, David. 1993. *Sacrificed for honor: Italian infant abandonment and the politics of reproductive control*. Boston: Beacon Press.

Kim, Jim Yong, et al. 2000. "Sickness amidst recovery: Public debt and private suffering in Peru." In *Dying for growth: Global inequality and the health of the poor*, ed. J. Y. Kim, J. V. Millen, A. Irwin, and J. Gershman, 126–53. Monroe, Maine: Common Courage Press.

Kirk, H. David. 1981. *Adoptive kinship: A modern institution in need of reform*. Toronto: Butterworths.

Kirton, Derek. 2000. *"Race," ethnicity and adoption*. Philadelphia: Open University Press.

Klarén, Peter F. 2000. *Peru: Society and nationhood in the Andes*. New York: Oxford University Press.

Kligman, Gail. 1992. "Abortion and international adoption in post-Ceausescu Romania." *Feminist Studies* 18: 405–419.

———. 1995. "Political demography: The banning of abortion in Ceausescu's Romania." In *Conceiving the new world order*, ed. F. D. Ginsburg and R. Rapp, 234–55. Berkeley: University of California Press.

———. 1998. *The politics of duplicity: Controlling reproduction in Ceausescu's Romania*. Berkeley: University of California Press.

Kopytoff, Igor. 1986. "The cultural biography of things: Commoditization as process." In *The social life of things: Commodities in cultural perspective*, ed. A. Appadurai, 64–90. Cambridge: Cambridge University Press.

Kottak, Conrad Phillip. 1986. "Kinship modeling: Adaptation, fosterage, and fictive kinship among the Betsileo." In *Madagascar: society and history*, ed. C. P. Kottak, 277–98. Durham, N.C.: Carolina Academic Press.

Ladrón de Guevara, Laura. 1998. *Diccionario quechua*. Lima: Editorial Brasa S.A.

Layne, Linda L. 2003. *Motherhood lost: A feminist account of pregnancy loss in America*. New York: Routledge.

LeBlanc, Lawrence J. 1995. *The convention on the rights of the child: United Nations lawmaking on human rights*. Lincoln: University of Nebraska Press.

Leinaweaver, Jessaca. 2001. "Kinship and adopting strategies in Peru." Special issue, "Children in Their Places 2001" Conference (Brunel University, West London, June 21–23, 2001). *Oriental Anthropologist* 1: 18–24.

———. 2005a. "Accompanying and overcoming: Subsistence and sustenance in an Andean city." *Michigan Discussions in Anthropology* 15: 150–82.

———. 2005b. "Familiar ways: Child circulation in Andean Peru." Ph.D. dissertation, Department of Anthropology, University of Michigan.

———. 2005c. "Mass sterilizations and child circulations: Two reproductive responses to poverty in Peru." *Anthropology News* 46: 13, 18.

———. 2007a. "On moving children: The social implications of Andean child circulation." *American Ethnologist* 1(34): 163–80.

———. 2007b. "Choosing to move: Child agency on Peru's margins." *Childhood: A Global Journal of Child Research* 14: 375–92.

——. 2008. "Improving oneself: Young people getting ahead in the Peruvian Andes." Special issue, "Youth, culture, and politics in Latin America," ed. Jon Wolseth and Florence Babb, 60–78. *Latin American Perspectives* 35(4) (July).

——. N.d. "Outsourcing care: How Peruvian emigrants meet transnational family obligations." Special issue on Peruvian emigration, ed. Karsten Pærregaard, Ayumi Takenaka, and Ulla Berg. *Latin American Perspectives*.

León Zamora, Eduardo, and María Andrea Staeheli. 2001. *Cultura escolar y ciudadanía*. Lima: Tarea.

Lévi-Strauss, Claude. 1983. *The Way of the Masks*. Trans. S. Modelski. London: Jonathan Cape.

Levitt, Peggy. 2001. *The transnational villagers*. Berkeley: University of California Press.

Lloyd, Peter. 1980. *The "young towns" of Lima: Aspects of urbanization in Peru*. Cambridge: Cambridge University Press.

Lobo, Susan. 1982. *A house of my own*. Tucson: University of Arizona Press.

Lockhart, James. 1968. *Spanish Peru, 1532–1560: A social history*. Madison: University of Wisconsin Press.

Lombardi, Francisco J., dir. 1990. *La boca del lobo*. New York: Cinevista Video.

López Basanta, Justo. 1997. "El salario." In *Instituciones de derecho del trabajo y de la seguridad social*, ed. N. de Buen Lozano and E. Morgado Valenzuela, 445–70. Mexico City: Universidad Nacional Autónoma de México, Instituto de Investigaciones Jurídicas.

Lorente, Sebastián. 1967 [1855]. *Pensamientos sobre el Peru*. Lima: Universidad Nacional Mayor de San Marcos.

Loza, Martha, et al. 1990. *Así, ando, ando como empleada*. Lima: IPEC (Instituto de Publicaciones Educación y Comunicación).

Ludeña Gonzalez, Gerardo F. 2000. *Un debido proceso de adopción para nuestros niños y adolescentes*. Lima: G&S Editores.

Mallon, Florencia E. 1995. *Peasant and nation: The making of postcolonial Mexico and Peru*. Berkeley: University of California Press.

Mann, Gillian. 2004. "Separated children: Care and support in context." In *Children and youth on the front line: Ethnography, armed conflict, and displacement*, ed. J. Boyden and J. de Berry, 4–22. New York: Berghahn Books.

Mannheim, Bruce, and Krista Van Vleet. 1998. The dialogics of Southern Quechua narrative. *American Anthropologist* 100: 326–46.

Martinez, Wilton, and Paul Gelles, prod. 1992. *Transnational Fiesta, 1992*. Berkeley: Berkeley Media LLC.

Mauss, Marcel. 1990 [1954]. *The gift*. New York: Routledge.

Mayer, Enrique. 1992. "Peru in deep trouble: Mario Vargas Llosa's 'Inquest in the Andes' reexamined." In *Rereading cultural anthropology*, ed. G. Marcus, 181–219. Durham, N.C.: Duke University Press.

Mead, Margaret. 1961 [1928]. *Coming of age in Samoa*. New York: Morrow Quill.

Medick, Hans, and David Warren Sabean. 1984. "Interest and emotion in family and kinship studies: A critique of social history and anthropology." In *Interest and emotion: Essays on the study of family and kinship,* ed. H. Medick and D.W. Sabean, 9–27. Cambridge: Cambridge University Press.

Méndez G., Cecilia. 1993. *Incas si, indios no: Apuntes para el estudio del nacionalismo criollo en el Peru*. Lima: Instituto de Estudio Peruanos.

Milanich, Nara. 2002. "Historical perspectives on illegitimacy and illegitimates in Latin America." In *Minor omissions: Children in Latin American history and society,* ed. T. Hecht, 72–101. Madison: University of Wisconsin Press.

——. 2004. "The Casa de Huérfanos and child circulation in late-nineteenth-century Chile." *Journal of Social History* 38(2): 311–40.

Miles, Ann. 2004. *From Cuenca to Queens: An anthropological story of transnational migration*. 1st ed. Austin: University of Texas Press.

Millones, Luis. 1981. *Tugurio: The culture of the Peruvian marginal population, a study of a Lima slum*. Trans. W. W. Stein. Buffalo, N.Y.: State University of New York, Buffalo, Council on International Studies.

Mintz, Sidney W., and Eric R. Wolf. 1950. "An analysis of ritual co-parenthood (compadrazgo)." *Southwestern Journal of Anthropology* 6(4): 341–68.

Modell, Judith S. 1994. *Kinship with strangers: Adoption and interpretations of kinship in American culture*. Berkeley: University of California Press.

——. 1998. "Rights to the children: foster care and social reproduction in Hawai'i." In *Reproducing reproduction: Kinship, power, and technological innovation*, ed. S. Franklin and H. Ragoné, 156–72. Philadelphia: University of Pennsylvania Press.

——. 2002. *A sealed and secret kinship: The culture of policies and practices in American adoption*. Public Issues in Anthropological Perspectives. New York: Berghahn Books.

Montecino, Sonia. 1996. *Madres y huachos: Alegorías del mestizaje chileno*. Santiago: Editorial Sudamericana.

Muñoz Cabrejo, Fanni. 2000. "La educacion femenina en la Lima de fines del siglo xix e inicios del siglo xx." In *El hechizo de las imágenes: Estatus social, género y etnicidad en la historia peruana*, ed. N. Henríquez, 223–49. Lima: Fondo Editorial Pontificia Universidad Católica del Perú.

Muñoz Nájar, Teresina. 2002. "ADN prueba final." *Caretas*, no. 1728, July 4, 18–21.

Needham, Rodney. 1971. "Remarks on the analysis of kinship and marriage." In *Rethinking kinship and marriage*, ed. R. Needham, 1–34. New York: Tavistock.

Neville, Gwen Kennedy. 1987. *Kinship and pilgrimage: Rituals of reunion in American Protestant culture*. New York: Oxford University Press.

O'Donnell, Alejandro. 2001. "The nutritional status of children in Latin America." In *The child in Latin America: Health, development, and rights*, ed. E. Bartell and A. O'Donnell, 5–47. Notre Dame: University of Notre Dame Press.

Oliver-Smith, Anthony. 1969. "The pishtaco: institutionalized fear in highland Peru." *Journal of American Folklore* 82: 326–63.

Onís, Paco de, prod. 2005. *State of fear.* New York: Skylight Pictures, New Day Films.

Orlove, Ben. 1998. "Down to earth: Race and substance in the Andes." *Bulletin of Latin American Research* 17(2): 207–22.

——. 2002. *Lines in the water: Nature and culture at Lake Titicaca.* Berkeley: University of California Press.

Ortega Matute, Palito. 1997. *Dios tarda pero no olvida.* Ayacucho, Peru.

——. 2000. *Sangre inocente.* Ayacucho, Peru.

——. 2005. *El rincón de los inocentes.* Ayacucho, Peru.

Ossio, Juan M. 1984. "Cultural continuity, structure, and context: Some peculiarities of the Andean compadrazgo." In *Kinship ideology and practice in Latin America,* ed. R. T. Smith, 118–46. Chapel Hill: University of North Carolina Press.

——. 1992. *Parentesco, reciprocidad y jerarquía en los andes: Una aproximación a la organización social de la comunidad de Andamarca.* Lima: Pontificia Universidad Católica del Perú.

Osterling, Jorge P., and Hector Martinez. 1983. "Notes for a history of Peruvian social anthropology, 1940–80." *Current Anthropology* 24(3): 343–60.

Oths, Kathryn S. 1999. "Debilidad: A biocultural assessment of an embodied Andean illness." *Medical Anthropology Quarterly* 13(3): 286–315.

Oviedo, José. 1999. *El Perú y su futuro: Dos paradigmas culturales sobre infancia.* Lima: IDL.

Paerregaard, Karsten. 1997. *Linking separate worlds: Urban migrants and rural lives in Peru.* New York: Berg.

Paley, Julia. 2001. *Marketing democracy: Power and social movements in post-dictatorship Chile.* Berkeley: University of California Press.

Palomino Vall, Efraín. 1986. "Ayacucho: 'Wawas y caballos' en Todos los Santos." In *Ayacucho: Su cultura viva: Ponencias presentadas al IX Congreso Nacional de Folklore* 3: 81–87.

Parker, D. S. 1998. *The idea of the middle class: White-collar workers and Peruvian society, 1900–1950.* University Park: Pennsylvania State University Press.

Parreñas, Rhacel Salazar. 2005. *Children of global migration: Transnational families and gendered woes.* Stanford: Stanford University Press.

Parry, Jonathan P., and Maurice Bloch. 1989. "Introduction: Money and the morality of exchange." In *Money and the morality of exchange,* J. Parry and M. Bloch, eds., 1–32. Cambridge: Cambridge University Press.

Paxman, John M., Alberto Rizo, Laura Brown, and Janie Benson. 1993. "The clandestine epidemic: The practice of unsafe abortion in Latin America." *Studies in Family Planning* 24: 205–26.

Peel, J. D. Y. 1978. "Ọlaju: A Yoruba concept of development." *Journal of Development Studies* 14(2): 139–65.

Platt, Tristan. 1986. "Mirrors and maize: the concept of yanantin among the Macha of Bolivia." In *Anthropological History of Andean Polities*, ed. J. V. Murra, N. Wachtel, and J. Revel, 228–59. Cambridge: Cambridge University Press.

Poole, Deborah. 1997. *Vision, race, and modernity: A visual economy of the Andean image world*. Princeton: Princeton University Press.

——. 2004. "Between threat and guarantee: justice and community in the margins of the Peruvian state." In *Anthropology in the margins of the state*, ed. V. Das and D. Poole, 35–65. School of American Research Advanced Seminar series. Santa Fe: School of American Research Press.

Portugal Catacora, José. 1988. *El niño indígena*. Lima: Artex.

Programa de Apoyo al Repoblamiento. 2001. *Censo por la Paz*, vol. 2003. Lima: PAR.

PROMUDEH (Ministerio de Promoción de la Mujer y del Desarrollo Humano). 2001. *Guia de Procedimiento Administrativo de Adopción*. Lima.

Ragone, Helena. 1994. *Surrogate motherhood: Conception in the heart*. Boulder: Westview Press.

Renne, Elisha P. 2003. *Population and progress in a Yoruba town*. Ann Arbor: University of Michigan Press.

Revollar Añaños, Eliana. 2001. "Los desplazados por violencia política en el Perú." *Allpanchis* 58(2): 9–31.

Reynolds, Pamela. 1996. *Traditional healers and childhood in Zimbabwe*. Athens: Ohio University Press.

Ritter, Jonathan. 2002. "Siren songs: Ritual and revolution in the Peruvian Andes." *British Journal of Ethnomusicology* 11(1): 9–42.

Roberts, Elizabeth F. S. 2006. "God's laboratory: Religious rationalities and modernity in Ecuadorian in-vitro fertilization." *Culture, Medicine and Psychiatry* 30: 507–36.

Romero, Raul R. 2001. *Debating the past: Music, memory, and identity in the Andes*. Oxford: Oxford University Press.

Roncagliolo, Santiago. 2006. *Abril rojo*. Mexico City: Santillana Ediciones Generales.

Rousseau, Jérôme. 1970. *L'adoption chez les Esquimaux Tununermiut, Pond Inlet, T. du N.-O.* Québec: Centre des Etudes Nordiques, Université Laval.

Rubin, Gayle. 1975. "The traffic in women: Notes on the 'political economy' of sex." In *Toward an Anthropology of Women*, ed. R. R. Reiter, 157–210. New York: Monthly Review Press.

Rugh, Andrea. 1981. "Orphanages and homes for the aged in Egypt: Contradiction or affirmation in a family oriented society." *International Journal of Sociology of the Family* 11 (July–December): 203–33.

Salazar Vega, Elizabeth. 2006. "Investigan cuántos niños fueron llevados a Francia." *El Comercio* (Lima), July 12, A1.

Salomon, Frank. 1982. "Chronicles of the impossible: Notes on three Peruvian indigenous historians." In *From oral to written expression: Native Andean chronicles of the early colonial period*, ed. R. Adorno, 9–39. Latin American Series 4. Syracuse, N.Y.: Syracuse University, Maxwell School of Citizenship and Public Affairs.

——. 1986. *Native lords of Quito in the age of the Incas: The political economy of north-Andean chiefdoms*. Cambridge: Cambridge University Press.

——. 1999. "Testimonies: The making and reading of native South American historical sources." In *The Cambridge history of the native peoples of the Americas*, ed. F. Salomon and S. B. Schwartz, 3: 19–95. Cambridge: Cambridge University Press.

Sanjek, Roger. 1990. "Maid servants and market women's apprentices in Adabraka." In *At work in homes: Household workers in world perspective*, ed. S. Colen and R. Sanjek, 35–62. American Ethnological Society Monograph Series. Washington: American Anthropological Association.

Sargent, Carolyn, and Michael Harris. 1998. "Bad boys and good girls: The implications of gender ideology for child health in Jamaica." In *Small wars: The cultural politics of childhood*, ed. N. Scheper-Hughes and C. F. Sargent, 202–27. Berkeley: University of California Press.

Scheper-Hughes, Nancy. 1992. *Death without weeping*. Berkeley: University of California Press.

Scheper-Hughes, Nancy, and Carolyn Sargent. 1998. *Small wars: The cultural politics of childhood*. Berkeley: University of California Press.

Schildkrout, Enid. 1973. "The fostering of children in Ghana." *Urban Anthropology* 2: 48–73.

——. 1978. "Age and gender in Hausa society: Socio-economic roles of children in urban Kano." In *Sex and age as principles of social differentiation*, ed. J. S. La Fontaine, 108–37. London: Academic Press.

——. 1980. "Children's work reconsidered." *International Social Science Journal* 32: 479–89.

Schneider, David M. 1980. *American kinship: A cultural account*. Chicago: University of Chicago Press.

——. 1984. *A critique of the study of kinship*. Ann Arbor: University of Michigan Press.

Schrauwers, Albert. 1999. "Negotiating parentage: The political economy of 'kinship' in central Sulawesi, Indonesia." *American Ethnologist* 26: 310–23.

Schweitzer, Peter. 2000. *Dividends of kinship*. Monographs of the European Association of Social Anthropologists. London: Routledge.

Seligmann, Linda. 1995. *Between reform and revolution: Political struggles in the Peruvian Andes, 1969–1991*. Stanford: Stanford University Press.

——. 2004. *Peruvian street lives: Culture, power, and economy among market women of Cuzco*. Urbana: University of Illinois Press.

Sharp, Lesley A. 2002. *The sacrificed generation: Youth, history, and the colonized mind in Madagascar*. Berkeley: University of California Press.

Simon, Rita James, and Howard Altstein. 2000. *Adoption across borders: Serving the children in transracial and intercountry adoptions*. Lanham, Md.: Rowman & Littlefield.

Simpson, Bob. 2001. "Making 'bad' deaths 'good': The kinship consequences of posthumous conception." Journal of the *Royal Anthropological Institute* 7: 1–18.

Sims, Calvin. 1998. "Using gifts as bait, Peru sterilizes women." *New York Times*, February 15, A6.

Skar, Harald. 1982. *Warm valley people: Duality and land reform among Quechua Indians of highland Peru.* Oslo: Universitetsforlaget.

Skar, Sarah Lund. 1994. *Lives together, worlds apart: Quechua colonization in jungle and city.* Oslo: Scandinavian University Press.

Smith, Gavin. 1989. *Livelihood and resistance: Peasants and the politics of land in Peru.* Berkeley: University of California Press.

Smith, Margo L. 1973. "Domestic service as a channel of upward mobility for the lower-class woman: The Lima case." In *Female and male in Latin America: Essays*, ed. A. Pescatello, 191–207. Pittsburgh: University of Pittsburgh Press.

Sørensen, Ninna Nyberg. 2002. "Representing the local: Mobile livelihood practices in the Peruvian central Sierra." In *Work and migration: Life and livelihoods in a globalizing world*, ed. N. N. Sørensen and K. F. Olwig, 23–44. London: Routledge.

Stack, Carol B. 1974. *All our kin: Strategies for survival in a Black community.* New York: Harper & Row.

Starn, Orin. 1992. "Missing the revolution: Anthropologists and the war in Peru." In *Rereading cultural anthropology*, ed. G. Marcus, 152–80. Durham, N.C.: Duke University Press.

Stein, William W. 1961. *Hualcan: Life in the highlands of Peru.* Ithaca: Cornell University Press.

Stepan, Nancy Leys. 1991. *The hour of eugenics: Race, gender, and nation in Latin America.* Ithaca: Cornell University Press.

Stephens, Sharon, ed. 1995. *Children and the politics of culture.* Princeton: Princeton University Press. See esp. "Children and the politics of culture in 'late capitalism,'" 3–48.

Stepputat, Finn. 2002. "The final move? Displaced livelihoods and collective returns in Peru and Guatemala." In *Work and migration: Life and livelihoods in a globalizing world*, ed. N. N. Sørensen and K. F. Olwig, 202–24. London: Routledge.

Stern, Steve J. 1982. *Peru's Indian peoples and the challenge of Spanish conquest: Huamanga to 1640.* Madison: University of Wisconsin Press.

——. 1998. "Beyond enigma: An agenda for interpreting Shining Path and Peru, 1980–1995." In *Shining and other paths: War and society in Peru, 1980–1995*, ed. S. J. Stern, 1–9. Durham, N.C.: Duke University Press.

Stoler, Ann Laura. 1991. "Carnal Knowledge and Imperial Power: Race and Morality in Colonial Asia." In *Gender at the crossroads: Feminist anthropology in the postmodern era*, ed. M. di Leonardo, 51–101. Berkeley: University of California Press.

Strathern, Marilyn. 1991. *Partial connections.* Savage, Md.: Rowman & Littlefield.

——. 2005. *Kinship, law, and the unexpected: Relatives are always a surprise.* Cambridge: Cambridge University Press.

Strocka, Cordula. 2006. "Growing up in the 'Corner of the Dead': Youth gangs, identity, and violence in the Peruvian Andes." Ph.D. thesis, Queen Elizabeth House, University of Oxford.

Strong, Pauline Turner. 2001. "To forget their tongue, their name, and their whole relation: Captivity, extra-tribal adoption, and the Indian Child Welfare Act." In *Relative values: Reconfiguring kinship studies*, ed. S. Franklin and S. McKinnon, 468–93. Durham, N.C.: Duke University Press.

Swanson, Kate. 2007. " 'Bad mothers' and 'delinquent children': Unravelling anti-begging rhetoric in the Ecuadorian Andes." *Gender, Place and Culture: A Journal of Feminist Geography* 14(6): 703–20.

Tate, Tim. 1990. "Trafficking in children for adoption." In *Betrayal: A report on violence towards children in today's world*, ed. C. Moorehead, 143–65. New York: Doubleday.

Theidon, Kimberly Susan. 2004. *Entre prójimos: El conflicto armado interno y la política de la reconciliación en el Perú*. Lima: Instituto de Estudios Peruanos.

Thurner, Mark. 1997. *From two republics to one divided: Contradictions of postcolonial nationmaking in Andean Peru*. Durham, N.C.: Duke University Press.

Toledo Brückmann, Ernesto. 2003. *Retablos de Ayacucho: Testimonio de violencia*. Lima: Editorial San Marcos.

Torres, María de los Angeles. 2003. *The lost apple: Operation Pedro Pan, Cuban children in the U.S., and the promise of a better future*. Boston: Beacon Press.

Torres Rodríguez, Oswaldo. 1999. *Los menores trabajadores de los Andes centrales*. Huancayo, Peru: EDIMUL S.A.

Trautmann, Thomas R. 1987. *Lewis Henry Morgan and the invention of kinship*. Berkeley: University of California Press.

Trawick, Margaret. 1992. *Notes on love in a Tamil family*. Berkeley: University of California Press.

Trouillot, Michel-Rolph. 1990. *Haiti, state against nation: The origins and legacy of Duvalierism*. New York: Monthly Review Press.

Tucker, C. Joshua. 2005. "Sounding out a new Peru: Music, media, and the contemporary Andean public." Ph.D. dissertation, Department of Music, University of Michigan.

Twinam, Ann. 1999. *Public lives, private secrets: Gender, honor, sexuality, and illegitimacy in colonial Spanish America*. Stanford: Stanford University Press.

UNICEF (United Nations International Children's Emergency Fund). 2007. *At a glance: Peru*. http://www.unicef.org/infobycountry/peru—statistics.html.

United Nations. 1995. "The United Nations Convention on the Rights of the Child." In *Children and the politics of culture*, ed. S. Stephens, 335–52. Princeton: Princeton University Press.

———. 2000. "Protocol to prevent, suppress, and punish trafficking in persons, especially women and children, supplementing the United Nations Convention against Transnational Organized Crime." http://www.unodc.org/.

United States. 2006. *Code of Federal Regulations.* Vol. 8 (Aliens and Nationality), 68–132. Washington: National Archives and Records Administration.

Urban, Greg. 1996. *Metaphysical community: The interplay of the senses and the intellect.* Austin: University of Texas Press.

U.S. Committee on Foreign Relations. 2000. *Convention on Protection of Children and Co-operation in Respect to Intercountry Adoption.* Washington: U.S. Government Printing Office.

U.S. State Department. 2004. International Adoption—PERU. http://travel/state.gov/family/adoption/.

Uzendoski, Michael. 2005. *The Napo Runa of Amazonian Ecuador.* Urbana: University of Illinois Press.

Valderrama, Ricardo, and Carmen Escalante. 1996. *Andean lives: Gregorio Condori Mamani and Asunta Quispe Huamán.* Austin: University of Texas Press.

——. 1997. "Ser mujer: Warmi kay—la mujer en la cultura andina." In *Mas allá del silencio: Las fronteras de género en los Andes,* ed. D. Arnold, 153–70. La Paz: CIASE.

Valenzuela, Abel, Jr. 1999. "Gender roles and settlement activities among children and their immigrant families." *American Behavioral Scientist* 42: 720–42.

van Deusen, Nancy E. 2001. *Between the sacred and the worldly: The institutional and cultural practice of "recogimiento" in colonial Lima.* Stanford: Stanford University Press.

Van Vleet, Krista E. 1999. "Now my daughter is alone: Performing kinship and embodying affect in marriage practices among native Andeans in Bolivia." Ph.D. dissertation, Department of Anthropology, University of Michigan.

——. 2002. "The intimacies of power: Rethinking violence and affinity in the Bolivian Andes." *American Ethnologist* 29(3): 567–601.

——. 2008. *Performing kinship: Narrative, gender, and the intimacies of power in the Andes.* Austin: University of Texas Press.

Vargas Llosa, Mario. 1975 [1969]. *Conversation in the cathedral.* Trans. G. Rabassa. New York: Harper and Row.

——. 1983. "Inquest in the Andes: A Latin American writer explores the political lessons of a Peruvian massacre." *New York Times Magazine,* July 31, 18–23.

Vásquez H., Enrique, and Enrique Mendizabal O., eds. 2002. *Los niños . . . primero? El gasto público social focalizado en niños y niñas en el Perú, 1990–2000.* Lima: Universidad del Pacífico Centro de Investigación and Save the Children Suecia.

Vincent, Susan. 2000. "Flexible families: Capitalist development and crisis in rural Peru." *Journal of Comparative Family Studies* 31: 155–70.

"Voces que buscan ser oídas." 2001. *Expreso* (Lima), October 22.

Volkman, Toby, ed. 2005. *Cultures of transnational adoption.* Durham, N.C.: Duke University Press.

Walker, Charles. 1999. *Smoldering ashes: Cuzco and the creation of republican Peru, 1780–1840.* Durham, N.C.: Duke University Press.

Weismantel, Mary. 1988. *Food, gender, and poverty in the Ecuadorian Andes.* Philadelphia: University of Pennsylvania Press.

———. 1995. "Making kin: Kinship theory and Zumbagua adoptions." *American Ethnologist* 22(4): 685–709.

———. 1997. "White cannibals: Fantasies of racial violence in the Andes." *Identities* 4: 9–43.

———. 2001. *Cholas and pishtacos: Stories of race and sex in the Andes*. Chicago: University of Chicago Press.

———. 2006. "Ayllu: Real and imagined communities in the Andes." In *The seductions of community: Emancipations, oppressions, quandaries*, ed. G. W. Creed, 77–99. Santa Fe: School of American Research.

Weston, Kath. 1991. *Families we choose: Lesbians, gays, kinship*. New York: Columbia University Press.

White, Ben. 1994. "Children, work, and 'child labour': Changing responses to the employment of children." *Development and Change* 25: 849–78.

Whitehead, Tony L. 1978. "Residence, kinship, and mating as survival strategies: A West Indian example." *Journal of Marriage and the Family* 40(4): 817–28.

Whitten, Norman E. 1981. *Cultural transformations and ethnicity in modern Ecuador*. Urbana: University of Illinois Press.

Willis, Paul. 1981. *Learning to labor: How working class kids get working-class jobs*. New York: Columbia University Press.

Wogan, Peter. 2004. "Magical writing." In *Salasaca: Literacy and power in highland Ecuador*. Boulder, Colo.: Westview Press.

Yanagisako, Sylvia Junko. 2002. *Producing culture and capital: Family firms in Italy*. Princeton: Princeton University Press.

Yngvesson, Barbara. 2003. "Going 'home': Adoption, loss of bearings, and the mythology of roots." *Social Text* 74: 7–27.

Young, Grace. 1987. "The myth of being 'like a daughter.'" *Latin American Perspectives* 14(3): 365–80.

Zelizer, Viviana A. 1985. *Pricing the priceless child: The changing social value of children*. Princeton: Princeton University Press.

Index

Note: Non-English words and names of interlocutors are italicized.

Some of the material included here has appeared previously in somewhat different form. Portions of the arguments from the introduction, chapters 2 and 4, and the conclusion appear in "On moving children: The social implications of Andean child circulation," *American Ethnologist* 1(34) (2007): 163–80. Material from the chapter on *superarse* appears in "Improving oneself: Young people getting ahead in the Peruvian Andes," *Latin American Perspectives* 35(4) (2008) and in "Accompanying and overcoming: Subsistence and sustenance in an Andean city," *Michigan Discussions in Anthropology* 15 (2005): 150–82.

Jessaca B. Leinaweaver is an assistant professor in the Department of
Anthropology at Brown University.

Library of Congress Cataloging-in-Publication Data

Leinaweaver, Jessaca B.
The circulation of children: kinship, adoption, and morality in Andean Peru
/ Jessaca B. Leinaweaver.
p. cm. — (Latin America otherwise)
Includes bibliographical references and index.
ISBN 978-0-8223-4181-9 (cloth : alk. paper)
ISBN 978-0-8223-4197-0 (pbk. : alk. paper)
1. Indian children—Peru—Ayachucho—Social conditions.
2. Children—Peru—Ayacucho—Family relationships.
3. Indians of South America—Kinship—Peru—Ayacucho.
4. Kinship—Peru—Ayachucho.
5. Adoption—Peru-Ayachucho.
6. Social structure—Peru—Ayachucho.
7. Interpersonal relations—Peru—Ayachucho.
8. Ayacucho (Peru)—Social conditions.
9. Ayacucho (Peru)—Moral conditions.
I. Title.
F3429.1.A9L45 2008
362.70985'32—dc22   2008013529